'Is it possible to build a vibrant community of readers in schoc
given here is yes. This book is a timely reminder of why readin
the role schools can play in fostering engaged readers. It demc
it is possible to build a vibrant community of readers amongst , ,
ing reading from a private and individual pursuit to a visible and valuable activity that
can be shared. The book passes on insightful strategies and approaches that others can
follow to put reading for pleasure back at the heart of schooling. Along the way teachers
and pupils reflect on what matters to them about reading and the choices they make
about what and where to read. This is reading as a reciprocal activity, in which deliberate
and sustained activity transforms what schools do. Read the book and be inspired.'

Gemma Moss, *Professor, Institute of Education, University of London, UK*

'An important and timely text for teachers, school leaders, administrators and policy
makers. Teacher knowledge and student motivation, and the dynamic role they play in
student learning are too often diminished in this era of high stakes testing and scripted
curricula. In contrast, Cremin and her colleagues provide a compelling argument for
increasing teachers' knowledge of literature and use of interactive book sharing strategies.
Their research demonstrates that such knowledge impacts positively on students' enthusiasm for reading and enhances their achievement. A comprehensive study that should be
shared widely.'

Victoria J. Risko, *Professor Emerita, Vanderbilt University and 2011–2012 President,
International Reading Association*

Building Communities of Engaged Readers

Reading for pleasure urgently requires a higher profile to raise attainment and increase children's engagement as self-motivated and socially interactive readers. *Building Communities of Engaged Readers* highlights the concept of 'Reading Teachers' who are not only knowledgeable about texts for children, but are also aware of their own reading identities and prepared to share their enthusiasm and understanding of what being a reader means. Sharing the processes of reading with young readers is an innovative approach to developing new generations of readers.

Examining the interplay between the 'will and the skill' to read, the book distinctively details a reading for pleasure pedagogy and demonstrates that reader engagement is strongly influenced by relationships between children, teachers, families and communities. Importantly it provides compelling evidence that reciprocal reading communities in school encompass:

- a shared concept of what it means to be a reader in the 21st century;
- considerable teacher and child knowledge of children's literature and other texts;
- pedagogic practices which acknowledge and develop diverse reader identities;
- spontaneous 'inside-text talk' on the part of all members;
- a shift in the locus of control and new social spaces that encourage choice and children's rights as readers.

Written by experts in the literacy field and illustrated throughout with examples from the schools involved in the project, it is essential reading for all those concerned with improving young people's enjoyment of and attainment in reading.

Teresa Cremin is Professor of Education (Literacy), The Open University, UK.

Marilyn Mottram was, at the time of the project, Senior School Improvement Adviser in an urban authority; now she is HMI and Ofsted's Deputy National Lead for English and Literacy.

Fiona M. Collins is Principal Lecturer, University of Roehampton, UK.

Sacha Powell is Reader in Early Childhood, Canterbury Christ Church University, UK.

Kimberly Safford is Senior Lecturer in Education, The Open University, UK.

Building Communities of Engaged Readers

Reading for pleasure

Teresa Cremin, Marilyn Mottram,
Fiona M. Collins, Sacha Powell
and Kimberly Safford

LONDON AND NEW YORK

First published 2014
by Routledge
2 Park Square, Milton Park, Abingdon, Oxon OX14 4RN

and by Routledge
711 Third Avenue, New York, NY 10017

Routledge is an imprint of the Taylor & Francis Group, an informa business

British Library Cataloguing in Publication Data
A catalogue record for this book is available from the British Library

Library of Congress Cataloging in Publication Data
Cremin, Teresa.
Building communities of engaged readers: reading for pleasure / Teresa Cremin, Marilyn Mottram, Fiona M. Collins, Sacha Powell, Kimberly Safford
pages cm
1. Reading. 2. Language arts.
LB1050.C754 2014
428.4—dc23
2013050807

ISBN: 978-1-138-77747-7 (hbk)
ISBN: 978-1-138-77748-4 (pbk)
ISBN: 978-1-315-77258-5 (ebk)

Typeset in Bembo
by Book Now Ltd, London

Contents

Illustrations

Figures

Tables

About the authors

Teresa Cremin is a Professor of Education (Literacy) at The Open University. She is a past President of the United Kingdom Literacy Association (UKLA), joint coordinator of the British Educational Research Association (BERA) Special Interest Group on Creativity and a member of the Economic and Social Research Council (ESRC) Peer Review College. Teresa is also an Academician of the Academy of Social Sciences, a Fellow of the English Association, a Trustee of UKLA and the Society for Educational Studies, a Director of the Cambridge Primary Review Trust and a Board Member of Booktrust and The Poetry Archive. Teresa's socio-cultural research, her teaching and consultancy focuses mainly on teachers' literate identities and practices, the pedagogies of reading and writing for pleasure and creativity in teaching and learning from the early years through to Higher Education. Additionally, working with teachers as co-participant researchers she has explored the everyday literacy practices of young people in the twenty-first century. Her recent projects have involved exploring contemporary enactments of Vivian Gussin Paley's work with young children scribing and enacting their own narratives, and the literary discussions of extracurricular reading groups, the members of which were shadowing the Carnegie and Kate Greenaway Medals. Teresa has written and edited over 25 books and numerous papers and professional texts, most recently publishing with Debra Myhill *Writing Voices: Creating Communities of Writers* (2012, Routledge) and editing with colleagues Kathy Hall, Barbara Comber and Luis Moll *The International Handbook of Research into Children's Literacy, Learning and Culture* (2013, Wiley Blackwell).

Marilyn Mottram was a primary teacher for many years and has taught in a variety of contexts. She has had extensive experience of leadership and improvement work in schools across a number of local authorities. At the time of the project, Marilyn was working as a senior School Improvement Adviser in Birmingham local authority and leading developments in curriculum and pedagogy. She was formerly a Senior Lecturer in Education at Birmingham City University and Head of Primary English. She works closely with practitioners and pupils and is passionate about offering space for teachers to be researchers of children's learning. Her own research interests include exploring the connections/disconnections between literacy practices and events in homes, schools and communities and the implications for literacy pedagogies and approaches. Marilyn is currently HMI and Deputy National Lead for English with Ofsted.

Fiona M. Collins is a Principal Lecturer at the University of Roehampton where she convenes the MA English Education pathway. She teaches on a range of modules linked to English Education and children's literature at both undergraduate and post-graduate level. She has co-edited two books on children's literature: *Historical Fiction: Capturing the Past* and *Turning the Page: Children's Literature in Performance and the Media* and, with a colleague Alison Kelly, has been involved in an ESRC series of lectures in which they presented research on student teachers' confidence in using children's poetry on school placements. In recent years she has also been involved in a number of externally funded research projects. Projects such as two EU Comenius funded projects, Images and Identity and currently Creative Connections, which explore links between creativity and identity as well as the two UKLA/OU research projects: Teachers as Readers: Building Communities of Readers and Building Communities: Researching Literacy Lives, on which she is a member of the research team.

Sacha Powell is a Reader in Early Childhood at Canterbury Christ Church University. She currently leads the Research Centre for Children, Families and Communities – a specialist, interdisciplinary unit dedicated to critical, ecosystemic approaches to researching the lives of children and young people using methodologies that fore-ground participation, co-construction and public involvement. Her own work falls within the broad spectrum offered by the area of Early Childhood studies and in particular it focuses on policy and services for children from birth to three with a babies' and young children's rights/agency perspective. Recent studies include The Baby Room Project, which emphasises a dialogic approach to early childhood professional education and practice and the importance of talk in babies' lives. This led to the development of new work, which explores and supports practitioners to theorise the role of singing with babies as a component of a pedagogy of care. Both projects have been co-directed with Dr Kathy Goouch and funders include the Esmée Fairbairn Foundation and the Froebel Trust. She is also co-editor with Kathy and Tricia David of the *Routledge International Handbook of Philosophies and Theories in Early Childhood* and *An Introduction to Early Childhood Studies* with Trisha Maynard (Sage 2013). She lectures on a range of undergraduate and postgraduate programmes in Education and Health and supervises doctoral students from diverse disciplines. She is a convenor of the Parents in Education Research Network and a member of The UK Froebel Research Committee and Executive Committee of TACTYC, the association for early childhood educators.

Kimberly Safford is a Senior Lecturer in Education at The Open University where she developed a foundation degree in Primary Teaching and Learning that now has over one thousand students. She also creates open educational resources for teachers, teaching assistants and teacher educators in India, Sierra Leone and Malawi, including a pan-Africa module on the teaching of early reading. She was formerly a Senior Lecturer in English Education at Roehampton University, and research officer at Centre for Literacy in Primary Education. She is currently researching the impact of spelling, punctuation and grammar testing in primary schools for UKLA.

Acknowledgements

The project team would like to acknowledge and thank both the UK Literacy Association (UKLA) and the Esmée Fairbairn Foundation for their generous funding of this work, without which the projects Phase I, *Teachers as Readers* and Phase II, *Teachers as Readers: Building Communities of Readers* would not have taken place. In addition, the team are indebted to a number of colleagues: in Phase I, those UKLA members working in local authorities who administered and returned the teacher questionnaires, and Ruth Rogers from Canterbury Christ Church University who undertook considerable data analysis; in Phase II, the members of the project's Steering Committee, the Local Authority Coordinators who led the II work in their authorities, the project's Literature Consultant Prue Goodwin, and the Primary National Strategy for supporting the dissemination work. In addition, and significantly, the team recognise the rich contribution made by Dr Eve Bearne, a member of the Phase I team, who also contributed richly to the Phase II data analysis, bringing her own unique lens to the data and Dr Judy Durrant the External Evaluator of Phase II from Canterbury Christ Church University whose perceptive report so encouraged us to extend our work. Finally, the many teachers, headteachers and children involved in both phases of this research deserve our particular thanks for their involvement.

With thanks to the publishers of the following to reproduce data and arguments first developed within:

Cremin, T., Bearne, E., Mottram, M. and Goodwin, P. (2008a) Primary teachers as readers. *English in Education,* 42(1), 1–16.

Cremin, T., Bearne, E., Mottram, M. and Goodwin, P. (2008b) Exploring teachers' knowledge of children's literature. *Cambridge Journal of Education,* 38(4), 449–464.

Cremin, T., Mottram, M., Collins, F. and Powell, S. (2008c) *Building Communities of Readers.* London: UKLA and the Primary National Strategy.

Cremin, T., Mottram, M., Collins, F., Powell, S. and Safford, K. (2009a) Teachers as readers: Building communities of readers. *Literacy,* 43(1), 11–19.

Cremin, T., Bearne, E., Mottram, M. and Goodwin, P. (2009b) Teachers as readers in the 21st century. In M. Styles and E. Arizpe (eds) *Acts of Reading: Teachers, Text and Childhood.* Stoke on Trent: Trentham Books, pp. 201–218.

Cremin, T. (2010a) Reconceptualising reading in the 21st century. In T. McCannon (ed.) *Reading in the 21st Century.* Dublin: Reading Association of Ireland.

Cremin, T. (2010b) Poetry teachers: Teachers who read and readers who teach poetry. In M. Styles and M. Rosen (eds) *Poetry and Childhood*. Stoke on Trent: Trentham Books, pp. 219–227.

Cremin, T. (2010c) Motivating children to read through literature. In G. Gillon, J. Fletcher and F. Parkhill (eds) *Motivating Literacy Learners in Today's World*. New Zealand Council for Educational Research.

Cremin, T. (2013a) Exploring teachers' positions and practices. In S. Dymoke, A. Lambirth and A. Wilson (eds) *Making Poetry Matter: International Research on Poetry Pedagogy*. London: Bloomsbury, pp. 9–19.

Chapter 1

Introduction

Setting the context

Teresa Cremin

For teachers working in accountability cultures, the development of children's engagement as readers and their pleasure in reading is too often seen as an optional extra in education; a desirable goal, not a core professional responsibility. Expected to foreground the teaching of reading skills (in particular phonics instruction) and concerned to raise reading standards, some primary teachers set aside little space and time in the curriculum to foster children's enjoyment in reading. Some confine this to the margins of the school day or frame it within periods of silent reading when children are expected to read (and enjoy) the books assigned to them. Some practitioners also view reading as a solitary practice and commonly associate reading for pleasure with keen and able readers devouring fiction at home and at school.

Yet other professionals, working in schools which recognise the value of developing readers who not only can but do choose to read independently, afford a higher profile to fostering children's (and teachers') pleasurable engagement as readers. In such schools, nurturing positive attitudes to reading and the affective engagement of all readers is profiled, and what is recognised and validated as reading is likely to be broadened as teachers seek to build upon children's everyday reading lives. Nonetheless, creating an effective balance between reading instruction and reading for pleasure is neither simple nor straightforward. International evidence from the Programme for International Student Assessment (PISA) shows ongoing deterioration in young people's enjoyment of reading (OECD, 2009). In England and Scotland, for example, in the 2006 Progress in International Reading Literacy Study (PIRLS), both countries experienced a significant decrease in the number of 11 year olds who expressed highly positive attitudes towards reading and a reduction in the number of children reading stories or novels outside school daily (Twist *et al.*, 2007). Although in the 2011 PIRLS, reading enjoyment and motivation had improved, in England, a fifth reported that they did not like reading (Twist *et al.*, 2012) and a UK survey showed attitudes to reading were more negative (Clark, 2013).

Additionally, the gender gap continues to widen, and book ownership in children and young people has fallen (OECD, 2010; Clarke and Douglas, 2011). This represents cause for concern and a significant challenge for the profession. Indeed, PISA concludes:

> Being a frequent reader is more of an advantage than having well educated parents and finding ways to engage students in reading may be one of the most effective ways to leverage social change.
>
> (OECD, 2002: 3)

In response to this complex context and informally expressed concerns about teachers' knowledge of children's literature, the United Kingdom Literacy Association (UKLA) undertook two studies upon which this book is based:

- Phase I, *Teachers as Readers* (2006–7): A survey of 1,200 teachers' knowledge and use of children's literature and their personal practices, preferences and habits as readers.
- Phase II, *Teachers as Readers: Building Communities of Readers* (2007–8): A project with 43 teachers seeking to develop their knowledge and use of children's literature and other texts and build communities of readers in school.

The UKLA Phase I survey *Teachers as Readers* drew on questionnaires from 1,200 primary teachers from 11 local authorities; none was a literacy coordinator in their school. The survey showed that the majority were committed readers, readers who made time for their own independent reading and found pleasure and satisfaction in so doing. However, it also revealed that the teachers relied upon a very limited canon of children's authors, and in particular, knew only a narrow range of picture fiction creators and contemporary poets writing for children (Cremin *et al.*, 2008a, b).

These findings, which received considerable media and policy interest, raised the question of whether primary-phase teachers are familiar with a sufficiently diverse range of writers to enable them to foster reader development and make recommendations to readers with different needs and interests (Cremin *et al.*, 2008a). Placed alongside the documented decline in reading for pleasure and the reduction in primary-phase book spending (Hurd *et al.*, 2006), this lack of teacher knowledge of children's literature revealed the need for improved professional development and support in this area.

The UKLA Phase II project *Teachers as Readers: Building Communities of Readers* (undertaken in the National Year of Reading 2007–8), responding to the Phase I findings, involved 43 primary teachers from 27 schools in 5 local authorities (LAs) in the research, supported by 5 LA coordinators. The project aimed to improve teachers' knowledge and use of literature in order to help them increase children's motivation and enthusiasm for reading, especially those less successful in literacy (Cremin *et al.*, 2008c, d, 2009a). In focusing on pleasure in reading literature and other texts, the project provided a potent alternative to the dominant discourse about literacy in primary education, namely the standards agenda. This agenda, prevalent in accountability cultures of most Western countries, foregrounds attainment as measured by national tests. It has been shown to lead to narrowed curricula, more limited classroom practice and a sense of professional disempowerment (Assaf, 2008; English *et al.*, 2002). Ironically, although the Phase II work did not focus on standards, one of the effects of the project was to improve children's performance as readers, as well as improving their attitudes to and engagement in reading.

Viewing reading from a socio-cultural perspective, as a social practice in which meaning is tied to the events in which it occurs (Barton *et al.*, 2000), the research team were aware that what is absent from the PISA and PIRLS (and missing in the Phase I survey) is any evidence from actual classrooms, teachers' applied use of literature and teachers' and children's interactions around reading. As a consequence, the team planned that the Phase II work would include case studying a group of 16 teachers from 10 of the 27 schools across the project year. Classroom observations and interviews with children, teachers and headteachers enabled a richer picture of the lived experience of readers in classrooms to be developed (see Chapter 3).

In addressing teachers' knowledge of and pleasure in children's literature and other texts, the project deviated from the more usual concerns regarding teachers' linguistic knowledge and instructional practices related to teaching children to read. In foregrounding teachers' experience of texts and their pleasure in them, the project also ensured commitment to a richer conception of reading and literacy education and highlighted a potential dynamic between teachers and children as readers. It identified a multi-layered Reading for Pleasure Pedagogy, and subtle, but significant distinctions between reading instruction and reading for pleasure (Cremin et al., 2008c, d, 2009a). These distinctions and the interplay between children's desire to read and their capacity as readers – the will and the skill – were central to the project and are examined through the book. Additional insights identified through the Phase II research, include the following: that reading and talk are mutually supportive learning experiences; that reading urgently needs reconceptualising in the twenty-first century; that reading for pleasure is strongly influenced by relationships between teachers, teachers and children, children and families, and children, teachers, families and communities; and that a reading for pleasure agenda can be developed effectively through the creation of classroom reading communities of reciprocity and interaction. Such communities are most effectively led by 'Reading Teachers – teachers who read and readers who teach' (Commeyras et al., 2003: 4). These professionals appear to recognise the significance of reader identity in reader development and frame their practice in responsive ways, encouraging interaction, choice, autonomy and increased reading for pleasure.

Arguably, this UKLA research focused on reader engagement and reading for pleasure has contributed to policy and practice in England. The team presented Phase I and II findings at DCSF policy seminars, to the DCSF English Board, to the Primary National Strategy (PNS) Regional Consultants and to conferences of Initial Teacher Educators run by the PNS in both 2008 and 2009. A National College for School Leadership E-discussion on reading for pleasure in 2011 was also prompted by the project and led by a member of the team. In addition, there has been considerable interest by national organisations, local authorities and schools, with presentations made at over 50 professional and academic conferences. Both phases of the research are extensively quoted in the All-Party Parliamentary Literacy Group's Boys' Reading Commission, compiled by the National Literacy Trust (APPLG, 2012) and in the Education Standards Research Team's Review of Research on Reading for Pleasure (ESARD, 2012). The work is also afforded attention in Ofsted's Poetry in Schools: A Survey of Practice (Ofsted, 2007) and Excellence in English (Ofsted, 2011). It could thus be argued that the research has served to influence the current government's position on wider reading and contributed to the high profile afforded reading for pleasure in the current National Curriculum (DfE, 2013), which for the first time in history recognises the pleasure offered by reading within its core aim:

> The overarching aim for English in the National Curriculum is to promote high standards of literacy by equipping pupils with a strong command of the written and spoken word, and to develop their love of literature through widespread reading for enjoyment.
>
> (DfE, 2013: 13)

This book seeks to continue to influence the reading agenda by documenting both phases of this influential UKLA work in order to reveal to teachers, student teachers, advisers and policy-makers, both the underpinning theoretical argument and a range of research-informed strategies and practical classroom approaches that effectively build reciprocal reading communities of engaged readers within and beyond the classroom.

Chapter 2

Reading for pleasure and reader engagement
Reviewing the research

Teresa Cremin

Do children in the early twenty-first century choose to read for pleasure at home and in school? If so, what are they reading and how frequently? Are they reading for themselves, for their own personal satisfaction or to please their teachers or parents? Perhaps they are merely reading to succeed in their country's assessment system? Additionally, what influences their engagement as readers? What impacts upon their desire to read or lack of it? And what, if any, are the benefits?

This chapter seeks to respond to these and other pressing questions. It examines the extent to which reader engagement and reading for pleasure represent cause for concern internationally, with particular reference to England, the site of the research projects upon which this book is based. The chapter commences by exploring the concept of reading for pleasure, and the evidence regarding the benefits to young people's cognitive, social and emotional development, then reviews a range of studies which document children and young people's engagement as independent readers. The significance of intrinsic and extrinsic motivation, the diversity of children's twenty-first century reading, gender differences, the role of choice, the impact of book ownership and parental involvement are all considered as influential factors, alongside consideration of school provision and practice. It is argued that the profession needs to pay more attention to children's attitudes, their preferences, pleasures and practices and their perceptions of themselves as readers in order to help ensure that they develop as readers who not only can, but *do* choose to read, for pleasure and for life.

Exploring the terms 'reading for pleasure' and 'reader engagement'

The term 'reading for pleasure' is often used interchangeably with the term 'reading for enjoyment'. Such reading can involve any kind of text – novel, magazine, comic, non-fiction – in electronic as well as in printed form. It can take place anywhere – at home, at school, in the community, on a bus (or any other form of transport), on a beach, in the park (or any other leisure location). It is often characterised as a personal solitary experience conducted in privacy, yet even when readers read alone, the act of reading remains profoundly social. At the core of reading for pleasure is the reader's volition, their agency and desire to read, their anticipation of the satisfaction gained through the experience and/ or afterwards in interaction with others. In the USA, such reading is often described as 'free voluntary reading' or 'independent reading', capturing the reader's sense of agency and choice (Krashen, 2004). It has also been described as 'recreational reading' (Ross *et al.*,

2006), reading undertaken for the personal satisfaction of the reader, in their own free time. The National Literacy Trust (NLT) in the UK, recognising that such reading is underpinned by the free will of the reader, further suggests it can encompass reading which, whilst it began at someone else's request, is sustained by the reader, in response to their interest (Clark and Rumbold, 2006).

Reading engagement is often associated with reading for pleasure: arguably, engaged readers are those who want to read, who choose to read and who find satisfaction in the process. Additionally, engaged readers tend to display positive attitudes to reading and are interested in it. Motivated to read on, to turn the page or open up new screens, engaged readers make time to read and read widely with the purposeful intention of making meaning which further supports their developing reading habit. The US study by Ross *et al.* (2006) highlights that the experience of reading is in and of itself a motivator, prompting readers to return in search of more. As Sanacore observes, when individuals read for pleasure frequently, they 'experience the value of reading for efferent and aesthetic processes, thus, they are more likely to read with a sense of purpose' (2002: 68). The PISA international survey (see next section) makes use of the term 'reader engagement', framing it as a complex variable that encompasses elements such as frequency of leisure reading, attitudes and interest in reading, and 'depth' (measured by the comprehension strategies that the 15 year olds report using) as well as diversity of reading (Marks, 2000). Other self-report surveys make use of single elements to define reading engagement, including, for example, behavioural engagement, emotional engagement and cognitive engagement (Fredricks *et al.*, 2004), these are sometimes accompanied by teachers' observations and assessments (Lutz *et al.*, 2006). Ellis and Coddington (2013: 228) argue that reading engagement is 'a meta-construct that crosses research disciplines and is studied in the context of schools and schooling, but also in out-of-school contexts such as families and the workplace'.

Engaged readers tend to be focused on finding, making and thinking about meaning. A purposeful activity, reading is related to the human need to make sense of the world, the desire to understand, to make things work and to make connections. Nell (1988) describes reading for pleasure as a form of ludic play, enabling a temporary escape from everyday life and the possibility of learning through vicarious experience and imaginative engagement, relating this to the human propensity to narratise experience and think through story. In addition to offering enjoyment, literature in particular develops the imagination and supports personal, emotional and cultural development (Cliff Hodges, 2010). In finding textual resonances, whether inter-personal, intra-personal or inter-textual (Smith, 2005), readers make meanings and think and talk about them informally with friends, family, work colleagues and even strangers, conferring over news items or sharing views on a popular novel on a train, for example. Different readers find satisfaction in different ways, through perhaps revisiting childhood favourites, reading magazines, newspapers, travel texts, recipes or Facebook pages, or trying out new and recommended authors and non-fiction. Many will experience pleasure in the affective engagement often involved and, in discussing the themes and issues which arise, others may also find pleasure in the social interaction around it.

In the UKLA Phase II project *Teachers as Readers: Building Communities of Readers*, on which this book draws, the term 'reading for pleasure' was used to refer to the volitional act of reading undertaken by individuals and groups, and by children and adults, and was thus closely associated with reader engagement. The 43 teachers involved, identified three disaffected readers in their classes to case study. These focus children were identified using Moss's (2000) category of 'can but don't' readers, that is, they could read but did not choose to do so; this is in line with the finding that whilst many primary learners in England can read, compared with their peers internationally, they find somewhat less pleasure in reading (Twist *et al.*, 2003, 2007). The project teachers identified children who presented as 'disaffected and reluctant' readers, with mostly negative attitudes to reading; they were unmotivated to use their competence as readers and often sought to avoid engaging in it. However, as discussed in Chapter 9, it was found that some of these children did of their own volition read, but at home, not in school.

An international and national cause for concern

In the early twenty-first century, the results of student performance on international literacy tests such as the Progress in International Reading Literacy Study (PIRLS) and the Programme for International Student Assessment (PISA) are seen as key reference points for policy makers. Students' performance in these assessments is seen as a measure of individual countries' comparative success on a worldwide scale. The PIRLS study is a five-year survey of 10–11 year olds' reading behaviour, attitudes and attainment from over 50 countries and nation states across the world, whilst PISA, an assessment of 15 year olds from almost 70 countries, involves assessment of reading, mathematics and science attainment on a regular basis. PIRLS has two strands, a paper-based individual comprehension exercise (focusing on literary reading and reading for information) and questionnaires for children, their parents and teachers on young people's wider experience of literacy. These include questions such as whether and how often they 'read for fun' (books and other texts) outside school, and the number of books at home. Statistical analyses of the two strands relate individual's test scores to the questionnaire data (Trong and Kennedy, 2007). Layered upon pre-existing national assessment systems, which many researchers perceive constrain quality professional practice (e.g. Goodwyn *et al.*, 2014), PIRLS may also serve to constrain what counts as reading. As Maybin (2013) observes, this large-scale international study is unable to include any documentation of what children actually do with texts, their interactions around reading, whether at home or at school. Arguably, reading seen through the lens of such large-scale surveys is framed more as a measurable result than a lived experience and a process. The complex factors which interact to develop young readers and the myriad of elements which characterise the experience tend to be ignored in such work. Such studies inevitably emphasise numerical reading scores and measurable data regarding young people's self-reports on multiple factors within the survey's options. Nonetheless, alongside PISA data, PIRLS results can afford insights about the role of reading in the lives of children and young people and can record shifts over time with regard to commonly used measures.

Over the last decade, international evidence from PIRLS and PISA tends to suggest that: the gender gap has not significantly altered; girls continue to outperform boys in reading achievement; and a worrying number of young people report that they do not like reading (Mullis *et al.* 2012; OECD, 2010). PISA data in particular show a decline in both enjoyment and frequency of reading for pleasure among the young, especially boys (OECD, 2010). European analyses of PISA results confirm a decline in reading engagement over the past decade; from 68 per cent of students in 2000 to 63 per cent in 2009 (Eurydice, 2011). In England, for example, 13 per cent of the children in the 2002 PIRLS study disliked reading compared with an international average of 6 per cent (Twist *et al.*, 2003). In the 2006 PIRLS study, a sharp drop in reading attainment accompanied a further decline in terms of attitudes; 15 per cent of English children had unfavourable attitudes to reading, and England was ranked thirty-seventh out of the 45 countries/provinces in terms of attitudes (Twist *et al.*, 2007). Additionally, 42 per cent reported that they rarely read literature for pleasure, a figure more than a third higher than the international average (Twist *et al.*, 2007). In the 2011 PIRLS study, whilst enjoyment in and motivation for reading had improved slightly in England, 20 per cent of the English children responded that they did not like reading, compared with an international average of 15 per cent (Twist *et al.*, 2012).

These results are largely in line with PISA data, which in 2000 showed that in relation to 'engagement in reading' England ranked twentieth of 27 OECD countries involved (OECD, 2002). In this study, engagement included reading for pleasure, reading widely and attitudes to reading. Nearly 30 per cent of English 15 year olds reported that they never or hardly ever read for pleasure, 19 per cent felt it was a waste of time and 35 per cent said they would only read if they were obliged to do so. This was despite high average scores in terms of attainment (OECD, 2002). In the 2009 PISA study, deterioration in enjoyment of reading was again notable compared with the OECD average. British teenagers read for pleasure much less than their peers in other countries and an increasing number report never reading for pleasure and feeling that it is a waste of time (OECD, 2010).

These large-scale comparative research studies are mirrored by UK research, affirming evidence of a decline in reading for pleasure in England. For example, in the Nestlé Family Monitor research (2003), whilst most of the 11–18 year olds reported reading books in their spare time, a third said they had better things to do than read books and a quarter suggested that they would be disappointed if someone gave them book. Comparative work by Sainsbury and Schagen (2004) showed a fall in children's attitudes to reading between 1998 and 2003: although the majority of children in this study still reported enjoying reading stories, their desire to do so had markedly decreased across this period. This was seen to be related to the introduction of the National Literacy Strategy (DfEE, 1998), although the complexity of the issue in the context of rapid technological advances and the changing nature of childhood, homework expectations and leisure activities is acknowledged. A number of other UK-based studies have also shown attitudes to reading declining with age, alongside young people's interest in choosing to read (e.g. Clark *et al.*, 2005; Maynard *et al.*, 2007; Clark, 2011; Clark, 2013).

The National Literacy Trust's annual UK surveys of young people's reading suggest that reading for pleasure is being side-lined by other activities (Clark, 2011, 2012, 2013). The most recent survey undertaken in the autumn of 2012 drew on the voices and views of 34,910 young people from 8 to 17 years in 188 schools. Based on this, Clark (2013) claims that whilst levels of enjoyment in reading remain static or 'stagnate' (with roughly half of those surveyed reporting enjoying reading), compared with previous years, reading has declined and attitudes to reading have become more negative. There was a particularly significant drop in the proportion of 8 to 11 year olds who read for pleasure and who read daily compared with earlier surveys. Over a fifth of children and young people reported rarely or never reading in their own time, and nearly a third agreed with the statement 'I only read when I have to' (Clark, 2013). It is not the case, though, that the young are turning to digital texts; with the exception of text messages, reading across most formats, (including for example magazines, comics, websites and emails) was reported to have fallen between 2005 and 2013 (Clark *et al.*, 2005; Clark, 2013). The UK situation is summarised as follows:

Not only are children and young people reading less and developing more negative attitudes towards reading, but there is also a clear correlation between this and their performance in reading tests.

(Clark, 2013: 8)

The benefits of reading for pleasure and reader engagement

Whilst reading for pleasure is seen as a worthwhile activity in its own terms, it has also been associated, directly and indirectly, with reading attainment. There is considerable international evidence that reading for pleasure (independent choice-led reading) and reading engagement are strong predictors of reading attainment (e.g. Anderson *et al.*, 1988; PIRLS, 2006; OECD, 2002, 2010). A positive relationship between frequency of reading for pleasure and scores on PIRLS literacy tests has been reported (PIRLS, 2006) and endorsed by PISA data (OECD, 2002, 2010). In all three annual NLT surveys, Clark (2011, 2012, 2013) found relationships between reading enjoyment, behaviour and attitudes and reading attainment. In 2012, young people who enjoyed reading very much were four times as likely to read above the expected level for their age compared with their peers who did not enjoy reading at all (Clark, 2013). Whilst claims for causality cannot easily be assigned, Stanovich (1986) posits the presence of the so-called Matthew effect, in that he argues better readers tend to read more because they are more motivated to read, which, in turn, leads to better reading. However, those who do not succeed as quickly, he argues feel neither confident nor capable and tend to read less, thus they practice less, are likely to be less engaged and less positively inclined toward reading. They are more likely to enter a downward spiral and fall behind their more successful peers. The OECD (2010) too asserts that the relationship between reading achievement and positive attitudes to reading is bi-directional.

There is also evidence of reading achievement impacting upon wider academic attainment across the curriculum (e.g. OECD, 2002) and the suggestion that it can diminish the effects of socio- economic status (e.g. OECD, 2002; Topping *et al.*, 2003) and support social mobility (Clark and Rumbold, 2006). Recent longitudinal work endorses this, demonstrating the significant influence of children's engaged leisure reading on test scores in maths, spelling and vocabulary; the researchers found that children who read for pleasure made more progress in these areas (between the ages of 10 and 16 years) than those who rarely chose to read (Sullivan and Brown, 2013). In relation to cognitive development, this work, in alignment with the OECD (2002) indicates that reading for pleasure is more important than parental educational levels. As such, enhancing independent reading it is argued can help raise educational standards. Research also points to a multiplicity of other personal and academic advantages of reading for pleasure, including, for example: improved general knowledge (Cunningham and Stanovich, 1998); increased self-confidence as a reader (Guthrie and Alvermann, 1999); a richer vocabulary and increased accuracy in spelling (Sullivan and Brown, 2013); an improved capacity for comprehension (Cox and Guthrie, 2001); and greater pleasure in reading in later life (Aarnoutse and van Leeuwe, 1998). Furthermore, reading allows young people to gather information about the world and how they fit into it, thus supporting identity explorations, for example: Rothbauer (2004) shows how independent reading can mediate the challenges of understanding and negotiating non-mainstream identities; Appleyard

(1990) reveals the kind of pleasure to be found in finding oneself in the text; Arizpe *et al.* (2014) demonstrate the myriad benefits, personally, culturally and in relation to literacy learning, of immigrant children reading wordless picturebooks; and Schoon *et al.*, (2010) show that high levels of reading engagement in preschool children can help to diminish the impact of language disorders.

In addition and significantly, the experience of reading literature and the deep emotional engagement which can be engendered needs to be more fully acknowledged and explicitly valued as a palpable benefit of independent reading. Children's literature research highlights the particular power of literary texts to help the young as they journey through other worlds, taking on other roles and experiencing engagement with, as well as distance from, the fictional characters they encounter (e.g. Benton and Fox, 1985; Arizpe *et al.*, 2014). This deserves to be acknowledged as an often profound and tangible benefit of reading fiction (Clark and Osborne, 2008; Cliff Hodges, 2010). As Landay and Wootton (2012) show, bringing a literary text to life, either in one's mind or through layered multi-sensory engagement via combinations of drama, artwork, writing, discussion, dancing and singing, not only enables readers to engage in interpretation, but inspires them to want to read, by provoking curiosity about the narrative or poetic content. The experience of 'living through the text' (Rosenblatt, 1978) and engaging affectively and reflectively often connects to children's positive attitudes to reading and the pleasure and satisfaction they find in it (Cliff Hodges, 2010; Hitchcock, 2010; OECD, 2002). Reading literature distinctively excites and develops the imagination, which is one of Alexander's (2010) key aims for the primary curriculum, in order that children can

> advance beyond present understanding, extend the boundaries of their lives, contemplate worlds possible as well as actual, understand cause and consequence, develop the capacity for empathy, and reflect on and regulate their behaviour... [W]e assert the need to emphasise the intrinsic value of exciting children's imagination. To experience the delights – and pains – of imagining, and of entering into the imaginative world of others, is to become a more rounded person.
> (Alexander, 2010: 199, quoted in Cliff Hodges, 2010)

This statement, as Cliff Hodges (2010) observes, could equally apply to reading literature, which many would argue is itself a key creative skill and one which can support children's personal, social and moral education, and can strengthen, challenge or alter the ways in which they see the world and engage with it (e.g. Landay and Wootton, 2012; Ross *et al.*, 2006). Additionally, recent US research suggests that high-quality literary fiction that requires intellectual engagement and creative thought enables young readers to develop the complex social skill of 'mind-reading' in order to understand others' mental states (Comer Kidd and Castano, 2013). Such empathy and mindfulness of others is a valuable personal and social asset. The Phase II project documented in this book also highlights the power of fiction to foster empathy and create bonds between readers.

Additionally, reading is linked to writing, as through independent reading, young people absorb a range of models for writing (Barrs and Cork, 2001; Corden, 2003; Cremin and Myhill, 2012) and develop a wider vocabulary, as well as more secure spelling habits (Sullivan and Brown, 2013). There are also, Clark (2013) asserts, robust links between reading and writing in relation to enjoyment, attitudes and behaviour. The last NLT survey not only confirmed an expected link between high achievers in reading and writing, but also a relationship between reading and writing frequency and revealed that young people who enjoy reading, tend also to enjoy writing (Clark, 2013).

Children's reading practices in the twenty-first century

Over the last decade the nature and form of what children can choose to read has altered radically, partly as a consequence of rapid technological advances and the increasing ascendancy of the image. Children take their multi-media world for granted, as from birth they are surrounded by multi-modal texts that combine images, words and sound, voices, intonation, stance, gesture and movement, as well as print on screen and on paper. Such texts, Bearne argues 'have changed the ways in which young people expect to read, the ways they think and the ways they construct meaning' (2003: 98). A great deal of what children choose to read in their leisure time beyond the school gates is not book based; for example, in the UK comics/comic books and newspapers were popular in 2007 (Twist *et al.*, 2007), whilst in 2011, text messages, magazines, websites and emails were found to be the most popular choices, with fiction being read outside school by 40 per cent of those surveyed (Clark and Douglas, 2011).

Fears and assumptions about the influence of popular cultural texts and TV competing with book reading remain. The UKLA Reading on Screen research (UKLA/QCA, 2007) showed a higher preference for multimodal screen-based texts over those composed mainly of words in relation to leisure reading, although there was no lack of interest in sustained book reading at home; the children surveyed appeared to be aware that they could gain different reading satisfactions from different types of text. Additionally, these data, alongside the evidence presented by Mackey (2002), suggest that reading on screen often boosts the reading of paper-based texts, with frequent indications of crossovers or links between screen texts and written texts. Online multimedia spin-offs from conventional fiction texts can support rather than undermine the extended reading of the original, since different forms of reading such as magazines, computer games, online material and fiction feed off each other. 'Reading for pleasure should be seen as part of a whole "pattern of entertainment" which supports and is supported by other media' (Hitchcock, 2010: 14–15). Research has also shown that the processes involved in reading print and TV have similarities as well as differences (Robinson and Mackey, 2003), that children's reading skills can be developed through reading film and that moving image texts can enhance learners' motivation to engage in print related texts (Marsh, 2000). This raises the question of how such reading for pleasure can be successfully resourced and supported in school.

The challenge for teachers is to find out about and capitalise on children's self-chosen informal everyday reading practices, practices they choose to undertake of their own volition for the pleasure and satisfaction they offer. In the project *Teachers as Readers: Building Communities of Readers*, teachers sought to do just this (see Chapters 4 and 6 for more details).

Gender differences

Internationally, girls remain more likely to report reading for pleasure than boys (OECD, 2010). This trend has also been documented in the UK (e.g. Nestlé Family Monitor, 2003; Clark and Douglas, 2011; Clark and Foster, 2005; Clark and Osborne, 2008;

Maynard *et al.*, 2007; Clark, 2013). In both the most recent NLT surveys (Clark, 2012, 2013), nearly twice as many boys as girls report not enjoying reading at all and never reading outside of class. Although Clark (2013) suggests the gender gap may be beginning to narrow slightly, widespread gender differences in reading persist into adulthood, with males being less likely to read than females (EU, 2012). When teenage boys do read for enjoyment, PISA data indicate that they tend to read newspapers or comics, whereas girls are more likely to read fiction or magazines (OECD, 2010). Topping's (2010) UK data, from young people aged 5 to 16 in 664 schools, found that boys tended to read easier books than girls in the same year. Moss's (2003) earlier work in England suggested that when boys read, they tend to read fiction, but, in order not to be perceived as struggling readers, status-conscious low-attaining boy readers may select non-fiction texts as these are not as readily associated with reading levels or abilities and may enable them to take part in reading networks and conversations by reading small chunks. However, such reading, as Moss (2003) notes, may not be as influential on reading attainment and reading engagement in the longer term.

Research also suggests that boys' motivation to read is generally lower than girls (Baker and Wigfield, 1999). This connects to attainment, with PISA 2002 showing girls had more positive attitudes, read more often and outperformed teenage boys in reading (OECD, 2002). More recently, the PISA 2009 results show that boys are the equivalent of one year's schooling behind girls (OECD, 2010). Lafontaine and Monseur (2009) argue part of the difference may be related to the PISA test characteristics as boys show lower scores in test items requiring written answers to open-ended questions. Motivation and engagement are key to understanding the gender gap. Research shows there is a closer reciprocal relationship between intrinsic motivation, competency beliefs and reading skill with boys than there is with girls (Logan and Medford, 2011). This study suggests that either boys' motivation and self-belief about their abilities as readers are more dependent on their success as readers or that boys' lower motivation and less assured self-beliefs about their competence as readers influence the effort they put into reading, thus holding them back.

This is a complex issue and likely to relate, amongst other factors, to boys' conceptions of reading, the choices they are offered and the gap between self-selected reading materials and those validated by teachers in schools (Moss, 2000). All young readers deserve to encounter texts which are relevant, interesting and personally engaging, such that they are intrigued and inspired; motivated to read of their own free will. But the gap between the texts affirmed as appropriate reading material by teachers and the range of texts accessed by boys elsewhere may well be growing. Nonetheless there are a number of strategies which teachers can employ in order to motivate boys (e.g. Younger and Warrington, 2005; APPLG, 2012; Guthrie *et al.*, 2006). Many of these relate to enhancing engagement through connecting to boys' individual interests, offering more choice in reading material, more male reader role models, stronger home–school links and making reading more interactive and fun. Many of these strategies will benefit both boys and girls. As the All-Party Parliamentary Literacy Group assert in the recent Boys' Reading Commission in England:

> A refreshed commitment in schools to promoting reading for enjoyment will strongly benefit boys, who want to read around their interests. To enable this to happen reading for pleasure needs to be an integral element in a school's teaching and learning strategy and teachers need to be supported in their knowledge of

relevant quality texts that will engage all pupils. There is a specific danger that a predominantly female workforce will unconsciously privilege texts that are more attractive to girls.

(APPLG, 2012: 4)

In the Phase II project, through widening their own repertoires of children's texts, transforming what counts as reading in school, and connecting to peer group cultures in the classroom, as well as developing a Reading for Pleasure Pedagogy, the project teachers gradually altered the attitudes of young male readers. Over time the focus group boys and others boys in their classes began to find more pleasure in reading.

Motivation

Those who read for pleasure exercise their own independent judgement about what they want to read and about the kind of readers they are/wish to become. Such readers are also often purposeful in their endeavours, and read in anticipation of some form of satisfaction. As the EU Expert Panel on Literacy recognise:

> The emphasis should be not just on reading well, but also on reading for pleasure, as one supports the other. Children should be given free time for pleasure reading for relaxation and escape .... In this process, intrinsic motivation is key – reading for its own sake rather than for reading other rewards.

(EU, 2012: 68)

Intrinsic motivation, which Sainsbury and Schagen (2004: 374) suggest encompasses a positive self-concept, a desire and tendency to read and a reported enjoyment of an interest in reading, is crucial. Readers who are intrinsically motivated are more likely to be reading for their own pleasure and satisfaction. Research suggests these readers may be reading more widely and more frequently and enjoying their reading more (Cox and Guthrie, 2001) and that such highly engaged readers who are interested in the text and are confident in their capacity as readers are more likely to persevere when they encounter more challenging texts (Schunk, 2003). The aspects of intrinsic motivation identified by Wigfield and Guthrie (1997) which, according to their study, predicts both reading breadth and comprehension, include importance, curiosity, involvement and a preference for challenge. It would appear then that keen independent readers believe reading is a worthwhile activity and continue to challenge themselves, reinforcing and developing their competence as readers in the process (for a more extended examination of reading motivation see Guthrie and Wigfield, 2000). Extrinsic motivation, by contrast, involves reading for recognition, reading for grades and for competition (Wigfield and Guthrie, 1997). Studies have found that the greater the emphasis placed on performance and grades, the less students are motivated to read (Guthrie and Davis, 2003) and that extrinsic motivation has a detrimental effect on reading comprehension (Schaffner et al., 2013).

Whilst reading for pleasure is more closely related to intrinsic than extrinsic motivation, as Clark and Rumbold (2006) note, the relationship between intrinsic and extrinsic motivation is not straightforward or a simple 'good versus evil' scenario, since children may well be motivated by both intrinsic and extrinsic aspects; they may read for their own pleasure and be obliged to (and derive some satisfaction from) reading for others' purposes (Lepper and Henderlong, 2000) and constructive teacher feedback, for example, can be a valuable extrinsic motivator (Wang and Holcombe, 2010). However, excessive extrinsic motivation and pressure to perform may drown a child's intrinsic desire to read. As Bernard Ashley, the author, observes 'because children have to sweat so much over books, reading for recreation for some is like going for a leisure swim in their own dirty bathwater' (2003: 4).

Low achievers often have limited intrinsic motivation to read and indifferent or negative attitudes towards reading; they may see reading as a chore. For struggling readers, one of the most demotivating factors is a lack of interest in the available reading material, so acknowledging textual diversity and enriched access, as noted earlier, is essential. As the EU Expert Panel on Literacy recognise, low achievement may reduce children's desire to read and lead to disengagement which further lowers their achievements and self-efficacy – a vicious circle – often compounded by sustained experience of perceived 'failure' and a lack of self-efficacy as a reader (Ivey and Guthrie, 2008). In Meek's (1991) words, 'poor inexperienced readers' have not yet found 'what reading is good for'. Moreover, since motivation to read appears to decrease with age (Clark and Osborne, 2008), ensuring commitment in the primary years is important.

Unmotivated, disaffected readers fail to benefit from reading teaching (Guthrie and Wigfield, 2000), so teachers need to plan to foster learner engagement and motivation, recognising the social, emotional and cultural dimensions of being a reader and finding out about the interests and preferences of the young. Children report that they would read more if only they enjoyed it more, if they had more time and if books were cheaper or about subjects they were interested in (Clark and Foster, 2005). Readers deserve to encounter texts which have particular salience for them, as caught in a web of fiction or in widening their knowledge of a favourite team for example, they become motivated to renew this rewarding experience. The affective dimension is seen by children as a vital motivator (Dungworth et al., 2004), a view which some adults also affirm (e.g. Spufford, 2002). This was demonstrated in the Phase II project (Cremin et al., 2009a), although in other research, young people additionally report that they read for reasons to do with learning and understanding (Nestlé Family Monitor, 2003; Clark and Foster, 2005).

Parental involvement

The impact of the home environment and parental involvement in their children's reading is widely accepted as influential on reading performance (OECD, 2010). Parental involvement is seen as a more potent force than other family background variables, such as social class, family size and level of parental education (Flouri and Buchanan, 2004). The beliefs held by children's parents about the purposes of reading and how children learn to read can shape children's motivation to read. For example, parents who believe that reading is a rich source of entertainment have children with more positive views about reading than parents who only emphasise the skills involved (Sonnenschein et al., 2000), and children whose parents view reading as a source of pleasure are more motivated than those whose parents hold less positive views (Baker and Scher, 2002). Worryingly, over a quarter of the nearly 35,000 8–16 year olds surveyed in the UK in 2012 reported that their parents did not care whether they spend any time reading (Clark, 2013).

However, research reveals that there is marked heterogeneity across the body of parents and that, within different ethnic and class groups, parents may have very different understandings/perceptions of the nature of reading and use it differently in their own lives. The work of Gregory and Williams (2000) for example, drawing on detailed ethnographic data collected in multi-ethnic communities in London, has shown the wealth of literacy practices and reading-related activities in the lives of those often considered by the establishment to be 'deprived' of literacy. This work also revealed the breadth of formal learning and reading experienced outside school by children in multilingual families, as well as the range of 'unofficial' reading matter found in monolingual families. It is clear that traffic between home and school is persistently one way, with reading materials moving from school to home (Marsh, 2003b). Also schools tend to have very stereotypical expectations of parents, expecting them to induct their children into school reading practices, and rarely attending to the assets that all children bring to school in their 'virtual school bags' (Thomson, 2002).

Parents and the home environment support both the early teaching of reading and the development of a love of reading, not only through book sharing and space for relationship building, but also through the use of books in playful activities(EU, 2012), and research suggests many parents want to be involved (Peters *et al.*, 2007). In this study, the desire to get more involved tended to be stronger amongst disadvantaged parent groups (e.g. those in lower social grades, ethnic minorities, respondents with a long-term illness or disability). As the authors suggest, more work is needed to understand how to involve parents and any barriers to involvement (Peters *et al.*, 2007).

Other evidence suggests that children are more likely to sustain their engagement as readers in homes where books are present and reading is valued (Baker and Scher, 2002), confirming the view of reading as a highly social activity that begins in the home (Holden, 2004). In the USA, one study showed that owning books influences children's expectations and experience of reading, as well as their preparedness to engage in reading (Allington *et al.*, 2010), and in a not unrelated manner, a UK survey showed that young people who had books of their own were twice as likely to report reading daily, whereas those without books of their own were more likely to say they never read (Clark and Douglas, 2011). In this study, 80 per cent of children who read above the expected level for their age had books of their own. Clark, *et al.* (2011) also found that the young people in their survey who had never received a book as present (19 per cent) were more likely to read below the expected level. More worryingly still, Clark's 2011 survey suggests that 3 per cent of UK children do not have any books in the home. Furthermore, international research indicates a relationship between book ownership and reading attainment: in the USA, through meta-analysis of 108 studies, Lindsay (2010) found that access to print material improves children's performance, encouraging them to read more and for longer, and in a longitudinal study across 27 countries, Evans *et al.* (2010) also found that having books in the home is as influential on a child's attainment as the education level of their parents.

To help ensure that reading becomes a lifelong habit, children need to see themselves as members of communities that view reading as a significant and enjoyable activity. It is therefore important that parents and teachers work together and are joined by librarians in order to understand the role of reading in children's everyday literacy lives. Libraries and the expertise of children's librarians can make a significant contribution to children being able to read independently and pursue their reading preferences (Ross *et al.*, 2006; Goodwin, 2011). Librarians, like teachers and parents can offer rich models to children and show what it is like to get pleasure from reading, though this can be problematic in the context of continued cuts to library provision.

School provision and practice

School provision and practice varies, but in countries where a narrow assessment of reading skills is foregrounded, children's free-choice reading is likely to be side-lined. From the inception of the National Literacy Strategy (NLS) in England in 1998 (DfEE), in which there was no specific mention of reading for pleasure, scholars predicted that children's independent reading would take a step backwards (Meek, 1998; Dombey, 1998; Furlong 1998; Burgess-Macey, 1999). As noted earlier, research across the following years that recorded a decline in voluntary reading affirms the accuracy of their prophecies. Additionally, classroom-based studies have documented a high degree of fragmentation of the reading experience in school, in part through the use of decontextualised text extracts, a lack of meaningful interaction in shared reading (Burns and Myhill, 2004), reduced opportunities to enjoy texts at length (Gamble, 2000; Fisher, 2005), a reduction in spending on books by schools (Hurd *et al.*, 2006) and a focus on text analysis and skills at the expense of pleasure and engagement (Frater, 2000; Cremin *et al.*, 2007; Lockwood, 2008).

Additionally, a narrow conceptualisation of reading and literacy underpins the curricula of many countries, including England. This views literacy as a set of cognitive skills owned by individuals, and as separable from both the text and the context in which a particular book, magazine or blog is being read, shared and potentially enjoyed. This 'autonomous' model of literacy (Street, 1984, 2008) has become popular with educational regimes driven by market-based notions of accountability. Such a model fails to take account of difference, of different learners, different texts, and different contexts. An alternative view of literacy is that it is richly embedded in social and cultural practice. Street's (1994) 'ideological model' emphasises the varied, situated and contingent nature of literate activity. This reveals that what constitutes reading will vary, depending on the institutional, social and cultural contexts in which reading 'events' occur (Barton and Hamilton, 1998). Such a model, which was adopted by the research team in the Phase II project, recognises difference and diversity and affords attention to learners' everyday reading practices and preferences.

Many studies show that when children select texts for themselves in school, this enhances their motivation and self-determination as readers (Krashen, 1993; Sanacore, 1999; Gambrell, 1996). Agency, interest and motivation are critical in fostering reading for pleasure, but those who struggle or who are less fluent are often given less autonomy as learners in school (Lupton and Hempel-Jorgansen, 2012) and less choice as readers (Schraw *et al.*, 1998). As a consequence they are less likely to find reading rewarding and may seek to avoid reading activities, perpetuating their sense of failure. Such children not only need support that enhances their motivation, engagement and self-esteem, they also need to be supported in making choices; indeed, Ross *et al.* (2006) argue that being able to choose successfully is an important skill that is never directly taught in school, but is learned through the experience of success fostered by early confidence.

Other research also confirms that choice, interest and reader engagement are closely connected (Clark and Phythian-Sence, 2008; Manzo and Manzo, 1995). Children are more likely to want to read material which connects to their personal interests, and may as a result discover what reading can offer them as individuals. To support children's engagement in reading, arguably therefore teachers need to know about them as individuals, and need to know about and be interested in what they are reading. In a UK study, Moss and McDonald (2004), through analysing school library borrowing, showed that reading networks (shown by the practice of friends borrowing the same titles at the same time or in close proximity), developed differently across two classes. One teacher afforded the children time and space to choose what they wished to read and showed interest in them as readers; the other teacher, in an effort to ensure breadth and maintain quantity, monitored the children's reading choices very closely. In the former's classroom, rich reader networks and positive reader identities developed; in the latter's, there was limited evidence of such networks, and Moss and McDonald (2004) suggest the children read because they were required to do so, not because they chose to.

However, to support reading engagement and enhance reading for pleasure, teachers not only need to know the child readers in their class (and what they like to read outside school), they also need to know a wide range of children's literature to read to and recommend to the young readers. The Phase I survey of teachers' repertoires of children's literature suggests that such knowledge may well be lacking (Cremin *et al.*, 2008a, b) (see Chapter 4). Additionally, professionals need to consider their own conceptualisation of reading and what counts as reading in school and question whether an implicit hierarchy of reading materials exists in their classroom. Through their involvement in the Phase II study, many teachers came to examine these issues (Cremin *et al.*, 2009a, Cremin, 2010a) and made significant changes in their practice as a consequence (see Chapters 6 and 7).

Where the diversity of children's home practices is under-recognised (Marsh, 2003a), their favourite reading materials are often unavailable in school (Clark and Osborne, 2008), and there appears to be a distinction between the reading matter that is enjoyed in the home and that which is sanctioned in school (Gregory and Williams, 2000; Hopper, 2005). In tending to reify the 'residual tradition' of fairy tales and approved or significant authors in schools, Luke (1988) argues that teachers fail to recognise 'the emergent alternate tradition' and as a consequence reduce the relevance and interest of much of the reading material presented to young learners. In England, whilst the new National Curriculum (DfE, 2013) recognises a need to promote reading for pleasure, digital and multimodal texts are not mentioned, yet these are an integral part of young people's reading diets. The emphasis on print texts (and by implication books) is likely to hold back the development of wider reading repertoires and further reduce the potential for pleasurable engagement in reading. As the EU Expert Panel on Literacy state:

> There should not be a hierarchical ranking of reading material. Books, comic books, newspapers, magazines and online reading materials are equally valid and important entry points to reading for children and adults alike. … Books and other printed texts are important. But in recognition of the digital opportunities, people should be encouraged to read what they enjoy reading, in whatever format is most pleasurable and convenient for them.
>
> (EU, 2012: 42)

Research regarding what children read in school and at home and the associations between different kinds of reading and reading attainment appears to offer contradictory messages. For example, it has been shown that regularly reading stories or novels outside school is associated with higher scores in assessments (PIRLS, 2006; OECD, 2010) and that compared with instruction in basic decoding and comprehension, reading and responding critically to literary texts leads to enhanced educational outcomes (Darling-Hammond, 2011). Furthermore, work in the UK indicates that young people who read above the expected level for their age read more of the traditional forms of reading, such as fiction, non-fiction, poems and plays, compared with those who are reading below the expected level for their age (Clark and Douglas, 2011). However, recent results from PISA suggest that, although compared with not reading for enjoyment at all, reading fiction for enjoyment appears to be positively associated with higher scores, it is the young people who read a wide variety of material who perform particularly well in reading assessments (OECD, 2010). Nonetheless, of these 'deep and wide' readers who perform highly, over 99 per cent report reading fiction several times a month or more, 53 per cent report reading non-fiction just as regularly (OECD, 2010: 55). Whilst the breadth of these readers' practices is evident, the markedly strong emphasis on literature deserves recognition, arguably such reading serves young people well, both as readers and as learners. This suggests that whilst recognition of diversity is important, a high profile for literature in school is needed to ensure young people are introduced to a wide range of literary texts which engage them, prompting them to try new authors and more challenging narratives and poetry. This is only possible however, if professionals keep up to date with contemporary writing for young people and have rich repertoires of literature on which to draw.

Conclusion

The accumulating evidence indicates that increased attention should be paid to reading for pleasure and reader engagement in schools. However, particularly in accountability cultures the dominant discourse is one of reading attainment alone. Few countries appear to recognise that their scores in PIRLS or PISA in relation to reading attitudes and engagement are likely to relate to the predominant educational focus in schools on basic reading levels, sounds, blends, fluency and comprehension. Few countries appear to acknowledge the potential potency of enhancing children's independent reading, their pleasure in reading and engagement as readers. As Steve Anwyll, the director of the NLS in England, acknowledged in 2004: 'If we're increasing the attainment of children at the expense of their engagement and enjoyment, then we're failing to do the whole job and we have to take that seriously' (quoted in Hall, 2004: 120).

A decade later the situation remains serious and needs to be taken seriously. Whilst countries and their cultures differ, the EU Expert Literacy Group, in identifying the skills and characteristics of outstanding teachers, note, amongst a longer list, that teachers' abilities to 'increase learners' motivation to read and write' and their 'strong personal interest in and passion for teaching and reading in particular' remain of crucial importance (EU, 2012: 43). Both international and national studies of children's attitudes to reading signal the value of volitional free-choice reading and of reading literature in particular. Such studies also suggest a need for qualitative research that does not rely solely upon large-scale quantitative self-report data. Whilst useful, such data have limitations; they cannot afford insights about what children actually do as engaged readers, nor can they document children's interactions around reading, whether at home or at school. Additionally, the numerical data collected in PISA and PIRLS, whilst highly influential, cannot afford insights about how teachers can foster reader engagement within or beyond the classroom. The Phase II project *Teachers as Readers: Building Communities of Readers* responded to these concerns and sought to increase children's reading for pleasure at home and at school. It also sought to widen teachers' knowledge and use of children's literature and other texts, and to associate reading with positive, interesting and satisfying experiences for both children *and* teachers.

Chapter 3

The UKLA projects

Teachers as Readers and Building Communities of Readers

Teresa Cremin

In response to the context detailed in Chapter 2, including international concerns about the decline in reading enjoyment, the UKLA research was undertaken in two phases: Phase I, *Teachers as Readers* (2006–7), and Phase II, *Teachers as Readers: Building Communities of Readers* (2007–8). This chapter briefly outlines these two UKLA projects upon which the book is based. It notes their different organisation and design, their relationship to each other, the teachers involved, and the methods used for collecting and analysing teachers' and children's knowledge and attitudes, practices and preferences as readers in the twenty-first century. It also describes the support afforded the teachers in Phase II and this project's explicit focus on developing their knowledge of children's literature and their personal, as well as professional pleasure in reading. Their voices and views, and the shifts in practice and attitude which were evidenced over the year are shared in later chapters; this chapter in particular documents the underpinning principles, methodology and dataset from which the project's findings regarding the development of motivated and socially engaged communities of readers was derived.

Phase I, *Teachers as Readers*

Project aims

This Phase I research, funded by the UKLA, ran across the year 2006–7 and sought to explore:

- primary teachers' personal reading habits and preferences;
- their knowledge of children's literature;
- their reported use of children's literature in the primary classroom;
- the extent of their involvement in local area/school library services.

Project sample

Linking into UKLA regional networks, the research team collected questionnaire responses from 1,200 primary teachers in 11 local authorities (LAs) in England and a smaller number of student teachers in five initial teacher education institutions. The LAs represented a spread of inner city, rural and urban areas, reflecting a broad range of socio-economic status. Approximately half the respondents worked with children aged 5–7 years and half with children aged 7–11 years. Teachers participating in the survey had varying lengths of teaching experience, ranging from 0–5 years (21.4 per cent) to over 21 years in the profession (18.4 per cent); there were fewer teachers with 16–20 years' experience than any other category (7.6 per cent). The teachers held a diverse range of responsibilities within their schools, none was a literacy coordinator.

Data collection and analysis

The questionnaire was piloted with several groups of teachers in different LAs and then adapted and finally administered on continuing professional development short courses across the period October–December 2006. As a result, the teachers' answers were not unduly affected by the summer holidays, when they might have had more time for reading than any other time of year. Each authority appointed a designated research coordinator who attended a briefing session to ensure the questionnaires were administered in a common manner; they also completed context sheets providing details of the professional development course, the setting, LA, number of teachers present and number of questionnaires returned. The coordinators also noted if any children's books had been used or referred to within the particular course and detailed these where appropriate. For the LAs involved there were several benefits, including:

- detailed information about their classroom teachers as readers and their classroom practice, essential for professional development planning;
- information about the use made of local library services and the potential for development of these in relation to literacy reading;
- collaboration over research with the UKLA, which is recognised as a national voice in literacy education.

The questionnaires were administered at short courses which were not literacy related. This meant that the teachers who completed the survey were responsible for a number of different areas of the curriculum; they were not deemed to be literacy specialists and were not leading literacy within their schools. This enabled the research team to avoid undue bias in the results since school literacy coordinators, who are often responsible for book buying, interact more regularly with publishers and others about children's reading materials and are more likely to have an enhanced knowledge of children's literature. In avoiding literacy specialists, the team were able to gather a more general picture of primary classroom teachers' habits, knowledge, experience and reported use of children's literature.

The questionnaire was completed and returned on the same day ensuring a very high response rate and a wealth of data from teachers in different parts of the country, thus increasing the validity and reliability of the study. The questionnaire (see Appendix) began with four questions about teachers' personal reading preferences and practices, including one which invited respondents to note when they had last read a book for pleasure. These were followed by two questions about use of libraries. Three key questions asked the respondents to name six 'good' children's writers, six poets and six picturebook authors. The term 'good' was explained as referring to writers whose work the teachers had found both valuable and successful with primary-aged learners. There were six questions which sought information about teachers' use of children's literature in their teaching and one question which involved ranking statements about the value of literature in learning. In addition, several questions focused on teachers' use of library services.

Thus both qualitative and quantitative information about teachers' views, knowledge and practices with regard to literature and to reading was sought; the former was subjected to categorical analysis (Strauss and Corbin, 1998), the latter was inputted and analysed by a research assistant making use of the quantitative software package SPSS (no. 13). Information was also gathered about length of teaching experience, responsibilities in school and the age of the learners with whom the teachers were currently working. Potential connections and relationships between the various strands of the research, namely the teachers' personal reading habits and preferences, their knowledge of children's literature, their reported use of such literature in the classroom and their involvement in library services were examined.

The results of the analysis of the 1,200 anonymous questionnaires are detailed in Chapter 4, though it is worth noting here that the evidence suggests that whilst personally teachers are readers, professionally there is cause for concern; teacher knowledge of children's literature was narrow. In selecting books to work with in the classroom 85 per cent of the teachers relied upon their own limited knowledge and made extensive use of their own childhood favourites. Teachers' knowledge also needs broadening in other ways, to encompass both the knowledge that develops through being a reader, and the rich pedagogical content knowledge that can support the development of independent young readers. Links with libraries were seen to be relatively few and under developed.

The research suggested the need for action to extend teachers' knowledge of texts and to build and sustain new partnerships between schools, families, libraries and LAs. The UKLA, as a professional subject association with extremely strong links with LAs, with researchers, teachers, library services, publishers and national organisations, was well placed to undertake such development work.

Therefore, following Phase I, *Teachers as Readers*, the Phase II project, *Teachers as Readers: Building Communities of Readers*, was developed in the DCSF National year of Reading.

Phase II, *Teachers as Readers: Building Communities of Readers*

Project aims

The core goal of the Phase II project, which was funded by the Esmée Fairbairn Foundation across the year 2007–8, was to improve teachers' knowledge and use of literature in order to help them increase children's motivation and enthusiasm for reading, especially those less successful in literacy.

The project, developed in collaboration with five LAs, aimed to develop:

- teachers' knowledge of children's literature in order to support independent reading for pleasure;
- their confidence and skilful use of such literature in the classroom in order to foster reading for pleasure;
- their relationships with parents, carers, librarians and families in order to support independent reading for pleasure;
- Reading Teachers – teachers who read and readers who teach in order to support independent reading for pleasure.

In order to identify the key messages of this project for policy and practice, the research team collected data about each of the above aims and explored the effects of the teachers' increased subject and pedagogical content knowledge (Shulman, 1987), new partnerships with parents and librarians, and the development of the practitioners as 'Reading Teachers – teachers who read and readers who teach' (Commeyras *et al.*, 2003), on children's pleasure in reading.

Project sample

Five LAs in England participated in the project: Barking and Dagenham, Birmingham, Kent, Medway and Suffolk. Each allocated funding to support the involvement of up to ten schools per area and to provide the support of an adviser to coordinate the local activities, including professional development. The five LA coordinators were themselves a source of research evidence for the research team. They took part in individual interviews, informal discussions, and group discussions; they also completed written reports and evaluations of the project in relation to their schools.

The schools involved in the project were recruited opportunistically, in one of two ways:

1   Some were approached by the LA coordinators because it was felt they would benefit from the development work. This was mostly because they were already receiving or needed support to improve their reading and/or literacy results, or because it was known the schools had identified reading for pleasure as part of their School Development Plan.

2   Some had heard about the project and had asked to be included. Sometimes this was because of low results, sometimes it was because of the enthusiasm for reading of a particular teacher or headteacher or because of concerns about the low numbers of children who were reading independently for pleasure. The numbers of schools and teachers recruited and retained throughout the project are shown in Table 3.1.

The sample of 27 participating schools involved one primary-level pupil referral unit (PRU), five infant schools, two junior schools and 19 primary schools; 41 of the teachers were female and two were male. Their teaching experience ranged from newly qualified teachers to 31 years in the profession with the average among case study teachers being 9 years. Of the sample, 20 per cent were teachers with responsibility for literacy within their school, and 80 per cent were classroom teachers with other responsibilities, but not for literacy.

Table 3.1 Schools and teachers recruited by local authority

LA	Schools	Teachers
Barking and Dagenham	5	10
Birmingham	6	10
Kent	6	8
Medway	5	9
Suffolk	5	6
TOTAL	27	43

Although the term 'teacher' is used throughout the book, it should be noted that two participants were teaching assistants who were not qualified teachers.

All the teachers undertook activities that involved at least one class of children. In one school (in Barking and Dagenham), two teachers were responsible for a Key Stage (each) and so worked with significantly more than 30 children. One teacher who worked at a PRU worked with far fewer. In total, more than 1,200 children (aged between 4 and 11 years) were directly involved in the project and many more were indirectly involved through the teachers' work to extend involvement in the work across their schools.

The teachers were invited to identify three 'focus' children in their classes. They kept termly records of notes and observations on these three children; the observational schedules were provided by the research team. To identify the focus children, the teachers used Moss's (2000: 102) threefold characterisation of readers: readers who *can and do* read freely; readers who *can but don't* read freely; and readers who *can't yet and don't* read freely. The teachers selected young readers from the second characterisation – those who, whilst able to read and adequately undertake most class-based reading tasks, were disinclined to read independently. They showed little commitment to or interest in reading, appeared to find little pleasure or satisfaction in the experience, sought to avoid it, and did not choose of their own volition to read over any other available activity in school. As such, it was agreed they were not reading for pleasure. However, as Chapter 9 details, on closer examination, teachers actually found that some of these disaffected readers (most of whom were boys), were engaged in volitional, free-choice reading at home.

Case study schools

From the overall sample of 27 schools, a random sub-sample of two schools per authority was selected for case study enquiries. These 10 schools gave permission for the research team to conduct in-depth research enquiries that involved the teachers, their classes, the pupils they had identified as focus children, and the headteachers. In some of these schools more than one teacher was involved in the project; 16 teachers in the 10 schools were involved in the case study enquiries. These teachers did not receive extra input from the research team or LA coordinators, they experienced the same support as the other teachers, though they did experience researcher visits to interview them, which may have supported their thinking and project motivation.

Forty-nine focus children were 'tracked' in the case study schools through their teachers' action research and by the core research team's case study activities. Some schools had elected to involve more than one teacher, and some teachers selected two or four children rather than three. These children were not the focus of additional/special activities or intervention, they experienced exactly the same as their classmates; they were only focus children in terms of extra data gathered about them. Thirteen (27 per cent) were girls and 36 (73 per cent) were boys, with the largest number of children being 10–11 years, and with more boys than girls across all but one age, 7–8 year olds (Table 3.2). It is noteworthy that the preponderance of boys identified as uninterested in reading is in line with international and national evidence that indicates boys fare less well in literacy activities, perceive reading as less interesting and read less frequently than girls, displaying much more negative attitudes (e.g. Clark and Foster, 2005; Twist *et al.*, 2007; Clark et al., 2008). The All-Party Parliamentary Commission on Boy's Reading (APPLG, 2012), whilst recognising this as an ongoing issue, is nonetheless clear that boys' underachievement

Table 3.2 Focus children from the case study schools by gender and age

Year group	Number		Percentage	
	Boys	Girls	Boys	Girls
Reception: 4–5 years	3	0	100	0
Yr 1: 5–6 years	0	0	0	0
Yr 2: 6–7 years	7	3	70	30
Yr 3: 7–8 years	4	4	50	50
Yr 4: 8–9 years	7	2	78	22
Yr 5: 9–10 years	5	2	71	29
Yr 6: 10–11 years	10	2	83	17
TOTAL	36	13	73	27

as readers is not inevitable. The marked shifts in attitude and attainment made by the 36 focus boys in the case studies in this project affirms this position. As will be shown, much depends upon teachers' knowledge and use of texts which interest, engage and motivate boys as readers; much also depends upon the inclusion of a Reading for Pleasure Pedagogy and the positioning of teachers as readers.

Phase II project organisation

Each LA worked within the given framework of the overall UKLA project and held regular local professional development sessions with their teachers. The teachers and their LA coordinators also attended three national day meetings in London. In addition to the 41 teachers and two teaching assistants from 27 schools who were directly involved, one family learning coordinator and one local librarian were involved throughout; many other librarians and support personnel were also involved but not in every session.

Whilst this book predominantly reports upon the findings from the data collection and analysis that was undertaken by the core research team, as these activities were closely associated with (and some data were derived from) the professional development events that were organised as part of the project, a brief outline of these activities is offered. As widening teachers' knowledge of children's literature was a core feature of the work, each of the LAs initially selected a particular literary focus (Table 3.3), although in every case the teachers' extended their knowledge beyond this starting point, particularly in response to recommendations from each other and interest shown by the children. Each LA coordinator had a linked team member to discuss project issues with and a researcher was allocated to each LA. The core team researchers' each case studied a sample of teachers, interviewing and observing them, their headteachers and the children across the year. As noted, the teachers also case studied three children in their classes. Thus the project combined professional development, teachers' action research and centrally coordinated research activities.

Local meetings

Each LA offered different provision to the teachers in terms of release from school and time to meet; this ranged from six one-day local sessions and several extended twilight

Table 3.3 Summary of project personnel and initial local authority foci

Local authority	LA project coordinator	UKLA linked team member	UKLA linked researcher	Initial focus of project
Barking and Dagenham	David Reedy	Fiona Collins and Kimberley Safford	Fiona Collins and Kimberley Safford	Challenging picture fiction
Birmingham	Sonia Thompson	Marilyn Mottram	Marilyn Mottram	Global literature
Medway	Ruth Wells	Teresa Cremin	Teresa Cremin	Poetry
Suffolk	Linda Dickson	Teresa Cremin	Sacha Powell	Picturebooks with 7–11 year olds
Kent	Sue Huxley	Fiona Collins	Sacha Powell	Short stories

meetings in one authority, to six mornings and several twilight meetings in another. Each LA funded their own teachers' supply and whilst the project team sought to ensure parity, this was not possible given the different funds available in LAs. Schools and libraries were often used as bases for these meetings. Each LA coordinator made time within their work as primary literacy consultants/literacy managers to run the project locally, most did this in addition to their other responsibilities.

The local professional development activities enabled the teachers to develop and maintain a mutually interested and supportive network, to discuss their current reading (both adult and children's texts) and to consider their school-based action research projects and other reading-related issues and theories. They also used these meetings to complete data requested by the core research team. The local events were organised and hosted by the LA coordinators of the project, who often involved members of the core research team as participant observers. The specific focus for each meeting was decided locally in line with the overall project structure (see below).

In order to widen their repertoires, teachers were encouraged to set themselves reading targets and each LA set up book boxes with children's and adult books. In addition, Walker Books gave each LA ten books linked to their specific focus and offered written guidance on planning from the Centre for Literacy in Primary Education (CLPE) about the books they gifted. This enabled teachers to lean upon the same resources and share the resultant work with each other. In addition, on the national days which were hosted at Scholastic UK in London, the teachers were given large 'goody' bags which included a number of proof copies of new books. Some of these books became 'texts in common' for the teachers and were widely read, discussed and swapped within each LA.

Each LA was visited by the project's children's literature consultant Prue Goodwin, who worked in response to need and focused upon their chosen theme. She ran development sessions which sought to widen teachers' awareness and understanding of poetry or global literature for example. All LAs involved local and school library services in various ways; some became permanent members of the LA group and afforded support of various kinds, including loaning additional material to teachers and schools.

National meetings

The three national meeting days sought to complement the local sessions, to provide opportunities for teachers from all the authorities and LA coordinators to come together, to listen to presentations, discuss literature and other texts, consider their reading histories and current practices as readers and as teachers of reading. In each of the national development days significant time was dedicated to teachers' sharing their recent reading, both adults and children's texts. Each teacher brought one children's and one adult book to each of the meetings, and each was invited to share in different groups their thoughts and views upon the texts they had brought. The ways in which they engaged with and talked about these texts, and the ways in which they positioned themselves as readers in the project groups, both local and national, was a focus for the research team. The days also afforded space to consider the implications of their own and the children's everyday reading practices; there was considerable ongoing discussion and consideration of the consequences of the teachers' new insights gained through reading and reflection upon reading, both in relation to the teaching of reading and the development of children's reading for pleasure.

The national days meetings were led collaboratively by the core team and the literature consultant. Time to meet with the team of LA coordinators was always set aside and visitors joined the project days: on one occasion Kate Wilson, the Director of Scholastic UK, spoke about the diversification of children's reading choices and publishers' responses, on another the author Sally Nicholls talked about her debut novel *Ways to Live Forever* (2008).

In both local and national meetings, the project teachers engaged in a range of professional development activities specifically related to the project's core aim to foster children's reading for pleasure. These included a focus on:

- *teacher knowledge of children's literature and other texts*, to widen and deepen teachers' knowledge;
- *children's reading practices*, to encourage a wider knowledge of children's everyday literacy lives and reading practices and preferences, and their individual interests and attitudes;
- *pedagogic practices*, to foster reading for pleasure;
- *family reading practices and links with librarians*, to foster adult involvement in children's reading and enable children to access a wider range of texts;
- *teachers' reading lives*, to raise awareness of their identities as readers and their reading habits, preferences and practices, as well as the influence of others upon their choices.

Steering committee

The project steering committee comprised senior colleagues from the Primary National Strategy (PNS), National Literacy Trust (NLT), the Association of Senior Children's and Education Librarians (ASCEL), the Schools Library Association (SLA), the Reading Agency (RA), Ofsted and the Qualifications and Curriculum Authority (QCA). Steering committee members' expertise and networks were beneficial, for example, the RA enabled all the project teachers to gain early access to the Summer Reading Challenge materials, and opportunities for advocacy work through ASCEL, NLT and the PNS were enabled. The PNS also part-funded a UKLA practical professional development text to help their consultants run Building Communities of Readers projects nationally (Cremin *et al.*, 2008d). This has also been widely used by teachers' wishing to implement the project in their schools.

Phase II project structure

The structure of the project is outlined in Table 3.4. The work commenced with an audit of the teachers' knowledge and use of children's literature and all involved completed the questionnaire used in Phase I, which also invited them to consider their practices and preferences as adult readers (see Appendix).

   Initially in the first term, following analysis of the questionnaires (the results of which were in close alignment with the Phase I data) (see Chapter 4), the focus was on widening the teachers' repertoire of quality children's authors and nurturing their own reading for pleasure as adults. It was recognised that the teachers needed to value reading themselves and to increase their awareness of their own reading habits and practices, in order to develop children's pleasure as readers. In this way they began to explore positioning themselves as Reading Teachers – teachers who read and readers who teach (Commeyras *et al.*, 2003). In this term they also identified the three focus children, children who could read but did not choose to do so as they lacked the motivation, and began to document children's reading practices in school. As the spring term commenced, this focus was retained and broadened

Table 3.4 Termly priorities for the project process

Term	Main focus
Autumn	*Phase 1: Getting Started and Planning*
Local and national sessions supported teachers with Aims 1, 2 and 4 in centre-based sessions. Priority was given to Aim 1 Forms A1, A2, B1, B2 at the start of term, and A3, B3, B4, to be completed by the end of the term	• Extend teachers' subject knowledge of children's literature (Aim 1) • Enhance teachers' confidence and skilful use of such literature in the classroom (Aim 2) • Enable teachers to understand the value of becoming a Reading Teacher (Aim 4) In this phase, teachers were gathering a range of start data from their focus pupils and their own professional learning. They were also reflecting on their one practices and experience as a reader Teachers planned a programme of action to start at the end of the autumn term/early spring term in school
Spring	*Phase 2: Implementing the Plan*
Local and national sessions afforded opportunity for teachers to spend time in critical reflection and peer discussions Forms A3, B3 and B4 to be completed by the end of the term	• Continue to extend teachers' knowledge and use of literature (Aims 1 and 2) • Develop clear links/relationships with parents, carers, librarians and families (Aim 3) • Explore strategies to enable teachers to develop as Reading Teachers (Aim 4) In this phase, teachers were trying new strategies, reviewing and evaluating their effectiveness As the term progressed, teachers were documenting any evidence of impact on the pupils' reading behaviours and attitudes and any change in community relationships

Summer	Phase 3: Continued Implementation and Examining Outcomes
Local and national sessions afforded continued opportunities for critical reflection and peer discussion, leading to the gathering of end of project data and final presentations Forms A1, A2, A3, A4, and B1, B3, B4, B5, B6 and B7 to be completed towards the end of the term	• Continue to extend teachers' knowledge and use of literature, their relationships with parents, carers, librarians and families and their role as Reading Teachers (Aims 1–4) In this final phase, at the end of the summer term teachers returned to their baseline data, and reflected upon, analysed and evaluated the impact of their project development, noting key issues and implications for further development

to encompass finding out about children's everyday reading practices at home and in the community, and considering their own pedagogic practice with regard to reading for pleasure. It was recognised that teachers needed to build relationships with parents, librarians and members of the community, and attention to this was also included in term two. In the summer term, it was planned for all four strands of the project to be sustained and developed.

The numbered proformas referred to in this structural summary (e.g. B1, B2) can be found in Cremin *et al.* (2008d). These reflective prompts, which were part of the project portfolio, helped to embed the practice of reviewing and evaluating progress in the project and supported the teachers in collecting and analysing evidence of impact.

Teacher involvement

Methodologically, the project adopted a collaborative research stance, positioning the teachers as action researchers, who were supported in documenting the responses of three focus children in their classes to their changing pedagogic practice. They were also supported in documenting their own learning journeys in multiple ways, for example through a number of project activities, as well as though their own research logs and reading journals. The teachers were actively supported in developing their action research projects focused on reading for pleasure, and invited through the use of the project portfolio to document, as noted above, the focus children's responses to any changes that they chose to make to their classroom practice.

In relation to the teachers' reflective involvement, the project also invited teachers to participate personally as well as professionally and to consider and document:

- their knowledge of children's literature;
- their understanding of themselves as readers and their classroom positioning in this regard;
- the pedagogic consequences of their personal/professional engagement and reflection;
- their evolving relationships with children, parents and librarians.

The project thus involved considerable reflection on learning and encompassed the development of new knowledge and identities, and new ways of teachers' positioning themselves in the classroom. The LA coordinators supported the teachers in developing systematic action research studies within the remit of the research and making use of the nationally provided tools and data collection sources. As Hitchcock and Hughes (1995: 27) note the principal features of action research are '*change* (action) and *collaboration* between researchers and researched'. As such, it was important that their research had clear aims and objectives, involved interrelated, overarching strands of data collection and analysis and stood up to ethical scrutiny.

The project's professional learning portfolio was designed for the LA coordinators, it was intended to help them to support their teachers' action research; it was used in local and national sessions and by teachers in school. It comprised guidance on doing an action research project, details of the aims and objectives of the project, and advice on ethical issues as well as the multiple core data collection instruments (e.g. observation schedule for documenting the focus children's engagement as readers) and proformas for reflection (e.g. consideration of professional positioning as Reading Teachers and activities under-taken in the classroom in this regard). The portfolio provided a common structural frame to guide the project process and enabled consistent data collection. Using this, the LA coordinators supported their teachers as action researchers as they case studied three less than enthusiastic readers in their classes. The teachers also documented their own learning journeys as Reading Teachers and engaged in regular reflections upon the impact of their work in relation to the project aims.

Phase II data collection and analysis

A combination of qualitative and quantitative data collection methods was employed so that the research team was able to explore numerical patterns and then look beyond these trends to qualitative evidence that might identify possible reasons or causes. There were two main approaches for the distribution, administration and collection of research tools: (a) instruments administered directly by the research team at national day meetings and in visits to case study schools, and (b) the teachers' use of standardised proformas/instruments in the portfolios. As can be seen in Table 3.4, the LA coordinators were provided with ongoing information and advice about what to distribute to or gather from teachers and when, and all the relevant paperwork was within the professional development portfolio. The termly interviews (early, mid and late phase) with the 16 case study teachers, headteachers and groups of children were all transcribed to enable cate-gorical analysis of key themes (Coffey and Atkinson, 1996).

The design of the data collection tools (e.g. questionnaires, proformas, interview schedules) was informed by the Phase I project, the early stages of the literature review and tools successfully used in previous UKLA studies involving children and/or teachers (Bearne *et al.*, 2004; UKLA/QCA, 2007). In order to capture rich data across the project, the research employed a case study strategy encompassing multiple methods of data collection demonstrating various perspectives and methods suitable for taking into account different aspects (Flick, 2006). The use of a range of sources and combined methods and tools also enabled triangulation of the data. The methods adopted included naturalistic observations in the classrooms of the 16 case study teachers, practitioner and university researcher reflections, and interviews with the case study teachers, their headteachers and their focus children, three times across the project year. In addition, observational data was gathered at national day project meetings and through standardised proformas. Thus the teachers' learning journeys as teachers, as readers and potentially as Reading Teachers were documented; data were gathered from several perspectives about their challenges, practices and positional shifts over time. In addition, all the project teachers gathered additional data about their focus children and their own classroom practice. So the multiple data collection activities included some undertaken by the university research team and others by the teachers working as action researchers in their classrooms.

Data collection activities undertaken by the university research team

Case study visits to schools

- Semi-structured interviews (×3) with project teachers ($n = 16$), early, mid and late phase;
- semi-structured interviews with the headteachers ($n = 10$), early, mid and late phase;
- semi-structured interviews/discussions with groups of focus children ($n = 49$) early, mid and late phase;
- structured observations (×2) of reading-related classroom activities in project teachers' classes, mid and late phase;
- drawing and discussion to explore children's ($n = 49$) constructs of 'a reader/readers', late phase.

Children's reading levels

- Reading levels for focus children were collected from teachers who recorded their scores for the beginning and end of the project. In some cases teachers provided reading levels data for additional children in their classes, as well as that for the focus children, and some also provided writing levels.

National day meeting information

- Teachers' own notes/drawings on their reading histories completed at the first national day ($n = 43$);
- notes made by the research team of teachers' group discussions of the children's and adults' books they brought to the three national day meetings (five groups per meeting, $n = 15$ sets).

Final reflections on impact at last national day

- Teachers' summative reflections on the overall and most significant impact from their perspective in their schools, completed at the last national day meeting ($n = 39$);
- LA coordinators' final reflections on impact across their authorities, just prior to the last national day meeting.

Data collection tools available to the research team in teachers' portfolios

Surveys (in the form of self-completion questionnaires)

- Baseline questionnaire of all participating teachers ($n = 43$) (see Appendix);
- end of project survey of all participating teachers ($n = 42$);
- baseline survey of all participating children ($n = 1,200$);
- end of project survey of all participating children ($n = 1,200$).

Reading levels and reading observations proformas

- All teachers maintained termly records (×3) on their focus children's reading habits and preferences, and recorded their reading scores at the beginning and end of the project.

Reflections on being a Reading Teacher proformas

- All teachers kept termly records (×3) of their reflections on becoming/being a Reading Teacher, including details of the books they had read during the term, their thoughts and reactions in reading journals, and their engagement in related classroom activities.

Reflections on impact proformas

- All teachers were invited to write termly reflections (×3) on their perceptions of the impact of the project's activities on themselves, the children they taught (including the focus children) and more widely across their schools.

Action plan proformas

- All teachers completed an initial action plan for the project in their schools and also wrote termly (×2) action plans for future activities and goals.

All the above data were used by the teachers for their own action research activities. The data were also copied by the research team (with prior written permission from participating teachers and children's parents as applicable) and gathered centrally for analysis. In many cases, teachers included a rich range of other material in their portfolios, such as research logs, reading journals, lesson plans and photographs. These were also copied with the teachers' permission. Additional data were gathered by the research team either at the project's national day meetings or during visits to case study schools. In project meetings, the research team were positioned as participant observers; for example, they too shared favourite texts, created reading histories and shared their reading lives, positioning themselves alongside the teachers as members of a professional learning community.

Data analysis

A mixed-methods approach was used for data analysis. The selection and segmentation of the wealth of data was undertaken through purposive sampling (Strauss and Corbin, 1990), and whilst material from all 43 teachers working in the 27 schools was analysed, the data collected from the 16 case study teachers working in 10 schools afforded more depth and detail. In this regard, each researcher initially worked independently and inductively to draw out themes from their own case studies through examining the case study interview transcripts with teachers, headteachers and the groups of focus children from each term, and the researchers' own observational notes made in the classroom, as well as analysing the teachers' observations and reflections and the case study children's drawings. The case study data were analysed for thematic content using the iterative process of categorical analysis (Coffey and Atkinson, 1996).

The process and findings were discussed in research team meetings to ensure reliability and clarity and with participants, LA coordinators and the steering committee as a means of quality assurance and checking authenticity. This process occurred after each round of visits to case study schools so that new questions might be added to the interview schedules for later visits. The responses to the closed questions from interviews and the questionnaire and surveys were coded and recorded quantitatively using Excel spreadsheets developed specifically for this purpose. Subsequently, and as appropriate, data were categorised under the key foci of the project and the new/sub-themes that emerged during the analytical process. In order to enhance the trustworthiness of the analysis (Lincoln and Guba, 1985), each research team member worked independently and then collaboratively to analyse data and all data were analysed by more than one team member and findings discussed by the team as a whole at regular meetings; with the steering committee; and with an experienced, independent educational researcher whose work both interrogated and enriched the analytic process.

In the chapters that follow, whilst the data draw upon the project's sample as a whole, the evidence frequently draws upon the case study materials and the smaller sample of participants that was involved in these in-depth enquiries. The case study data allowed the research team to gain a richer understanding drawn from observed evidence and a more detailed picture of the changing patterns in practice and perception in these schools over the project year.

Ethical considerations

The project gave rise to many ethical issues, not least due to the combination of action research by teachers and meta-analysis of their documentation (as well as core data) by the research team. The team adhered to the BERA Revised Ethical Guidelines (BERA, 2004), and informed consent and the right to withdraw was offered all participants. The researchers worked with an ethic of respect for all participants and in particular the children's rights to participate and have their views taken seriously, to opt out, to privacy and to protection from harm. They were mindful of the potential coercion that focus children might feel subjected to when asked to participate in interviews during school time, and sensitive to children's signals that they might wish to opt out. The team was also careful to ensure that parents' were fully informed of the project's aims and what children's participation would involve. Parental consent was obtained, including gaining repeat assurances of consent for the use of photographs of children in presentations and publications. Throughout the book pseudonyms are used for all project participants and schools involved.

Conclusion

Both the Phase I (2006–7) and Phase II (2007–8) research projects were systematically organised, professionally conducted and collaboratively undertaken with and through UKLA networks. Phase I, a quantitative survey, encompassed a broader picture which sought to establish primary teachers' knowledge and use of children's literature and to understand their practices and preferences as adult readers. Phase II employed quantitative and qualitative methods to develop new knowledge and understanding about the influence of teachers' subject knowledge, their metacognitive awareness of themselves as readers and of the nature of reading, and the consequences for classroom practice and reader relationships, within and beyond school.

Historically, in early 2006, members of the UKLA Children's Literature Special Interest Group had voiced their concerns about teachers' professional knowledge of appropriate literature for young learners and also discussed the possibility that teachers' repertoires, if limited, might be linked to the ongoing decline in children's reading for pleasure in England seen in PIRLS (Twist *et al.*, 2003). So the UKLA sought funding from the Esmée Fairbairn Foundation to undertake a research and development project in the area. However, this was declined due to the lack of a secure evidence base regarding teachers' knowledge of children's literature. The association therefore decided to undertake its own research to gather evidence on this issue. As soon as the Phase I results demonstrated there was considerable cause for concern (Cremin *et al.*, 2007, 2008a, b, 2009b), a second application for a new more focused project, Phase II, was submitted and was successful. Whilst the book draws on both these inter-linked UKLA studies, due to the breadth and depth of documentation gathered in Phase II classrooms and schools, and the impact of the findings, considerably more space is afforded the latter project on building communities of engaged readers (Cremin *et al.*, 2008c, d, 2009a, b; Cremin, 2009, 2010a, b, c, 2013a).

Chapter 4

Teachers' knowledge and use of children's literature

Fiona M. Collins

Knowledge of children's literature and of individual children and their reading interests is essential in order to develop young readers who can and do choose to read for pleasure. Those teachers who have a secure knowledge of a range of children's literature are not only more able to recommend the right text for the right child, but are also better positioned to create a community of readers in the classroom (Younger and Warrington, 2005; Kwek *et al.*, 2007). Children, like adults, develop reading preferences, and teachers need to be able to match texts to individual's interests and needs. Such focused advice not only widens reading repertoires, but increases the chances of young readers finding reading relevant. It can also foster shared knowledge of texts, prompting rich text talk between peers and between teachers and children who have read the same text. As Chambers stated over 40 years ago: 'Unless a school is staffed by people who enjoy books and enjoy talking to children about what they read then it is unlikely that they will be very successful in helping children to become readers' (1973: 22).

The focus for this chapter is the findings from the Phase I and II projects from which data were collected on teachers' personal reading habits and preferences and their knowledge and use of children's authors, poets and picturebook creators in the classroom. Quantitative data from Phase I, *Teachers as Readers*, reflect the knowledge base of 1,200 primary teachers who were teaching in 11 local authorities in England (Cremin *et al.*, 2008a, b). The data set for Phase II of the project was derived from 43 teachers working in 27 schools in five local authorities of England (Cremin *et al.*, 2009a) (see Chapter 3 for more details). The second data set predominantly confirmed the findings of the Phase I data, so references to Phase II data are only made where there were particular differences.

Effective teachers of reading

Internationally, studies have found that effective teachers of reading require sound subject knowledge of children's literature and reading development (Flynn, 2007; Dreher, 2003; Hunt, 1993) in order to support all children in becoming independent, fluent readers who make thoughtful choices about the texts they read. For primary-school teachers this means knowledge of a range of contemporary and classic children's authors, books, poets and picturebook creators. Medwell *et al.* (1998) also support this view; their research revealed that thoughtful use of a wide range of texts was noticeable in the practice of effective teachers: 'They include class novels, stories which illustrated particular narrative features and conventions of writing, information books with particular book conventions and good quality literature matched to the children's levels of individual and group reading ability' (p. 28).

This is confirmed by Shulman (1987) who argues that in order for practitioners to be effective they require sound subject knowledge. However, he also recognises the value of pedagogical content knowledge, which is arguably 'the craft of teaching' (Brown and McIntyre, 1993): knowing how to impart subject content to learners in an appropriate and accessible manner. The interplay between the two cannot be underestimated as one supports the other. In terms of using literature with young readers this interplay manifests itself in various ways, teachers of reading need to: suggest reading material to individual children in order to motivate them as readers; have a secure knowledge of a range of texts in order to have in-depth discussions with children; identify books which read aloud well and that their class would enjoy; and know which books will be fruitful for closer examination (Chambers, 1985, 1993). Considering subject and pedagogical content knowledge in relation to children's literature, three interlocking domains of teacher understanding and practice are required:

- knowledge of appropriate books, authors and poets (Meek, 1982, 1991; Styles, 1992; Cremin *et al.*, 2008a, b);
- understanding how and when to use these texts in the classroom, for example, in reading aloud, as support for writing or drama, recommending to individual children and author study (Medwell *et al.*, 1998; Hall and Harding, 2003; Cremin, 2007);
- understanding children's development as readers both in and out of school (Meek, 1988; Barrs and Thomas, 1991; Flynn, 2007) and how home, culture, personal interests and community influence reading practices (Gregory *et al.*, 1996; Waugh *et al.*, 2013; Villers, 2011).

Effective teachers of reading use literature to engage in wide-ranging discussions with children. Millard (1997) argues that children are more likely to become critical and discerning readers where teachers and children talk about their reading choices and how their reading is influenced by social relationships and processes. Chambers (1993) also explores the benefits of holistic reading routines and environments where teachers use their knowledge of texts to provide guidance to children on reading material, model reading practices and make time for independent reading and book talk. Wayne Mills, quiz master of the International Kids' Lit Quiz, confirms the importance of book talk between a knowledgeable adult and child reader:

> Kids love to talk to me about books because just as kids like to talk to parents or teachers about books, they know in me they've got someone that's probably read the book that they have read and as we know it is one of the most satisfying things on this planet to find someone that you can relate to and discuss the same book that you've read.... It's a meeting of minds.
>
> (Mills, cited in Harrington and Mills, 2011: 183)

In order to produce effective literacy teachers, initial teacher education needs to ensure that student teachers develop a secure knowledge of children's literature, especially as some may enter their courses with a less than wholehearted approach to reading themselves. In the USA, Applegate and Applegate (2004) found that pre-service teachers do not choose to read, have 'anaemic personal reading habits' and can be character-ised as unenthusiastic readers. Two other US studies, Sulentic-Dowell *et al.* (2006) and Nathanson *et al.* (2008), also found that most student teachers are not active readers, and many describe themselves as non-readers. Nathanson *et al.* (2008) identified that those who were enthusiastic readers, 'more frequently recalled discussions about litera-ture and opportunities for making interpretations in secondary classes compared with unenthusiastic readers' (2008: 319). They suggest that text discussion appears to act as a motivational strategy for readers from the earliest years right through to university education. In Canada, in similar research with pre-service teachers, Benevides and Stagg Peterson (2010) found that those who achieved higher test scores had stronger memories of being read to as a child, of visiting libraries frequently and of enjoying reading gener-ally. Drawing on a number of international studies, Dreher argues:

> Teachers who are engaged readers are motivated to read, are both strategic and knowledgeable readers, and are socially interactive about what they read. These qualities show up in their classroom interactions and help create students who are, in turn, engaged readers.
>
> (Dreher, 2003: 338)

In the UK, the research of Bowers and Davis (2013) into the personal reading habits of student teachers concurs with this sentiment; those student teachers who are readers and have a love of books aim to encourage this attitude in the children they teach. These researchers also found that those student teachers in Wales who were reading children's literature used it as a form of bibliotherapy; they claim that reading for pleasure can help alleviate professional stress through escaping into the pages of a book at the end of a busy day. However, carving out time within initial teacher education to focus on children's literature can represent a challenge, especially with increasing proportions of training being school based. In the UK for example, the 'Literature Matters' project, a partnership between different university education departments and school library services, successfully developed student teachers' knowledge of children's literature, but was found to be unsus-tainable because of the challenges and demands of teacher education (Bailey *et al.*, 2007).

Contextualising the teaching of reading in England

In recent years it has been argued that teachers' creative use of literature has been framed and controlled by the centralised system for teaching literacy in England (Grainger *et al.*, 2005; Marshall, 2001; Martin, 2003) and that teachers' confidence in knowing and using children's literature may be limited (Arts Council England (ACE), 2003; Bowers and Davis, 2013). The introduction of the National Literacy Strategy (DfEE, 1998) set out a 'detailed, proscriptive teaching programme where many teachers felt compelled to use text fragments to teach specific objectives' (Collins and Safford, 2008: 418). In order to cover the range of texts required, teachers did not perceive they had the time to explore texts in any depth or read complete novels to older readers (Frater, 2000; King, 2001). Alongside this, the government required student teachers' English subject knowledge to be audited, but as Graham (1997) observed this did not include children's literature or other creative aspects of the English curriculum. ACE clarified the situation which is still the case today:

> [L]iterature is neither detailed as an art form, alongside music, drama or dance, nor identified as a training need for English teachers.... There is in fact still no statutory requirement of trainee teachers to study children's literature. There are only a handful of colleges where children's literature is a part of the teacher training course.
>
> (ACE, 2003: 36)

Thus newly qualified teachers could be starting their careers with limited knowledge of children's literature and how to use it in their teaching. If this was the case it would be inadequate, and would severely prejudice their chances of becoming effective teachers of literacy.

It has also been argued that with the emphasis on teaching systematic synthetic phonics a more disconnected and skills-based approach to the teaching of reading developed, promoting decoding at the expense of reading for meaning and pleasure (Wyse and Styles, 2007). Additionally, the profession became over-reliant on text extracts to teach literacy (Dombey *et al.*, 2010), and the emphasis on improving literacy standards impacted on teachers' promotion of reading for pleasure (National Literacy Trust, 2012). For many years, no policy documents foregrounded reading for pleasure, although the inspection report *Reading for Purpose and Pleasure* (Ofsted, 2004) highlighted that some schools were giving insufficient consideration to children's independent reading and reading preferences. It found few schools successfully engaged the interests of those who, whilst competent readers, did not choose to read for pleasure. In a later report *Excellence in English* (Ofsted, 2011) which focused on 12 outstanding primary and secondary schools, inspectors noted the significance of teachers' subject and pedagogical content knowledge in supporting pleasure in reading.

> The schools all took reading for pleasure seriously. Teachers read and talked with enthusiasm, recommending books and planning opportunities for pupils to read independently outside the curriculum. Their success was seen in good test results and in children's enthusiasm for reading beyond the classroom.
>
> (Ofsted, 2011: 8)

It is encouraging that the new National Curriculum advocates the use of literature for reading aloud whole texts and by implication recommending writers:

> Pupils should continue to listen frequently to stories, poems, non-fiction and other writing, including whole books and not just extracts, so that they build on what was taught previously. In this way, they also meet books and authors that they might not choose themselves.
>
> (DfE, 2013: 36)

Teachers as adult readers

Research has shown that teachers who are readers have a significant impact on the children they teach as they model positive attitudes to reading (Sulentic-Dowell *et al.*, 2006; Cremin, 2010b). Yet, as already noted student teachers may not be active readers or, as Cox and Schaetzel (2007) found in Singapore, may read primarily for information rather than pleasure. Other research with practising teachers suggests for example that Kenyan teachers do not read much beyond newspapers and religious texts (Commeyras and Inyega, 2007), and that newspapers predominate teachers' reading in Nigeria (Babalola, 2002). In Botswana, research indicates teachers read mainly for information and self-enhancement (Commeyras and Mazile, 2009, quoted in Gennrich and Janks, 2013). Elsewhere, less attention has been paid to the personal reading habits of practising teachers. Early literature (Mour, 1977) and that pertaining to student teachers (Applegate and Applegate, 2004; Nathanson *et al.*, 2008), raises the question of whether teachers read sufficient high-quality literary works. In some countries, particularly developing countries, fewer people have been enabled to acquire literacy capital in relation to printed texts. Lack of access to reading materials in mother-tongue and limited numbers of libraries results in 'differential access' (Bourdieu, 1991: 133). The dominance of English as a language of learning and teaching further disempowers those whose mother-tongue is not English. These factors combine to result in an 'unequal distribution of the chances of access' (Bourdieu, 1991: 57), since although individual teachers will be differently literate, not all literacy practices are equally valued in education and in society as a whole. It is also argued teachers do not undertake much professional reading (Rudland and Kemp, 2004) and conflicts may exist between curriculum requirements and teachers' own reading choices.

In England in the Phase I survey of teachers' knowledge and use of children's literature, questions about their reading preferences practices and habits as readers were included in order to contextualise their responses (Cremin *et al.*, 2008a). In terms of current personal reading, 73.2 per cent respondents had read for pleasure during the last month and 20.2 per cent during the last three months (Figure 4.1), thus clearly illustrating that nearly three-quarters were regular readers. Popular fiction, including women's popular fiction, thrillers and crime novels, was the most frequent choice (40 per cent). Autobiography and biography (14 per cent) and other post-1980s novels (14 per cent) were the next most popular categories; a smaller percentage (6.5 per cent)

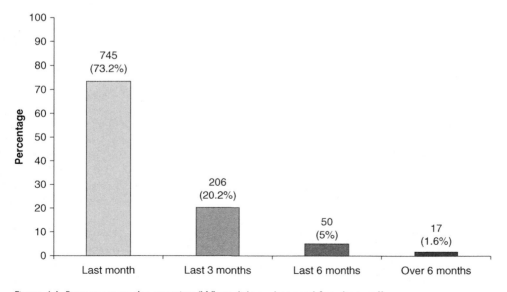

Figure 4.1 Responses to the question 'When did you last read for pleasure?'

had recently read children's fiction including books termed as 'crossover' books. Not surprisingly in this category, *Harry Potter* by J.K. Rowling was the most frequently mentioned and there were multiple mentions of Mark Haddon's prize-winning book about a boy with Asperger's Syndrome, *The Curious Incident of the Dog in the Night-Time*. The lowest recorded categories (2.5 per cent and under) were: newspapers and magazines; lifestyle/health; religious/spiritual; academic; educational; practical/factual; travel; short stories; poetry; and plays. It seems that for the majority of these UK-based teachers, reading remains a source of satisfaction. This tunes in with large-scale studies, which have consistently found that the vast majority of the population read (e.g. Reading the Situation, Book Marketing Ltd, 2000).

In terms of favourite childhood reading, the overwhelming majority of the Phase 1 respondents recorded popular fiction, often series fiction. Enid Blyton and Roald Dahl were by far the most-mentioned authors, reflecting their popularity in the 1960s and 70s. Younger teachers' knowledge of these two authors may be linked to their parents' and grandparents' recommendation of their own childhood favourites. There was a close connection between the teachers' favourite childhood reading and the texts they used in class, an issue returned to later.

Of the favourite childhood books mentioned, 10 per cent were nineteenth century classics such as *Black Beauty* (Anna Sewell) (23), *Heidi* (Johanna Spyri) (19), *Little Women* (Louisa M. Alcott) and *What Katy Did* (Susan Coolidge) (13 mentions each). These classic novels may well be regarded as female reading correlating with the proportion of female teachers both in the survey and the primary profession as a whole. Relatively high numbers were also recorded for twentieth-century classics such as *The Lion, the Witch and the Wardrobe* (C.S. Lewis) with over 50 mentions, *The Hobbit* (J.R.R. Tolkein) (16), *Swallows and Amazons* (Arthur Ransome) (15) and *Winnie the Pooh* (A.A. Milne) (14). Only 9 per cent of the respondents mentioned picturebooks with *The Very Hungry Caterpillar* by Eric Carle being the most mentioned (13). Only 1.5 per cent mentioned poetry as their favourite childhood reading, although this may, in part at least, have been as a result of the question which referred to a favourite 'book', where a broader question asking about childhood reading generally might have opened further memories of reading materials beyond fiction bound within books. Nonetheless, similar findings were found in a survey of student teachers' poetry knowledge, few of whom had any significant memories of reading poetry as a child (Collins and Kelly, 2013).

In selecting the most important book they had ever read, the highest percentage recorded (17 per cent) was for religious/spiritual books, with 12 per cent for significant recent novels (post-1980s) in second place. Following these, high-scoring categories, in order of importance, were: nineteenth-century and earlier classics; children's fiction; autobiography and biography; twentieth-century American classics; and twentieth-century European classics. There was an emphasis on affective content and many connections to books they had been introduced to in school, which were (and remain) on examination curricula, highlighting teachers' roles in bringing memorable literature to young readers.

In relation to sourcing books for their reading habit, 80 per cent of the Phase 1 teachers reported using local bookshops, 36 per cent buying on-line, some used both. Friends were mentioned by 56 per cent as a frequent resource. In contrast, libraries were not recorded as a frequent source, 34 per cent of the 1,200 teachers use libraries, suggesting that 66 per cent do not make use of a library in their adult reading lives, despite the fact that the majority are readers. Additional routes to finding reading material which were mentioned included advertising, 'Richard and Judy' TV recommendations and magazine/newspaper reviews.

What subject knowledge of children's literature do teachers possess?

In the light of the previous discussion, the following sections of this chapter discuss the insights from Phases I and II of the Teachers as Readers research in relation to teachers' knowledge and use of children's texts and the impact this has on the teaching of reading (Cremin *et al.*, 2008a, b, d). Within the Phase I questionnaire (see Appendix), three questions aimed to establish the teachers' current knowledge of children's literature. The questions asked them to name: six 'good' children's book authors; six children's poets and six picturebook authors/illustrators. The term 'good' was explained as referring to writers whose work the teachers found both valuable and successful to use with primary-aged learners.

Teachers' knowledge of children's writers

In response to being asked to name six 'good' children's writers, 64 per cent of the teachers in Phase I named five or six writers with 46 per cent naming six. Thus less than half of the teachers could cite six authors, which is disappointing when children's literature in the UK is so vibrant and a rich array of talent exists from which to choose. As with the teachers' favourite childhood author, Roald Dahl gained the highest number of mentions by far (744). The nearest four were: Michael Morpurgo (343); Jacqueline Wilson (323); J.K. Rowling (300); and Anne Fine (252). Others above a hundred mentions were: Dick King Smith (172); Janet and Alan Ahlberg (169); Enid Blyton (161); Shirley Hughes (128); C.S. Lewis (122); Philip Pullman (117); Mick Inkpen (106); and Martin Waddell (100).

Most of the authors who were mentioned by more than 100 respondents were very well known in 2006 at the time of completing the questionnaire and remain popular today. However, the dominance of these writers places in the side-lines numerous other significant writers of the time, such as: David Almond (20); Geraldine McCaughrean (10); Darren Shan (8); Berlie Doherty (5); and Eva Ibbotson (3). This reflects a limited knowledge base and suggests a scant palate of authors that could be made available to young, fluent readers by their teachers.

Few writers of novels for older readers were included in terms of range and diversity. Although the data were collected from schools located in a variety of culturally diverse educational areas, the authors cited were mainly white British. An exception to this was Malorie Blackman, a black British author (English Children's Laureate, 2013–15). She only received 24 mentions although she came twenty-third in the top 25 authors. In 2006, Blackman was a well-established author who had won a range awards for her writing and whose work had been adapted for television, but with 24 mentions she did not seem to feature significantly for the respondents. Beverley Naidoo, whose writing is largely set in Africa and often deals with issues of migration and child survival, was mentioned only three times. In relation to successful authors from other English-speaking countries, the US author Betsy Byars was mentioned 15 times and Louis Sachar had two mentions. This was interesting, as seven teachers stated they had read his novel *Holes* aloud recently to their class. However, no mention was made of Morris Gleitzman, the popular Australian author who had by then written *Two Weeks with the Queen* as well as multiple other novels. No authors in the top 25 were writing in any other language other than English. Both the emphasis on white British authors and the lack of authors in translation, suggest the teachers' knowledge of children literature was limited in relation to world literature, yet children need to see their lives reflected in literature, and need to develop their understanding of others' lives through literature.

In addition, given the current popularity of fantasy novels apart from Roald Dahl, Philip Pullman and J.K. Rowling few authors of this genre were noted. For example, only one record was made each for Philip Reeve, even though his first book in the *Mortal Engines Quartet* had won the Nestlé Smarties Children's Book award in 2002 and only one respondent mentioned William Nicholson, whose novel *The Wind Singer* had won the 2000 Nestlé Smarties Children's Book Award. Marcus Sedgwick, who was well established in 2006 and had been shortlisted for the Guardian Children's Book Award in 2002 for *The Dark Horse*, was not mentioned at all. The lack of knowledge of such writers is surprising as often prize-winners are displayed explicitly in book shops and made obvious on Amazon. This finding suggests that teachers are not keeping abreast of significant children's books (or their authors) and are thus not in the position to recommend them to children or purchase them for the school library.

In Phase II, the range cited was equally as limited, with the same established authors as in Phase I, namely Anne Fine, Dick King Smith, Michael Morpurgo, Philip Pullman, J. K. Rowling and Jacqueline Wilson. Thus in the 18 months between collecting data for Phase I and the beginning of Phase II, there was no noticeable difference, except that Roald Dahl was not quite as prominent in this group of 43 teachers.

Overall the breadth cited raises cause for concern. The high numbers recorded for Roald Dahl, Michael Morpurgo and Jacqueline Wilson may relate to how and where teachers access books they use in the classroom. It is likely that if teachers are not reading beyond school and class libraries, they will be obliged to rely upon their own childhood reading, as was evident here. It also seems likely that the national requirement to study 'significant' children's authors may have influenced the knowledge indicated, especially as the focus appears to fall on a few key authors. Additionally, the media profile given to the top five authors in the Phase I survey, three of whom have been Children's Laureates (Michael Morpurgo, Jacqueline Wilson and Anne Fine), may also have been influential.

Teachers' knowledge of poets

In both questionnaires naming six good poets represented a challenge. In Phase I, 58 per cent of the respondents named one, two or no poets, 22 per cent named no poets at all. Of the 1,200 teachers involved, only 10 per cent named six poets. The highest number of mentions was for Michael Rosen (452) with five others gaining over a hundred mentions: Allan Ahlberg (207); Roger McGough (197); Roald Dahl (165); Spike Milligan (159); and Benjamin Zephaniah (131). Some of the named poets were featured in the other categories such as Allan Ahlberg and Roald Dahl who had respectively written *Heard it in the Playground* and *Revolting Rhymes*.

As might be expected, there was a predominance of poets mentioned whose poetry might be seen as light-hearted or humorous, such as Michael Rosen and Spike Milligan. Also relatively well known were those poets whose work is commonly deemed classic:

Edward Lear (85), A.A. Milne (57) and Robert Louis Stevenson (32) were the most mentioned, with Lewis Carroll receiving 13 mentions and Christina Rossetti 11. For those classed as modern classic poets, Ted Hughes (58) and Charles Causley (37) gained the most mentions, though the figures are surprisingly low given their place in the history of children's poetry in the UK. Very few women poets were mentioned. In the top 20 in order of numbers of mentions, the last two were women poets. Numbers for woman poets cited were: Grace Nichols (16); Christina Rossetti (11); Eleanor Farjeon (9); Judith Nicholls (8); Pam Ayres (5); Floella Benjamin (3); Sandy Brownjohn (3); Sharon Creech (3); Carol Ann Duffy (3); Jackie Kay (2); Valerie Bloom (2); and Wendy Cope (1). Furthermore, with the single notable exception of Benjamin Zephaniah, very few black poets received any mention: John Agard (14) and James Berry (3), as well as previously mentioned Jackie Kay and Valerie Bloom.

In this category, the repeated mentions which the Ahlbergs received, and indeed Mick Inkpen, Shirley Hughes and Colin McNaughton, suggest that much of the most well-known work, whilst poetic in nature, is found within the pages of picturebooks. The 150-plus mentions that Roald Dahl received as a poet are presumed to relate to his collection *Revolting Rhymes* and need to be placed alongside the evidence of 'over dependence' on Dahl found in the author section. Unlike the picturebook category, few teachers named any actual poetry books, reflecting perhaps the current trend of anthologising in the world of poetry or that the covers and titles of poetry books are less memorable and significant than those of picture-based texts.

The apparent lack of knowledge of poets may indicate that teachers tend to select poetry, not poets, to read and study. Perhaps they use published poetry posters and other resources to teach particular forms and language features, or use poetry to link with a cross-curricular topic, rather than enjoying and savouring the language, form and message for its own sake. This may relate to the policy profile given to studying poetic form (such as haiku, ballad, cinquain), rather than responding to and enjoying poetry per se. An English inspection report on poetry teaching affirms this finding that the range of poets known to primary teachers is too narrow; it revealed that teachers rely on specific poems, many of which they were themselves taught in school (Ofsted, 2007). Similar poems with an overemphasis on classic poetry were identified both by Ofsted and by the Phase I teacher respondents, including for example: *The Magic Box* by Kit Wright; *On the Ning Nang Nong* by Spike Milligan; and *The Owl and the Pussy Cat* by Edward Lear. The limited knowledge of poets is in line both with the occasional mention of poetry as a childhood favourite in Phase I and with a Roehampton University survey on young people's reading (Maynard *et al.*, 2007). Well over half of the 4–16 year olds in the Roehampton survey did not answer the question about their favourite book of poems, while of those that did, many did not have a favourite, did not know or did not read poetry. This is hardly surprising if their teachers lack knowledge of poets and their work. Collins and Kelly (2013) identified similar findings in a project on the poetry journeys of student teachers; 69 per cent could not remember or were vague about their primary-school introduction to poetry. Some have positive experiences but others, as Collins and Kelly (2013) found, were alienated from poetry appreciation at secondary school because of the constant poetry analysis for examination purposes. In sum, the marked lack of knowledge of poets displayed by the practitioners in Phase I is seen as a matter of concern restricting children's access to the rich diversity of poetic voices and poetry written specifically for children.

Teachers' knowledge of picturebook creators

Considering that half the Phase I respondents were teachers of 5 to 7 year olds, it is very surprising that 62 per cent named only one, two or no picturebook creators. Of these, 24 per cent named no picturebook authors/illustrators at all, whilst only 10 per cent named six. The highest number of mentions by far was for Quentin Blake (423) with four others being mentioned over a hundred times: Anthony Browne (175), Shirley Hughes (123), Mick Inkpen (121) and Alan Alhberg (146). The artwork of Quentin Blake is well known through his picturebooks, such as *Zagazoo* or *Clown*, and his illustrations of Roald Dahl stories. Blake illustrated a range of Dahl's work including *The Twits*, *The Enormous Crocodile* and *The Giraffe and the Pelly and Me*, as well as re-illustrating *Charlie and the Chocolate Factory* in 1995. Other picturebook creators who received over 50 mentions were: Eric Carle (81); Julia Donaldson (80); Martin Waddell (80); Nick Butterworth (78); and Tony Ross (55). Perhaps unsurprisingly, the target audience for many of the cited picturebook creators were children in the early years of reading.

The second highest category noted was the many books whose titles were offered but whose authors/illustrators were not recalled by the respondent. Here, 302 book titles were specifically named; perhaps the picturebook creator was unknown or not remembered by teachers as they completed the questionnaire. The titles noted were very varied and included, for example *A Piece of Cake* (Jill Murphy), *Pumpkin Soup* (Helen Cooper), *Can't You Sleep Little Bear* (Martin Waddell, illustrator Barbara Firth), *Going on a Bear Hunt* (Michael Rosen, illustrator Helen Oxenbury), *Owl Babies* (Martin Waddell, illustrator Patrick Benson), *Catkin* (Antonia Barber, illustrator P.J. Lynch). A large number of titles of traditional tales were cited, e.g. *Goldilocks and the Three Bears* and *Jack and the Beanstalk*. These tales from the oral tradition are not necessarily picturebooks, though a variety of traditional tales are published, illustrated and retold by both unnamed writers and illustrators (in reading schemes for instance) and by named author/illustrator partnerships. Such tales are often subverted, for instance *Hansel and Gretel* by Anthony Browne and *The Pea and the Princess* by Mini Grey. By citing traditional tale titles the respondents showed once again a lack of knowledge of picturebook creators, with the implication that they are not aware of the actual books or writers whose work they use in class.

In relation to picturebook creators who were developing in popularity at that time, Lauren Child, author of the Charlie and Lola series, was mentioned by 23 respondents, prompted perhaps by the TV series. Patrick Benson received three and Mini Grey one mention; Emily Gravett was not mentioned at all. Emily Gravett and Mini Grey had respectively won the Kate Greenaway Medal in 2005 and 2006: Gravett for her picturebook *Wolves* and Grey for *The Adventures of the Dish and the Spoon*. Once again, as with the findings from the author survey, rather than keeping abreast of current picturebook creators, teachers appeared to be relying on their childhood reading, and in particular drawing on traditional tales and the work of Quentin Blake, probably influenced by his work with Roald Dahl.

The data show real differences in subject knowledge between teachers of younger and older readers, as can be seen in Table 4.1. Whilst the 6 per cent difference between the two groups of teachers who could cite six creators is perhaps explainable, it is worrying that the percentage who could not name any such books is relatively close in both groups. For 22 per cent of teachers of the younger children to not know any picturebook creators signifies a lack of understanding about the importance of this aspect of

Table 4.1 Teachers' picturebook knowledge according to age of children taught

No. of picturebook creators named	Teachers (%) of	
	5 to 7 year olds	7 to 11 year olds
Six	14	8
Two, one or none	52	66
None	22	25

subject knowledge. The regular sharing of picturebooks with young children should involve talking about the meta-language of books including authors/illustrators so that children can make links with the artists' other books and develop their preferences. If the teacher does not realise the significance of such knowledge they are unlikely to model this important aspect of being a reader for the young children that they teach.

There were fewer mentions of named picturebook creators/illustrators (apart from Anthony Browne) who offer complex polysemic texts for older readers. For example, negligible mention was made of the work of Gary Crew (4), Marcia Williams (3), Philippe Dupasquier (2) Shaun Tan or Neil Gaiman (1 each), and no mention at all of David Wiesner or Colin Thompson. Complex picturebooks and graphic novels make demanding reading and offer older readers an alternative way into the multimodal world of the twenty-first century. They deserve attention. The subject matter of many such texts deal with delicate issues such as homelessness, war and bereavement, issues which can be difficult for children to approach through words alone. Picturebooks such as *Rose Blanche*, *Way Home*, *A Monster Calls* and *The Scar* for instance, deal with such issues in sensitive ways. For struggling or reluctant older readers, sophisticated picturebooks can give them a way into reading complex narratives. Reluctant boy readers can often fall into this category and thus such texts need to feature in teachers' literary repertoires.

In the Phase II data, half of the 43 teachers named six picturebook creators, whilst a quarter named only one or two. These findings, whilst slightly better than Phase I, still presented cause for concern at the start of the research. Furthermore, two teachers admitted that they had resorted to using the Internet to find names of such artists, as it was such a challenge for them: 'If we're honest we cheated on the first questionnaire. We just couldn't complete it so we looked on the Internet' (Teachers, interview, Barking and Dagenham).

Early career teachers' lack of subject knowledge

Whilst teachers who had been teaching for more than 10 years, and practitioners who had been teaching for less than 16 years, displayed a lack of breadth in their knowledge of writers for children, teachers with the least number of years' teaching (0–5 years) named a significantly smaller number of texts in all three areas: authors, poets and picturebook creators. This limited repertoire might be traced back to their training and the authors and poets they were introduced to in teacher education, on school placement and in early-career continuing professional development. The lack of emphasis in initial teacher education requirements internationally on children's literature and its absence in the English audit in England are likely to have been influential in relation to this weak subject knowledge (Collins and Safford, 2008). Since 1998, the assessment of student teachers' competence in English has focused on grammar and phonic knowledge, the English test based on a very limited view of subject knowledge fails to encompass knowledge of texts to support reader engagement, development or pleasure (Collins and Safford, 2008). One teacher from the Phase II research, who had been teaching for two years, could not remember reading or studying any children's literature on his pre-service course and voiced the view at the outset that he was neither a reader of adult texts nor a reader of children's fiction. Other newly qualified teachers perceived themselves to be over-reliant on Roald Dahl and a small canon of celebrity writers, many of whom had been Children's Laureates. Many also recognised that in relation to using texts, they relied heavily upon texts promoted through commercially produced schemes and did not always have the actual books, as extracts from them for teaching literacy were provided.

Significant concerns about subject knowledge exist

Overall, the data presented for both phases of the research raised questions about teachers' subject knowledge. Teachers with weak subject knowledge are not in a position to support children adequately in making their own reading choices and choice and recommendations are important for all readers, particularly young developing readers (Court, 2011; Goodwin, 2011; Hughes-Hassell and Rodge, 2007). For children to become motivated enthusiastic readers they need be introduced to literature which will interest and inspire them to read. International research has shown the role of literature and its relationship to high reading scores (OECD, 2010). Through encountering a range of such texts, readers will for example expand their vocabulary, hear the tunes of language, develop stamina for reading and experience different fictional worlds and poetry. All children need teachers who have knowledge of a range of literature which they can recommend to them, either as a class, group or individual. According to Maynard *et al.* (2007), very few children aged 5–7 years (14 per cent) ask their teachers to help them choose books and only 14 per cent of those aged 7–11 said they would choose a book on a teacher's recommendation. It appears that children too may be aware their teachers are not in a position to make salient suggestions. The new National Curriculum in England (DfE, 2013) promotes wider reading and states that children should be introduced to a range of poems, stories and non-fiction which is not possible unless each class teacher has strong subject knowledge of children's literature.

Teachers' use of children's literature

However, subject knowledge alone will not make an effective teacher of literacy; it is the professional capacity to combine this with pedagogical content knowledge (Shulman, 1987) that marks out the most effective teachers. So within the Phase I survey several questions focused on teachers' pedagogical use of children's literature and their understanding of its role (Cremin *et al.*, 2008a).

Approaches and practices

Teachers were asked to comment on how they used children's literature in the classroom. The replies were categorised and a number of approaches identified, namely:

- *a holistic approach* where literature is used to offer imaginative and creative textual content for reading and is used as the basis for teaching reading and writing rooted in meaningful interactive contexts;
- *a functional approach* where literature is used to teach literacy skills at word, sentence or text level;
- *a partial approach* where respondents adopted a mixed approach (in part holistic in part functional) but were not explicit about the range of activities they used;
- *unspecific* where respondents did not or could not offer a rationale to underpin their use of literature in the classroom.

Worryingly, 11 per cent of the sample of 1,200 professionals offered no response to this question, raising the question as to whether literature was used at all in their teaching. Of those who did, the percentages reflect an inconsistent approach to the use of literature in primary classrooms from using literature in a creative way to using it as a tool to teach literacy skills and both.

Twenty-seven per cent took a holistic approach and responded enthusiastically about the ways they used literature in the classroom. They commented, for example:

- 'Books are studied and shared for a long period of time then we write stories, parts of stories or poetry in that particular style, or we do drama, or both'.
- 'Literature is used in our guided and independent reading times'.
- '... as a stimulus for all sorts of writing, using quality texts as models, reading for pleasure and writing for different purposes'.

Twenty-three per cent used literature in a functional way, noting for instance:

- 'For word and sentence work, to find verbs, adverbs, etc. and for comprehension'.
- 'Reading extracts as a starter to support the lesson objective on comprehension'.
- '... as a catalyst for phonic teaching, sequencing, grammar, etc.'.

Twenty-eight per cent of the responses were categorised as partial, for example:

- 'To read and enjoy identifying examples of interesting and effective vocabulary'.
- 'Use a big book as a focus for a week and this provides for all instructional activities for reading and writing in literacy'.
- 'For developing comprehension and punctuation, reading and writing'.

The remaining 22 per cent were unspecific, noting for instance:

- 'As a stimulus for topics'.
- 'Cross-curricular work and starters'.
- 'Shared text'.

In relation to using publishers' literacy materials, over a quarter of the teachers noted that they used these on a daily or weekly basis. Such materials can support teachers in exploring texts and can act as a platform for developing their pedagogical content knowledge; however, some are prescriptive and all may be employed in this way, foregrounding skills and functional approaches. Fewer than 10 per cent said they used them monthly, and nearly two-fifths reported using publishers' materials infrequently. Regarding this latter group, it is not known whether they developed their own teaching materials from literature that they knew themselves.

Reading aloud

Reading aloud is a significant pedagogical activity in relation to introducing children to different texts, genres and authors (see Chapter 7), so it was encouraging that 70 per cent of the teachers in Phase I reported having read a book aloud either during the previous month or that they were doing so currently. However, 152 teachers did not respond to this question, which might imply that they did not read aloud to their class, and 9 per cent stated that it was over six months since they had read aloud to the class or that they had never done so. Just under half of the teachers of 7–11 year olds had either only read a complete book to their class within the last 3–6 months or had never done so. This is of particular concern because independent readers need encouragement though introductions to the work of quality writers, as well as the experience of engaging with demanding and emotionally satisfying literature. The experience of sharing a novel cannot be under estimated in relation to developing the skills of inference and deduction and the simple enjoyment of hearing a book lifted off the page (Collins, 2005).

Teachers were also asked to name the last book they had read aloud for pleasure to a class. Picturebooks were by far the most frequently mentioned (35 per cent). Of the total number of book titles mentioned Roald Dahl again dominated with 143 mentions. Fourteen of his titles were noted with *Charlie and the Chocolate Factory*, *George's Marvellous Medicine* and *The Twits* being the most popular. His books are funny and entertaining, and his ability to play with language appeals to children. However, in relying on his work (favourites from their own childhood), teachers were not arguably introducing children to new authors. Over the years, Dahl's work has been criticised by many teachers and librarians, with Rees arguing that his worlds are 'two dimensional and unreal' (1988: 144) and Cameron (1972) criticising *Charlie and the Chocolate Factory* for being based on false humour and punishment. *The Twits* plays on Dahl's apparent dislike of people with beards and, alongside *George's Marvellous Medicine*, the feeding of negative characters with ill-tasting food. As read-alouds, it is questionable whether these books fall into the category of quality literature.

Other popular titles included several by Julia Donaldson and Francesca Simon's *Horrid Henry* series. The latter (31 mentions) is an easy read for newly fluent 7–8 year old readers and may, as with Dahl, have been suggested by children for their teacher to read. The novel *Holes* by Louis Sachar (7 mentions) may have been prompted by the film adaptation and *Goodnight Mr Tom* by Michele Majorian (16 mentions), may have been prompted by a World War II history focus, as a stimulus for learning about the period. However, there are many other war novels published for young readers. The novels mentioned as read-alouds fell into a range of genres, although fantasy (20 per cent) and mystery/adventure (14 per cent) predominated, with over a third falling into these categories. Smaller percentages were noted for fairy tales, short stories, war stories, school stories, poetry, non-fiction and nineteenth-century classics, in descending order of popularity.

Choosing literature and library use

In deciding which books to use in the classroom, teachers in Phase I reported using several criteria, the most important being 'personal knowledge and interest' (85 per cent), and 'children's recommendations' (64 per cent). For some, guidance from the school literacy coordinator is important (31 per cent), also librarians' recommendations (21 per cent). The finding that the majority rely on their personal knowledge of children's literature, however, raises concerns, since as noted earlier, this is both limited and limiting; many relied upon their childhood reading. To support and develop children as independent readers, teachers need to be able to recommend a richer range.

Questions about library use indicated that just over half of the teachers (52 per cent) use their local library facilities for school, mostly borrowing books for classroom use, but also for professional/personal reading and for visits to the library and from librarians. Teachers with fewer years of teaching experience were less likely to use library services. Sixty-two per cent of those who had taught between 0–5 years reported not using the local library for school purposes. When asked when they had last visited a library with their class, nearly a quarter of the teachers did not respond, and of those who did, 60 per cent noted they had visited over six months ago and 18 per cent noted they had never done so (Table 4.2). Perhaps not surprising, given recent financial cuts in public and school library services, this represents further cause for concern. Although the data will have been influenced by local conditions and arrangements, the overall figures drawn from 11 local authorities indicates at best infrequent visits and serious under-use of librarians' expertise for selecting contemporary literature for learners.

The perceived value of literature

When asked to rank five statements about the importance of literature, the Phase I respondents selected 'developing the imagination as the top priority, and second, 'engaging the emotions'. The role of literature in 'promoting reading' and 'developing knowledge' were ranked third and fourth, and 'developing writing' was rated as having the least importance (Figure 4.2). The lowest rating of the role of literature in developing writing suggests that teachers did not necessarily see the important links between reading and writing and raises further questions about their use of literature: were they divorcing literature from pedagogy? Had it become a mere tool to employ in the context of reading instruction, a resource for shared and guided reading alone?

In recognising the deep imaginative value and emotional engagement which literature can offer, the survey's respondents clearly seek such satisfactions, sustaining themselves

Table 4.2 Responses to the question 'When did you last visit your local library with a class?'

Frequency	Number	Percentage
Within last month	61	7.7
Within last 3 months	51	6.4
Within last 6 months	62	7.8
Over 6 months ago	479	60.1
Never	144	18.1
TOTAL	797	100

Note: There were 289 missing answers to this question.

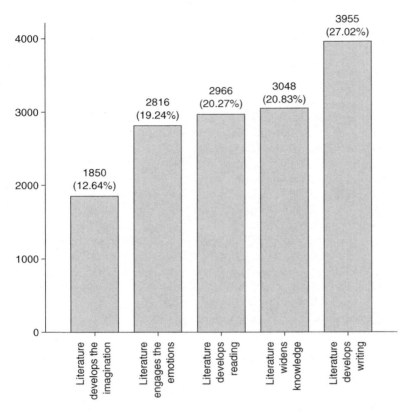

Figure 4.2 Responses to the ranking of five statements about the value of literature (NB. The LOWER the score, the HIGHER the ranking)

as adult readers. However, their apparently limited knowledge of children's writers (particularly of poets and picture fiction creators) and reliance upon this knowledge, without substantial recourse to librarians or literacy consultants, suggest some tensions and difficulties exist for these professionals. They may be able to successfully source their own reading habits, but they are not in a strong position to support younger learners in developing their own preferences. Nor are they arguably in a position to support children's imaginative and emotional engagement in literature or foster their intrinsic satisfaction as readers, despite recognition that literature is critical in this regard. In a not dissimilar manner, the National Curriculum in England notes that pupils need to develop 'culturally, emotionally, intellectually, socially and spiritually' and recognises that 'literature, especially, plays a key role in such development' (DfE, 2013: 14). In the absence of a rich repertoire of children's literature, such development will inevitably be severely constrained.

Conclusion

To motivate young readers and nurture the development of positive reader identities, a breadth of knowledge of good-quality children's literature is essential, as the All-Party Parliamentary Literacy Group argue in the Boys' Reading Commission (2012):

Teachers need knowledge of a range of texts to suit and engage the diverse profiles of children and young people they teach. They need to be comfortable and confident in using them within lessons and as material for pupils' personal reading outside of the classroom.

(APPLG, 2012: 13)

The data from Phase I suggest that personally, teachers read for pleasure as adults and read a range of materials (Cremin *et al.*, 2008a). Their own school experiences appear to have been influential in forming their choices of significant books, suggesting that the current generation of teachers have a vital role to play in promoting young people's enjoyment and commitment to reading. However, and more significantly, primary teachers do not appear to keep abreast of children's literature, they show limited subject knowledge of quality authors, picturebook creators and poets and seem to rely on their own childhood reading (Cremin *et al.*, 2008b). The dominance of the work of Roald Dahl across all areas further reduces the range and breadth of writers being introduced to children and suggests the profession is over-dependent upon a narrow range. The lack of knowledge of world literature and literature in translation is also a concern as is the lack of knowledge of poets, particularly women poets and poets from other cultures. Alongside this the significant number of teachers who cited the titles of picturebooks rather than their creators raises questions, as does the scant mention made of the creators of complex polysemic picturebooks whose work is most suitable for older readers. The relatively large number of teachers who reported relying on publishers' materials, and the few who reported visiting local libraries with their classes, represent further cause for concern.

The research reveals a tension between the personal reading habits and pleasures of the adult teachers and their knowledge and practice with regard to children's literature. It raises the question of whether teachers possess sufficient such knowledge to foster reading for pleasure, and whether they find it difficult to prioritise children's engagement and response as readers in school. It suggests there is an urgent need for increased attention to be paid to both teachers' knowledge and use of children's literature and speculates that increasing teachers' awareness of their own habits and practices as readers might also afford a complementary way forward.

Chapter 5

Enhancing teachers' knowledge of children's literature and other texts

Fiona M. Collins

> The project has given us the confidence to choose how we want to teach literacy. Our subject knowledge – well we see the whole thing of subject knowledge differently now – it's more about knowing how we can put reading at the heart of literacy. We can tell you now about the children's tastes in reading – where they are coming from. I can't believe we didn't know these things. Knowing this has a great impact on the way we use our knowledge of literature.
>
> (Teacher, interview, Birmingham)

This chapter documents the development of teachers' subject knowledge of children's literature and other texts during the Phase II (*Teachers as Readers: Building Communities of Readers*) project year. It is organised according to the key findings of the research in that teachers' subject knowledge developed alongside their willingness to take risks in relation to their choices of texts. Arguably this occurred as a result of an increased confidence and independence in researching new and different reading materials and increased awareness of children's own reading practices and preferences. In turn, this new confidence and wider knowledge impacted on the teachers' use of a richer, more diverse range of books and other texts and enabled them to develop a Reading for Pleasure Pedagogy.

Initial situation in relation to the teachers' subject knowledge

As with Phase I, *Teachers as Readers*, the Phase II teachers were asked to complete a questionnaire which explored their subject knowledge of children's literature (see Appendix). The data showed that the teachers were at different starting points in relation to their subject knowledge. A small number were knowledgeable and enthusiastic about such literature, while most were over-dependent on their childhood reading, had not kept up with current publications or were only familiar with texts linked to published literacy units and schemes, thus reflecting findings from the Phase I data set. The following comments by teachers and self-ratings (out of 6) indicate the diversity of perceived subject knowledge at the beginning of the project year across the group of 43 professionals:

> I am pretty good so I think I would say a 5, people say I'm good and I'm passionate about it .... Probably less so about picturebooks.
>
> (Teacher, interview, Suffolk)

I think I have good knowledge of children's literature from, say, when I was young, but my problem is that I haven't got knowledge of more contemporary children's authors. ... I read a lot when I was younger; I think I'm still stuck in the 1980s.

(Teacher, interview, Birmingham)

I can't say I'd ever read many children's books before this project – being Key Stage 2 and all that – I know that's terrible but it's the truth – I just read the one we were doing in the unit and not, if I'm honest, always all of that! It wasn't ever profiled at college really and I'm not sure I saw the point then.

(Teacher, interview, Kent)

The last comment of the three reflects the unsaid sense that for many teachers of older primary children, knowledge of children's literature may not be seen as a priority, which, given children of this age (8–11 years) have recently been shown to hold increasingly negative attitudes to reading (Clark, 2013), raises cause for concern.

Enhancing teachers' subject knowledge through reading and book talk

A particular focus of the first term of the project was to immerse the teachers in children's literature both in the national and local meetings. Time and space to read, talk and develop their subject knowledge was prioritised. As the local authority (LA) coordinator for Kent said of her teachers:

All the teachers on the project were not readers of children's fiction and although not averse to reading, only read for pleasure occasionally – almost guiltily. They felt strongly that the time spent in the autumn up until Christmas without pressure to 'do' anything other than read was crucial.

(LA coordinator, Summer term report, Kent)

Talking about books brings the text alive for readers through extending their understanding and relationship with the narrative. Both adults and children enjoy talking about what they read and through this 'explore what has happened to us by talking it through' (Chambers, 1985: 11). Regular book talk sessions can help readers understand how they interpret or give shape to a text in different ways; a valuable lesson for teachers to learn. The planned book talk sessions within the project gave the teachers an opportunity to share their thoughts and emotions, about their reading, within a safe environment. As Maybin and Moss (1993: 139) state:

Talk about texts is one of the key ways in which readership networks are established. It is through talk about texts that what it means to read and to be a reader are jointly negotiated.

Book talk time in the national meetings

At the national meetings members of the research team, librarians and the projects children's literature expert shared various books alongside pedagogic approaches designed to support the project research aims. These sessions were extremely popular and the impact of them was that teachers made recommendations to each other. The teachers were asked to bring two texts on each day, one adult and one for children, which they were reading for their own interest and pleasure. This sharing of these texts established reading communities, linking readers with different interests and passions. Teachers responded positively to the personal and social dimensions of professional development within the project and commented on how these approaches helped them to consider their roles as models and teachers of reading. It also became clear in the book talk discussions, and in the teachers' responses in their written reflections and reading journals, that they began to consider books as rich material for generating thinking and reading, rather than just viewing them as pedagogical tools to teach literacy skills in extended units of work:

> I identified really early on in the project that one of the reasons the children didn't read for pleasure in my class was that … the way I was delivering – or teaching – was kind of taking the fun out of books … we never really discussed reading with them or said, well you could read a book by such-and-such an author, that kind of made me think, well actually I've got a role to play here. Some of the days we went to in London and some of the [LA] centre-days, we spent time talking about books, enjoying books and I thought 'I need to change my approach here. I need to think about how I introduce books as 'tasks' to them'.
>
> (Teacher, interview, Birmingham)

At the first national day the project teachers were given a proof copy of *Ways to Live Forever* by Sally Nicholls. This amusing and sensitively written book debut novel about an 11 year old boy dying of leukaemia won the Waterstones' Children's Book Award in 2008 and has subsequently been adapted into a film. Many of the teachers started reading the book on the way home from the meeting and when they met again at the second national day they were eager to discuss the narrative and its impact on them personally:

> I couldn't put it down – I loved it. I read an extract to my son because his godmother has leukaemia.
>
> (Teacher, national meeting, Barking and Dagenham)

> I read it and cried, read it to my daughter, she cried, then read it to my class, we shed some tears together. Several couldn't wait to read it to themselves. When I brought in a signed copy of the final version I was almost attacked.
>
> (Teacher, interview, Kent)

At the final national meeting, the publishers Scholastic organised for Sally Nicholls to talk to the group. The reading of this text in common gave the teachers a rich base to engage in book talk which allowed them to question, negotiate and explore the content of the story with their colleagues.

Book talk time in the local meetings

In their local groups, teachers were encouraged to broaden their subject knowledge, set themselves reading targets and keep lists of what they were reading (see Chapter 3 for more details). Local practices varied, for example in Suffolk and in Barking and Dagenham, teachers were asked to bring a picturebook by a creator they were unfamiliar with and introduce it to the group. In Medway, 'speed dating' was developed with teachers bringing six texts (adult and children's) and speaking to six people about each of these individually. The formal and informal dialogue which occurred about the books prompted the teachers to read more. Book swapping between them became common practice as they recommended books they had read and enjoyed to each other. Through these and other practices, communities of readers developed and teachers learnt from each other.

In each LA, teachers were provided with new books related to their chosen theme – poetry, world literature, picture fiction and short stories. Some were funded by the LA, others by Walker books, Scholastic publishers and local libraries. The Medway teachers were also supported in responding aesthetically as 'there was a general feeling that there was a lack of knowledge on ways to provide opportunities to respond to poetry' (LA coordinator, Autumn term report, Medway).

The project's children's literature consultant, Prue Goodwin, visited to offer support centred on the specific texts being explored by the teachers. For instance in the two LAs focusing on picturebooks, the session covered 'an in-depth consideration of symbolic, iconic and realistic realisation in picturebooks and time spend on practical interactions with some outstanding books' (Goodwin, Internal report). Goodwin noted that at both of these sessions 'there was considerable difference between individual's knowledge of children's books but it was clear that gaps in experience were narrowing quickly' (Goodwin, internal report). These sessions enthused teachers and introduced them to new and contemporary children's books impacting on their subject knowledge.

The book talk sessions in local groups provided a model for in-depth discussion about texts and through the power of recommendation, the popularity of certain texts developed, these circulated widely between the five LAs: picturebooks such as *Big Blue Sofa* by Tim Hopwood, *The Snow Dragon* by Vivien French and *The Little Mouse* by Emily Gravett became widely known, as well as John Boyne's novel set in Germany during World War II, *The Boy in the Striped Pyjamas*. In several schools, the picturebook artist Marcia Williams became very popular and Alan Bennett's adult book *The Uncommon Reader*, not surprisingly, was widely read. It was recognised that their own reading and the pleasure to be found in it was important:

> There is something comforting in reading for yourself something that you are already familiar with as part of a community.
>
> (LA coordinator, national meeting, Medway)

> We are sharing books that we have read and looked at ourselves. That's different to finding books from a list. That's what we have been able to do this year – at the centre sessions with Sonia [LA coordinator] and at the national days – it's been great to share with other teachers. Not just what works in the class but what books we ourselves have enjoyed.
>
> (Teacher, interview, Birmingham)

Developing teachers' knowledge of children's literature

A premise of the project was that subject knowledge development is critical to the development of rich pedagogic practice and necessary to support children's reading for pleasure. Thus at three stages through the year the teachers were asked to rate their subject knowledge, as can be seen in Table 5.1. An interesting point to note in the table is the dip in the mode in Term 2. This may reflect that some participants had begun to appreciate the limits of their knowledge in relation to the breadth and diversity of contemporary children's literature and had come to understand potential gaps in this.

As in the beginning of Phase II, the teachers, 80 per cent of whom were not literacy coordinators in their schools, were asked to note six 'good' authors, poets and picture-book creators in the questionnaire (see Appendix). At the end of the project, this was repeated and in all three categories, the teachers named more authors, poets and illustrators. Those named showed that the teachers had moved away from a 'canon' and reliance upon their childhood reading and were able to identify a wealth of established and contemporary authors and recent prize-winners. Through reading beyond the known and in some cases out of their comfort zone, the teachers noted many authors who were new to them individually. The selection included those noted in Table 5.2.

Some teachers took risks in other ways and challenged themselves to research and use books and texts that connected to children's popular culture. For example, one reception teacher in Barking and Dagenham focused on the work of the picturebook creator Lauren Child, as she knew that the children in her class enjoyed the *Charlie and Lola* animated television series. She acknowledged that before the project she was unaware of the breadth of work of this postmodern picturebook creator and as result she researched and read all of Lauren Child's work. She then used the children's prior knowledge and enthusiasm for the TV series as a springboard to introduce them to Lauren Child's books and characters, and created a Lauren Child author box for the children to read independently.

Table 5.1 Teachers' self-ratings for subject knowledge across the project year

	Average	Median	Mode
Term 1	3.8	3.8	3.5
Term 2	4.2	4.0	3.0
Term 3	5.0	5.0	5.0

Table 5.2 A selection of 'new' writers noted in the end of project questionnaire

Authors	Poets	Picturebook creators
Malorie Blackman	Grace Nichols	Emily Gravett
Frank Cottrell Boyce	Claire Bevan	Lauren Child
Siobhan Dowd	Tony Mitton	Polly Dunbar
Linda Newberry	Judith Nicholls	Anthony Browne
Jenny Nimmo	Roger Stevens	Mini Grey
Philip Reeve	Kit Wright	Oliver Jefferies

Through the year the project teachers began to respond more thoughtfully to the books they read. As they read more and shared their reading in book talk sessions with one another, they talked increasingly about the impact that the texts had upon them personally. The conversation in the national day book talk sessions developed significantly across the year. Teachers gradually started to respond to texts in a more aesthetic manner and came to consider how reader's responses relate to their life experiences, knowledge, culture and context (Rosenblatt, 1978). They began to respond to children's books as readers, not just as teachers, and the focus of their discussions shifted from being about how a book could be used to teach specific literacy objectives to being focused upon how it affected them as readers. The following comment about *The Boy in the Striped Pyjamas* by John Boyne reflects such a response: 'Very cleverly written – with repeated phrases. The realisation and innocence of it all. There's a moment in the book when he has his hair cut and the realisation of what could happen hits you' (Teacher, national meeting comment, Suffolk). This teacher's thoughtful comment reflects her understanding of the significance of the seemingly simple act of a haircut in the concentration camps of World War II. Through this response she brought together her knowledge of the atrocities of World War II with her reading of a modern children's novel, reflecting the power of narrative on the reader (Protherough, 1983).

Towards the end of the year, teachers demonstrated that their new knowledge and accompanying passion for particular authors, poets and narratives was a valuable and easily shared commodity, one upon which they came to depend:

> It has made me look again at new books, authors, illustrators – all of which has given me enthusiasm to share with the children in the class.
>
> (Teacher, written reflection, Barking and Dagenham)

> The project has had a massive impact on my knowledge of children's books which was previously over-reliant on Dahl! I'm now using a range including picturebooks, poetry, choose your own adventure, comedy, mystery and multicultural literature and have a large bank of recommended books to use with my class.
>
> (Teacher, written reflection, Birmingham)

A deeper understanding of poetry

Medway's focus on poetry meant that teachers in this LA developed their knowledge in a specific way. Poetry books came 'out of the cupboard' and were regularly read and shared rather than just being a focus of standalone units of work in school. Teachers were challenged to read both adult and children's poetry and many commented that this was demanding and involved: '[G]oing the extra mile – for me at least since I've never really found any poetry I liked until this year' (Teacher, interview, Medway).

The teachers shared and developed their knowledge together, swapped books or borrowed anthologies from each other, making copies of favourites and working towards two poetry festivals, one for younger and one for older primary-age children, at which children from across the project schools gathered. These celebratory afternoons involved the children and their teachers in performing and swapping poems and sharing their pleasure in language.

> The teachers have become more aware of poets and their poetry. This has arisen as a result of encouraging the teachers to focus on poets rather than poems with their class …. All the teachers have discovered new poets – some of these are popular, but are 'new' to the teacher.
>
> (LA coordinator, Summer term report, Medway)

Teachers discovered a range of poets, which, whilst not new to some were unknown to others, for example Tony Mitton, Paul Cookson, Valerie Bloom, Roger Stevens, Sheree Fitch, Judith Nicholls and Claire Bevan, and authors who also write poetry, such as Sharon Creech and Berlie Doherty. More women poets were in evidence; concerns about practitioners' knowledge of female poets had been identified in the Phase I questionnaire (Cremin et al., 2008a, b). Several teachers who traditionally focused on classic poetry started to read and enjoy a wider range of more modern poets. Poets' lives and work were also learnt about and teachers were invited to introduce and promote a chosen poet to the rest of the group which proved to be an effective way of enabling teachers to develop a deeper knowledge of the work of particular poets. The teachers read favourites aloud to one another and began to talk more reflectively about poetry, its distinctive patterns, forms, meaning and content. The LA coordinator noted, 'The project has 'freed' the teachers. They have explored poetry through art, music and action but predominately through talk'. This exploration reflects a deeper understanding of poetry and a confidence to explore the poetic form more widely. As the year progressed, so the teachers' developing knowledge and enthusiasm impacted on the children who reciprocated with suggestions, for example: 'The children themselves have helped me to widen my own knowledge, by their own browsing of books (poetry) and then choosing some to read aloud' (Teacher, written reflection, Medway).

A deeper understanding of picturebooks

In Barking and Dagenham and in Suffolk, challenging picturebooks for older, as well as younger primary-age children, were the initial focus. Some of the project teachers of older children had not previously considered working using picturebooks with them. Therefore the challenge was to extend their understanding of how to read multi-layered picturebooks which interlink visual images with written text. However, with time and tailored support, the teachers' knowledge, experience and enjoyment of such picturebooks grew greatly. These teachers not only developed their repertoire of complex picturebooks appropriate to the age group, but they also began to understand the motivating power and rich possibilities inherent in such visual texts: 'I am reading and using a wider range of picturebooks. I now know the importance of pictures and their impact on the story' (Teacher, written reflection, Barking and Dagenham).

In both LAs, teachers were invited to read a wide range of picturebooks and particularly through working with the projects' literature expert, they developed a deeper understanding of the construction of picturebooks in relation to the role of images, and of the complex juxtaposition of words and images (Panteleo and Sipe, 2008; Arizpe and Styles, 2003; Lewis, 2001). Challenging picturebooks such as *Rose Blanche* by Roberto Innocenti and *Flotsam* by David Weisner were read, enjoyed and discussed with older primary age children. The LA coordinators were extremely positive about the impact of the project in relation to their teachers' subject knowledge, book and text talk and awareness of the layers of meaning found in such texts:

The group's knowledge of picturebooks and how to support children to understand the interplay between work and text has been greatly enhanced.... They are more confident in their own ability... to engage reluctant readers and are actively selecting more challenging books for use in cross-curricular units and classroom libraries.

(LA coordinator, Summer term report, Suffolk)

For example, at the beginning of the year, Sue was reluctant to use picturebooks as the basis for teaching and revealed that she had no knowledge of such texts and their use. Her presentations show that she now has the confidence to use such texts in creative and practical ways with her class, enabling them to create their own multi-modal texts.

(LA coordinator, Summer term report, Barking and Dagenham)

The teachers recognised the children's use of higher level thinking skills and the quality of their interaction when talking about the pictures. This resulted in heightened awareness of the impact on learning of visual texts.

(LA coordinator, Summer term report, Suffolk)

A richer awareness of world literature

Across the whole project teachers read and enjoyed novels and short stories aimed at older children. One commented she enjoyed reading Malorie Blackman's work (currently Children's Laureate, 2013–15), and appreciated they appeal to a range of readers with different interests, another that she particularly valued the work of the prize-winning American author Sharon Creech whose book *Walk Two Moons* she had enjoyed so much, she had ordered a set for the school. In recognition of such examples, the External Evaluator stated in her report: 'Teachers described the "freedom" that they experienced in exploring unfamiliar genres and authors, encountering new literature' (Durrant, 2008: 10).

In Birmingham the initial focus was on world literature with the aim to link to children's experiences, lives, and cultural heritage. The Phase I questionnaire data had identified that often the authors and books known and used by teachers did not reflect a pluralistic society (Cremin *et al.*, 2008a, b) and this was recognised as an area for development. The Birmingham teachers challenged themselves to extend their knowledge of literature to include books and texts which represented a more realistic view of England and the world. As teachers noted:

We did really want to do lots more around global literature, our school is in a white working class area and there is a racist element in the community so we were keen to develop the global theme...

(Teacher, interview, Birmingham)

Now we are moving away from the traditional British authors.

(Teacher, interview, Birmingham)

One school bought copies of *The Breadwinner* by Deborah Ellis for the older children. The story follows 11 year old Parvana as she is forced by circumstances to become the breadwinner for her family in a war-torn Taliban-era Afghanistan. Also on World Book Day the school invited an African storyteller to tell traditional stories to the children. Over time the teachers increased their knowledge of global literature and became more aware of the need to use this to ensure that they reflected and built upon the experiences of the pupils in their classes. This led some of the teachers to reap the benefits of introducing their classes to the lives/cultures of children around the world through literature. This impacted on both the children and their teachers, though across the project it remained an area for further development. However, in Birmingham, the coordinator noted:

> The project has given the teachers the confidence and the knowledge to move outside of their 'comfort zone' when it comes to children's literature. This was achieved through introducing the 'global' aim early on in the project. At first, the teachers were a little reticent, but through consistent reinforcement, purchasing a range of books from publishers, including Letterbox Library, and sign-posting specific texts at our meetings, this has proved to be extremely effective.
>
> (LA coordinator, Summer term report, Birmingham)

Knowledge of children's reading practices and preferences

As the project year progressed, the teachers were introduced to various activities on the national meeting days which aimed to develop their subject knowledge more widely, particularly their knowledge of children's reading practices. This work was significant and began to transform teachers' understanding of reading, prompting some to reconceptualise reading in the twenty-first century (Cremin, 2010a).

One key activity, which had a particular impact on the project, was Rivers of Reading, though as professionals the practitioners developed this, adapting it in their own contexts. Based on an idea explored by Burnard (2002) and then further developed by Cliff Hodges (2010), Rivers of Reading is an activity which invites readers to create a river collage reflecting their reading over a specific period of time; this could be 24 hours, a weekend or much longer. Children were invited to draw, stick on/write about anything they read over the weekend – comics, magazines, football programmes, television pages, DVD cases, computer games, cereal boxes, chocolate bars and so on, and were encouraged to invite their parents and brothers/sisters/nans/granddads (anyone who was interested) to join in and write their name next to their entry on the Reading River. These were then brought to school so that the children could share all the reading they had done.

As a result of this experience the project teachers not only came to realise the range of reading material that as adults they read, but also the range of texts that children and their families regularly engage with outside school. One Birmingham teacher used Rivers of Reading with her 5 and 6 year old children, noting that she had 'discovered so much more [about the children's reading] during this project' (Winchester, 2008: 21). Figure 5.1 shows two examples of children's Rivers of Reading. The first reveals the cover of the Shrek 3 DVD, reading a ketchup bottle label in a restaurant and the *Happy Horse* story, and has comments from both parents and the names of Jessica's family members. It reflects a range of literacy practices

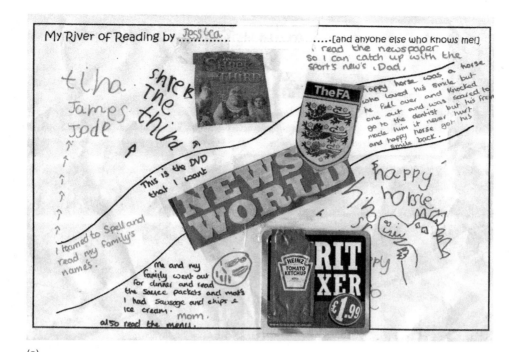

(a)

(b)

Figure 5.1 Examples of children's Rivers of Reading

carried out by all of the family. The second, in highlighting the range of environ-mental print encountered over a weekend, also positions Shifah's school bag, with her school book alongside it on the river, indicating that this is only a strand of the many reading practices in which she takes part. The third shows the magazine culture and more contemporary reading practices undertaken by 9 year old Afraa and her family (Figure 5.2).

The Rivers of Reading enabled teachers to learn more about the wealth of materials that children read out of school for personal enjoyment and prompted them to make connections to this breadth. It also impacted on their perspectives, for example:

> When we started the project we realised that our immediate challenge was actually getting children to read... anything. So we needed to start with where they were and that was the popular genres – comics – magazines – joke books – that was the way in for us.
>
> (Teacher, interview, Birmingham)

> The Reading Rivers made me personally reassess what children are reading in this high-tech age.
>
> (Headteacher, interview, Suffolk)

This move away from the literature of the classroom into exploring the mate-rial that children read beyond school was enlightening for many. In effect, through finding out about the children's practices and home-based preferences, the teachers began to appraise their often book-based conceptions of reading. Reading Rivers and other activities such as 24 Hour Reading, in which children (and their teach-ers) brought to school examples of all the reading they had undertaken in the last 24 hours, meant the teachers were prompted to consider this range. This encouraged the practitioners to widen the range of material that was welcomed in the classroom; for many this was a move away from a culture of teacher-selected literary texts. Some children also asked their parents to keep a 24 Hour Reading Record of what they were reading and this prompted conversations about what counts as reading in school and beyond. Furthermore, the teachers not only sought to find out what children read at home, but also sought to honour the learners by reading some of this and actively responding to it: 'The children have taken me on a journey into what they read outside school – I never realised really it was so wide – now we have a much greater choice in school' (Teacher, interview, Kent).

Over time the materials with which teachers became acquainted, and which they made newly available in school, encompassed magazines and comics, graphic novels and cata-logues, books, fiction and non-fiction, poetry, newspapers (both local and national), sports reports, junk mail and much more besides through the internet. The impact of reading visual texts such as comics and graphic novels not only extended teachers' knowledge, but also gave them greater understanding of the challenging nature of such reading. As one teacher noted: 'I'd never read a graphic novel before – it was quite demanding – the children love them' (Teacher, interview, Medway).

Comics and magazines are habitual reading matter for a great many children. The regular purchase of a weekly publication is important part of many children's reading for pleasure. A survey by the National Centre for Research in Children's Literature

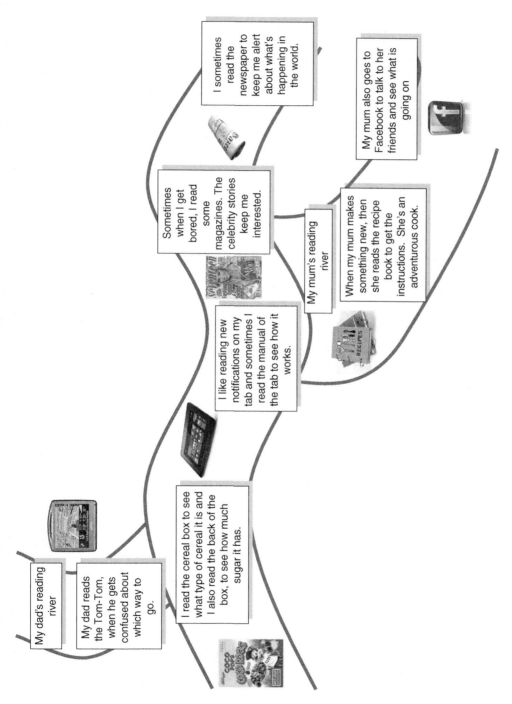

My dad's reading river

My dad reads the Tom-Tom, when he gets confused about which way to go.

I read the cereal box to see what type of cereal it is and I also read the back of the box, to see how much sugar it has.

I like reading new notifications on my tab and sometimes I read the manual of the tab to see how it works.

Sometimes when I get bored, I read some magazines. The celebrity stories keep me interested.

I sometimes read the newspaper to keep me alert about what's happening in the world.

My mum's reading river

When my mum makes something new, then she reads the recipe book to get the instructions. She's an adventurous cook.

My mum also goes to Facebook to talk to her friends and see what is going on

Figure 5.2 Afraa's Reading River

(NCRCL) in 2005 found that 71 per cent of primary children read comics regularly. In that year, the *Simpsons Comics* and *The Beano* were found to be the most popular comics for older primary-age children (Maynard *et al.*, 2007). Reading comics not only gives children immense pleasure but engages them in reading different types of texts and shows how humour is represented in both words and pictures. Children's enjoyment in comics is reflected in the way that they read and reread them at length; they 'command reader identification and involvement' (Bromley, 2000: 42). Teachers became much more aware of the significance of comics in children's reading repertoires and they became accepted/welcomed in most classrooms.

Teachers also became aware that they needed to keep more abreast of current trends in children's popular fiction. One teacher described how a lack of knowledge of specific book, author or genre can mean that teachers, are prevented from engaging in meaningful book talk with younger readers: 'Harry Potter is an example of this where children were talking about it and drawing upon it in their work but teachers hadn't necessarily read the books so were unable to participate in knowledgeable way' (Teacher, interview, Medway).

Together with this awareness, a growing understanding permeated the group that their personal childhood reading was not necessarily relevant today: '[B]ooks that I read as a child may not have the same impact [on today's children] and I really need to keep reading to keep up to date' (Teacher, interview, Barking and Dagenham).

This recognition was in stark contrast to the reliance upon favourite children's authors found in the Phase I research, in which Road Dahl was cited by many teachers as their favourite childhood author, he was also the most cited 'good' author and was the most popular author to read aloud in class (Cremin *et al.*, 2008a, b). Teachers also became aware that 'No two readers are the same' (Cliff Hodges, 2010: 182) and that in order to motivate young readers it is important to suggest texts which will engage and interest them; matching the text to the child. One teacher, Maya, who taught 9–10 year olds, recognised that no boys in her class read for pleasure; there was a stigma attached to boys' reading, which she reported was seen as 'nerdy, girly and uncool'. So she organised book boxes to engage and interest her reluctant boy readers and let her focus children (all of whom were male) run this 'boys' library'. Girls were denied access to this resource, which over time proved to be a fruitful strategy, not only for the young boy readers, but also for Maya, who realised that if she was going to be able to discuss these tales (which comprised mostly short Ginn Readers) with the boys, she would need to read them herself. However, as she observed, prior to her involvement in the project, she would never have considered reading a single one of them as they were 'books for boys'. Thus the project nudged her out of her 'comfort zone' and expanded her knowledge.

Taking responsibility for ongoing subject knowledge development

As the year progressed, the teachers' subject knowledge improved and their interest in and attitude to children's reading material became much more positive. In interviews and final reflections, most stated that the project had had a substantial impact on them and voiced the view that they were considerably more confident about their repertoires of children's literature and that they intended to try and keep up to date with the work of new authors.

Their involvement in reading, recommending and discussing texts with their fellow peers both nationally and locally, helped them continue to widen their knowledge, and as documented more fully in later chapters, the teachers began to share and talk about books in their schools and observed the impact that their 'coming out' as readers had on the children: '[T]he children see us swapping books and talking about books …. Sharing something like that in front of the children, quite naturally, is very powerful' (Teacher, interview, Barking and Dagenham).

The local reading communities which developed during the project year encouraged the teachers to take responsibility for sustaining their enhanced knowledge of reading. Teachers also organised themselves into informal reading groups in and between schools in order to share and discuss their reading. These groups varied and included informal conversations over lunch in staff rooms, regular slots before staff meetings and more developed semi-structured reading groups:

> The Kent group has begun to develop as a self-motivated adult reading group. They share adult and children's books both at meetings and through email, text messages and in unexpected contexts when they meet. They attend seriously to each other's recommendation and make a note of them so as not to forget.
>
> (Researcher, observational notes, Kent)

Another way in which the teachers took increased responsibility for developing their own knowledge was through widening their text selection sources. Many began to search out new and different books and authors through reading book reviews, researching the winners of book awards, such as the prestigious Carnegie and Kate Greenaway Medal Award scheme (Butler *et al.*, 2011), subscribing to the children's literature magazine *Books for Keeps*, visiting bookshops and exploring websites:

> I loved that, it was *Journey to the River Sea* I think it was called and I noticed when I went on the internet' cos I've started looking at sites, which is not me at all 'cos I hate going on the computer, but I did notice that there were a number of other Eva Ibbotson books as well. I desperately want to read some more of hers.
>
> (Teacher, interview, Birmingham)

The project not only encouraged teachers to extend and develop their own personal libraries of children's books, but also book collections in schools were considerably extended: new books were purchased and book boxes established as well as book loans organised from local library services. Increasingly, children were involved in this process and in decision-making about the books to be bought and borrowed. Increasingly too, the teachers' employed their newly acquired subject knowledge for planning and in their classroom practice. As Chapter 7 documents, this enabled them to establish a Reading for Pleasure Pedagogy. As one aptly summarised: 'Knowing more authors has made the world of difference to my teaching. I recommend books now to particular children and have begun to plan my own work using writers I never knew existed' (Teacher, interview, Suffolk).

Conclusion

Given that 80 per cent of the project teachers were not literacy subject leaders in their schools, the initial limitations in knowledge revealed by some were not perhaps surprising. Across the project year all the teachers markedly improved their knowledge of children's literature and other texts and this affected their confidence, understanding and pleasure in reading a wider range of texts. This occurred through project-led sessions and, significantly, through book talk and informal reader-to-reader recommendations. The strong emphasis on this supported teachers in developing more aesthetic responses to books for children. Thus, rather than thinking about how these texts could be used to teach specific learning objectives, teachers began more thoughtfully to consider their meanings and how these texts touched their lives. Teachers developed the habit of sharing their new reading discoveries with each other, both locally and nationally. Their increased knowledge of children's texts was frequently accompanied by an enthusiasm, which they passed onto young readers; as a result, reciprocal recommendations occurred in many classes where children and teachers recommended texts to each other and then discussed them. The power of this reader-to-reader support cannot be over-emphasised; it helped establish reading networks in project classrooms.

Teachers also recognised the value of knowing more about the children's everyday reading lives and practices, and sought to recognise and celebrate this diversity in school. Though the teachers were challenged by getting to know more world literature and poetry, and some teachers of older readers found it difficult initially to appreciate the value of picturebooks, over time this was mostly overcome. The newly qualified teachers had to work the hardest at widening their repertoires, but as they came to understand the significance of their subject knowledge they, like their more experienced colleagues, took increased responsibility for developing and sustaining this knowledge over time.

Chapter 6

Reading Teachers

Teachers who read and readers who teach

Teresa Cremin

Whilst a rich knowledge of children's literature and other texts is crucial to support reading for pleasure, teachers also need to be able to draw on deep knowledge and understanding of the nature of reading, developed in part through the experience of being a reader. Through reflecting upon their identities as readers, teachers can became more conscious of their reading practices, more aware of the passion, pleasure and pain involved and may begin to consider reading from the inside – as readers, not just as teachers of reading. Such professionals have been described as Reading Teachers – teachers who read and readers who teach (Commeyras *et al.*, 2003). In essence, these are teachers who not only value reading personally, but who actively seek to explore the potential of teaching from a reader's *and* a teacher's point of view. In order to develop positive reader identities in young people such practitioners consider their own and children's reading lives and practices, creatively adapting their pedagogy and positioning in the classroom as a result. They engage as role-models, but also as fellow readers; members of an engaged community of readers.

This chapter focuses upon the insights of the Phase II project, *Teachers as Readers: Building Communities of Readers*, regarding Reading Teachers (RTs); it notes the renewed pleasure in reading which teachers developed and reveals the challenges involved. Working in accountability cultures, with targets and tests predominantly focused on phonics and comprehension, professional practice is often constrained or compromised (Assaf, 2008; English *et al.*, 2002). These constraints, the project found, also served to limit teachers' engagement as readers in school. Nonetheless, some of the teachers who became more conscious of themselves as readers risked sharing their reading lives with younger learners and experienced the transformative potential of adopting such a stance in the classroom. Through supported reflection, these professionals became more mindful of the diversity of their reading preferences and practices, the ways in which they engaged emotionally and exercised their agency as adult readers, and began to appreciate the social nature of reading. Reviewing their reading practices and identities, and finding out more about the children's, prompted these teachers to challenge their assumptions about the solitary nature of reading, align their understandings with the lived experiences of learners, and broaden what was recognised and validated as reading in their classrooms.

Those teachers who developed most fully as RTs appeared to make more of an impact upon the children than their colleagues in the project did. They more markedly influenced disaffected readers' attitudes and attainment and in the process developed more overtly reciprocal reading communities in school, communities in which both adults and children were engaged as readers. This chapter shares the many ways in which, positioned as readers, these enhanced professionals began to develop children's metacognitive awareness as readers, made available new forms of participation and fostered the young people's pleasure and engagement as readers. It also suggests ways in which practitioners can develop as RTs.

Reading Teachers

Research on teachers' literate identities indicates that their engagement as readers (and writers) is important as it enables them to model the value, pleasure and satisfaction in leading 'a literate life' (Kaufman, 2002). If a teacher is visibly an active reader and writer, Kaufman (2002) argues, they will induct young literacy learners into 'living their own literate lives'. In supporting teachers' considerations of their identities as readers, the project adopted the view that identity is not something that one 'has', but that it is something one actively pursues, thus recognising the 'doing of identity' (Hall, 2008). Identity involves on-going work and roles are not fixed, but are constantly in the process of being produced in different contexts (Urrieta, 2007). Drawing on the work of Holland *et al.* (1998) and Holland and Lave (2001), the team saw identity as situated, positional and thus multiple and enacted in interaction (McCarthey and Moje, 2002). For example, when teachers seeking to position themselves as RTs constructed and enacted their identities as readers in the classroom, they did so in relation to others – children, other teachers, teaching assistants and parents for example. This notion of relational identity positioning is significant when considering how teachers both perceive themselves and are (or are not) perceived by children as readers in the classroom. Arguably, through sharing their home reading practices or memories of learning to read and presenting themselves as readers in various ways in school, they were helping themselves seem and feel literate (Bartlett, 2007).

Children's conceptualisations of what it means to be a reader are constructed at an early age through their interactions with significant others in the home and in school (Levy, 2009). They learn what counts as reading and what it means to be a reader in different contexts and rapidly come to appreciate the consequences (both positive and negative) associated with the various reading identities made available to them (McDermott *et al.*, 2006). Research suggests that teachers create and privilege their own understandings of available reading identities (Hall *et al.*, 2010). For example, in this US study, children were categorised as 'poor' readers, 'good' readers or 'becoming good' readers, and this had considerable consequence for the kinds of instruction and support they received. As Hall *et al.* note:

> Students were expected to ascribe to the dominant models of identity or risk being marginalized. Furthermore, teachers seemed unaware that students believed there was a social risk in trying to become a good reader and that working towards such an identity required first outing oneself as a poor one.
>
> (2010: 241)

Often identity models or positions in the classroom are not able to be questioned due to unequal power relations, so young people's identities as readers are at least in part framed and shaped by teachers' conceptualisations of readers and reading. However, if teachers become more conscious of their own identities as readers, more mindful of their own diverse practices and preferences, and more aware of the influence of text and context for example, then it is possible that this will prompt them to consider the younger readers' identities, practices and preferences also. They may additionally come to consider the identity positions made available to children in the classroom by their own routines, expectations, text organisation and wider pedagogic practice.

Studies focusing on teachers as readers indicate an apparent continuity between teachers and children as engaged and self-motivated readers (Commeyras et al., 2003; Cox and Schaetzel, 2007; Dreher, 2003). In the case studies documented by Rummel and Quintero (1997) for example, it is reported that the teachers' lives and classroom practices were strongly influenced by their pleasure in literature which nurtured both them and in turn their pupils. These studies suggest that being a reader frames and supports teachers of reading, who gain both personal and professional support as they seek to apprentice younger readers and model their own pleasure in reading.

However, whilst these mainly US studies assert the existence of a link between a teacher's reader identity and pedagogy, this remains little more than an unexamined assumption, and the available evidence relies almost entirely on potentially problematic self-reports of teachers' classroom practices. None of the studies noted above observes teachers and children together in classrooms, so they are not able to consider their positions, interactions and engagement as readers, nor are children's perspectives on their teachers as readers documented. The Phase II project responded to both these methodological weaknesses and, through the case studies (see Chapter 3 for more details), sought to gain more in-depth data about the teachers and the children's positions and perspectives as readers.

Teachers' increased pleasure in reading

The Phase I *Teachers as Readers* research revealed a tension between the personal habits and pleasures of the adult teacher readers and their lack of professional knowledge and assurance with children's literature (Cremin et al., 2008a). The teachers did read for pleasure, and were keen on both popular fiction and a wider range of texts, but knew relatively little children's literature (Cremin et al., 2008a, b) (see Chapter 4). As a consequence, in the Phase II project, the teachers were actively supported as readers: dedicated time was set aside for sharing their current reading (both adults and children's), texts were read aloud and recommended to them and local groups set up book boxes and explored various genres and authors/poets for children. Through finding both more material worth reading and others to share the reading experience with, the teachers made more time to read and rediscovered the satisfaction of reading: 'I've been introduced to so many good books – it's great – really reawakened my pleasure in reading. I always have a book in my bag now in case I get 5 minutes to read' (Teacher, interview, Kent).

Most of the teachers set themselves personal reading challenges; some celebrated their widening repertoires by displaying certificates in their classrooms when, for example they had read 10 self-chosen children's and/or adult texts. They frequently talked about this newly ignited interest in reading which encompassed texts of various kinds and formats, both for adults and children. The impact of their increased pleasure in reading on partners, families and pupils was also repeatedly mentioned, in conversations, reading logs and interviews, as was the making and receiving of recommendations and the myriad of classroom consequences of this renewed enthusiasm. For example:

> My new bedtime habits are being transferred to my husband as I bought him *Reach for the Sky* about Douglas Bader and he then bought a Ralph Fiennes – now we read together.
>
> (Teacher, interview, Kent)

> There's more quality time for reading so there's more enjoyment of reading. And we're not feeling guilty. Even my husband has started reading and we read on the weekends now – it's a real change.
>
> (Teacher, written reflection, Medway)

> Reading again has given me back my enthusiasm when I am reading to the children. Their enthusiasm has been rubbing off on me as they love their daily story time and so I've given myself more time for my own reading – it works both ways.
>
> (Teacher, written reflection, Barking and Dagenham)

> I feel like the project has given me permission to read again – to choose – connect and enjoy books for their own sake, in school and out.
>
> (Teacher, interview, Suffolk)

Challenges involved in developing as a Reading Teacher

However, whilst the teachers in the project found new satisfactions as readers and were keen to develop the children's desire to read, from the outset many expressed reservations about developing as RTs and taking time from teaching in order to share with the children something of their engagement as readers and their reading lives and practices. Many were unconvinced that such a stance would significantly influence the children's attitudes or attainment, for example: 'I'm not sure they need to know about me as a reader, after all my focus should be on them – on raising standards and so on' (Teacher, interview, Kent); 'I have found this hard and don't get it yet – I'm still not sure it would really make a difference' (Teacher, interview, Medway).

Understandably, after 10 years of prescribed reading practice, in line with English National Literacy Strategy (DfEE, 1998; DfES, 2006) expectations, practitioners found the open-ended and innovative nature of a RT stance created uncertainty. It was not part of the reading discourse (nor indeed was reading for pleasure at this time) and many were concerned that no specified reading objectives were being 'covered' when teachers and learners explored their practices, preferences and experiences as readers. For example: 'I'm not used to working without specific objectives' (Teacher, written reflection, Birmingham); 'It's hard to know what one is 'covering' if you know what I mean' (Teacher, interview, Medway).

The teachers, who were used to leaning on the explicit instructional pedagogies of shared and guided reading and working within well-known and defined literacy boundaries, clearly perceived themselves to be under pressure to focus on the named and framed skills-based objectives set out for each class/year group of children. Whilst prepared to make time and space for changes to their pedagogic practice in other ways, by setting up reading corners, establishing the practice of regularly reading aloud and creating time for independent reading and talk about books (see Chapter 7), several were reticent to take the risk of introducing this more personal dimension and sharing something of themselves as readers, for instance: 'I feel guilty I should not be talking about me' (Teacher, written reflection, Kent).

Initially, many voiced the view that taking time from instruction and the given curriculum in this way was probably not justified; they were unconvinced of the value of 'coming out as a reader' and were tentative about reflecting on their own reading histories and experiences as readers with young people. Whilst it is argued that the enthusiasm teachers show for reading and the pleasure they take in it acts to motivate young readers (Commeyras et al., 2003; Kaufman, 2002; Sanacore, 2002), and that teachers who lack this passion affect learners negatively (Applegate and Applegate, 2004), for some, stepping beyond sharing their enthusiasm for reading was hard. The sense of personal 'exposure' involved appeared to create a degree of discomfort for some professionals and challenged their perceptions of their roles as educators, for example: 'Surely as a professional I shouldn't be talking about my reading life, I need to focus on the children' (Teacher, interview, Kent); 'How far should we/could we allow our personal lives into the classroom?' (Teacher, interview, Barking and Dagenham).

The practical and conceptual challenges involved meant that not all of the 43 project teachers explored the transformative potential of this personal/professional identity shift. In one classroom, for example, a teaching assistant, commenting upon a discussion in which, alongside the teacher, she had talked briefly about her favourite childhood book, made it clear that such work was viewed as tangential, an optional extra: 'Children were also giving their views/memories of important books in the discussion, but as this was a digression from the main literacy lesson, the discussion was not extended upon' (Written reflection, Suffolk).

Several saw being an RT as simply being an enthusiastic teacher of reading and did not fully discover the scope of this arguably more personal, creative, discursive and reciprocal stance towards teaching reading. However, with support and through early positive feedback from children, some of the teachers began to respond to the challenge:

> It's strange talking about my reading – it feels odd, I'm so much older than them and we have different interests – but I have to admit they're always interested – keen to know about what I'm reading and how I go about it.
>
> (Teacher, written reflection, Suffolk)

> I feel like I have exposed part of myself to the children and have regained a love and pleasure of reading which had stopped – you have to make time to read and share it – it is vital.
>
> (Teacher, written reflection, Kent)

Critical of the testing regime and concerned to realise that they were positioned predominantly as instructors and assessors, some sought to experiment with the concept and positioned themselves overtly as readers in the classroom. As Pavlenko and Blackledge assert, teachers are 'agentive beings who are constantly in search of new social and linguistic resources which allow them to resist identities that position them in undesirable ways' (2004: 27). By the close of the project a continuum of practice existed: approximately 40 per cent of the teachers had actively grasped the concept and become RTs;

most made occasional forays into sharing their reading lives; a few had simply shared their growing enthusiasm for reading.

Reading Teachers re-conceptualising reading

Despite the recognised value of enhancing children's metacognition, teachers relatively rarely help children reflect upon their experiences as readers; rather they tend to focus upon developing and assessing the content/products of their reading (Hall *et al.*, 1999). However in this project, as teachers reflected more consciously on their own reading experiences, shared their thoughts with their peers in the local groups and found out about the children's everyday reading lives, they began to widen their conceptions of what counts as reading and being a reader in the twenty-first century. In particular, those who positioned themselves more consciously as RTs demonstrated increased awareness of the significance of all readers' personal preferences and practices, emotional engagement, the social nature of reading and the salience of readers' rights and agency. As they reviewed and redescribed reading, they also reframed their pedagogic practice in responsive ways to connect to and support the children and build communities of engaged readers.

The RTs' gradual openness to reflect upon themselves as readers also contributed to children's conceptions of reading. 'If reading is anything' as Meek (2002) observes, 'it is the ability to think about meaning'. Together, teachers and children in the project began to foreground just this – attention to the content and substance, meaning and purpose of the diverse texts they all chose to read. As one noted:

> As an infant school perhaps we are caught up in teaching early reading skills. We can underplay the next steps in becoming; in being readers who have a choice, readers who are making meaning, readers who are connecting with others in stories and poems in order to express themselves in a way they don't know or can't know how to. Readers who are seeking other lives and ways of being – just as we are as adult readers.
>
> (Teacher, written reflection, Medway)

Diverse preferences and practices

The issue of what counts as reading altered significantly across the year. Initially the project teachers mainly perceived the term reading to equate to the reading of fiction and fiction that was traditionally bound in books. This changed dramatically as the teachers reflected upon their own reading and began to find out more about the children's preferences and everyday practices beyond the school (Cremin, 2010a). Some teachers started the year not perceiving themselves to be readers, but then began to reconsider this. Reflecting upon the first national day book talk session, one observed:

> At first I didn't think I had a right to be there – they all had books and I thought I don't have the right to talk about reading, but then if you think about it – what counts as reading and who defines that? I did have a right to be there. I wondered too about my class, did they feel the same?
>
> (Teacher, interview, Birmingham)

Through discussions, reflections and keeping reading logs, the teachers became more conscious of their own preferences, although many underestimated the rich variety and diversity inherent in their reading lives and appeared, like those pre-service teachers in Nathanson *et al.* (2008) to measure their own reading against what they perceived as distinctive or 'literary'. Initially, some found it difficult to acknowledge or share their pleasure in reading magazines or the work of particular authors for example, and were tentative or even embarrassed to mention these. Discussions about implicit hierarchies, and the reification of the novel helped to ease these concerns and gradually the teachers came to recognise and challenge their assumptions about reading, for example: 'I never counted all that as reading, maybe I'm still too book bound' (Teacher, interview, Medway). In so doing they began to question their perceptions of children's preferences:

> My boys particularly are very keen on the Horrible History series, or they get the *First News* and look at sport so they're not necessarily reading books. Before this project I think we would of thought that's not reading, that's not proper reading.
>
> (Teacher, interview, Kent)

Recognising the diversity of texts which they chose to read for pleasure helped the RTs realise that their preferences were uniquely theirs, and influenced by purpose and context, for example browsing magazines to relax, seeking solitude and escapism in a novel and examining holiday websites with the family. The breadth of their preferences encompassed: work by particular authors; autobiographies; biographies; popular fiction; 'classics'; specific magazines and newspapers; travel books; online holiday information; and friends' Facebook pages, tweets and blogs. The RTs began to share some of the rich diversity of the texts and contexts they participated in as readers with children.

> I talk about myself as a reader now to the children – talk about my tastes as an adult reader – they know that I go for travel books – I like reading about different places and cultures – and also new children's fiction.
>
> (Teacher, written reflection, Suffolk)

> I have thought much more about my reading choices and myself as a reader and have talked about these with the children – I wouldn't really have thought about playing a part like this before.
>
> (Teacher, written reflection, Medway)

> My reading habits aren't something I'd ever really thought about. But it really made me think – why haven't I been reading much … 'well I have a lot to do, I'm busy – I need to just relax and do nothing sometimes. I'm tired. Then I thought well, these are Y6 children – they are busy, they go to Mosque school and they have things to do. And I thought – what works for me? I read magazines, short articles. I'm going to share this with the children – this is still reading – they can think about their pastimes, computer games, comics, magazines. Reading short things counts. A lot of them have started reading poetry.
>
> (Teacher, written reflection, Birmingham)

> I read the newspaper on the bus to work and I've started to talk to the children about that. I think they have quite a narrow view of what counts as reading.
>
> (Teacher, interview, Birmingham)

As the RTs moved away from privileging literature, whilst still recognising its power and potency, they began to find out more about the children's practices and interests as readers. The young people led their teachers into new textual territories and RTs developed their knowledge of individuals' reading tastes and choices. As Lutz *et al.* (2006) have shown, when teachers commit time and space to giving individual readers their attention, it fosters children's reading engagement; this was evident here also. Furthermore, the teachers often expressed surprise at the breadth and diversity of their reading beyond school, for example: 'Children are much more vocal about their reading habits and preferences now, we are often really surprised by what they know about and what they read at home – it's so much wider than we'd ever have credited' (Teacher, interview, Medway).

Profiling textual diversity in school became common practice and was shaped by RTs into various activities including, for example, 24 hour Reading, Reading Rivers (detailed in Chapter 8) and Desert Island Texts. Openness and reciprocity underpinned such activities; teachers shared their own reading preferences/practices and invited the children to recognise and share their own, connecting these vitally to purpose and context and their identities as readers. Carrie, who initially had not considered herself as a reader due to her preference for magazines and newspapers, developed the activity Desert Island Texts in order to recognise and share her fondness for such reading material. This involved Carrie explaining to her class which texts she would take to a desert island. These included: Gary Barlow's autobiography *Take That* (having been a teenage fan of the pop group), the current copy of *The Kentish Courier* (in which her school was profiled), *Fantastic Mr Fox* by Roald Dahl (the first book she remembered reading as a child) and the current copy of *OK!* magazine (because she wanted to read the spread on Wayne Rooney's marriage to Colleen McLaughlin). The 9–10 year olds were invited to select their own Desert Island Texts, and made 3D islands to display these with various inventive textual connections on land and sea. They undertook this with considerable enthusiasm and explained their preferences to each other. The three previously disaffected young readers' choices not only reflect their unique interests and preferences as readers, but afford evidence of the genuine acceptance of textual diversity in this RTs' class and their growing confidence as young readers to voice their preferences, these included:

- *Simpsons Comics, Terrible Tudors* and *Gorgeous Georgians* by Terry Deary, *Pig Heart Boy* by Malorie Blackman (Zak);
- *Top Gear Magazine*, Jeremy Clarkson autobiography, R. Hammond autobiography, *Terrible Tudors* by Terry Deary (Adam);
- *The Gift of Christmas, Animal Ark* by Lucy Daniels, *What's out There?* by Lynn Wilson, my phone (Chloe).

(Children, research observation, Kent)

In addition, as readers of fiction the RTs became more aware of their personal habits and strategies which they documented in their reading diaries, these habits were myriad and often extensively debated. For example, whilst some commonly chose to read the end of a novel (e.g. last page/ paragraph/chapter) well before they reached it, others perceived this to be anathema, a practice which 'defies the point' in one teacher's view. Likewise, some found doodling and mark making satisfying, whilst others were offended by it, perceiving it was 'defacing the book or whatever you're reading'. Several referred to skipping descriptive passages, to 'flicking forwards into the action' or 're-reading bits to get going again'.

Teachers came to realise individual tendencies and habits were differently employed depending upon the text and their engagement in it. These included for example:

- folding down corners;
- doodling and/or writing in texts;
- using post-it notes;
- using multiple bookmarks;
- reading several books at once, dipping into each at will;
- reading the end of a novel early on;
- re-reading passages/chapters;
- skimming through the start to get into a story;
- skipping long, descriptive passages.

The RTs shared their habits with children in various ways, triggering new conversations about the experience of reading. For example, one teacher told her class that she had read the first 100 pages of *Northern Lights* by Philip Pullman before she had felt really involved or keen to read on. She acknowledged she had only persevered because so many people had recommended it. Eventually, however, she stayed up late into the night reading it and 'simply couldn't put it down'. As a consequence, her class discussed the value of perseverance and stamina for reading 'books that deserve it', as one boy noted. This conversation led the 10–11 year olds to create a list of such books, not all of which were lengthy, but which they perceived demanded stamina.

Social and affective engagement

In the local and national groups, sustained time was set aside for the teachers to read and talk about their reading. On national days they brought in an adult's and a children's text to recommend to each other, and had over an hour to discuss these in small groups. The speed with which the teachers collectively engaged in these reading groups was remarkable, as were the significant shifts in the teachers' discourse during the year. In the autumn term, teachers' talk about their self-chosen children's literature was dominated by a professional focus. They concentrated on what the book was good for in relation to set literacy objectives (e.g. relating to teaching character, plot, setting and particular language or literary devices) and on how long the book would sustain a literacy focus and the amount of work it could generate. For example:

- 'It's great for character and there are loads of alliterations too so you could work on those'.
- 'It'll keep you going for a month as it does settings really well with all the changes'.
- 'I've used it for history too so it double counts if you know what I mean'.

(Teachers, comments, national day)

This was largely at the expense of almost any mention of the content or meaning of the narrative, or of how individual books affected them personally or might affect younger readers. Virtually all the connections that were made were professional and related to using literature as a tool to deliver assessable literacy skills in specific year groups.

In contrast, in discussing their self-chosen adult books, meaning and affect were fore-grounded; teachers' voiced personal views and emotional responses about the narrative or non-fiction and discussed emerging cultural, social or moral issues for example. Additionally, life-to-text and text-to-life connections were frequently shared. The power of texts to reveal new things about themselves and the world and evoke their curiosity was also discussed. Comments were also made about writing style, the language and the author's interests and/ or skill, although these were not as numerous. Making meaning and affective connections tended to be privileged when reading and discussing their adult reading, in alignment with Rosenblatt's (1978) 'aesthetic reading' which, she notes, occurs when the literary reader 'also pays attention to the associations, feelings, attitudes and ideas that the(se) words and their referents arouse' (p. 24). In the early months, the teachers appeared to adopt a more effer-ent stance to the children's texts, which Rosenblatt (1978) describes as occurring when a readers 'attention is directed outward ... towards actions to be performed after the reading' (ibid.).

However, as the year progressed, more children's literature was read and the experi-ence of reading and being a reader was explicitly considered, teachers' talk about texts for the young began to alter. They gave increased attention to the layers of meaning and personal response to children's texts and whilst still aware of the potential of these texts to support literacy teaching, they began to talk more about such literature not just as a resource to be studied, but as literature worth reading for its own sake. Texts to be experienced and enjoyed, not merely read, analysed and examined in order to fulfil prescribed literacy goals.

The RTs in particular came to see affect and engagement as crucial to motivating themselves as readers and began to voice their thoughts and feelings in class about texts they were reading, many for the first time. For example, several spontaneously shared with their classes that they had cried whilst reading books such as *Ways to Live Forever* by Sally Nicholls, *Elsewhere* by Gabrielle Zevin and *The Boy in the Striped Pyjamas* by John Boyne. As one teacher observed: 'It's ok to be moved by a book – if it makes you cry in public then it shows you're human'. Others talked about their anger at the actions of fictional characters in *A Thousand Splendid Suns* by Khaled Hosseini and of current politi-cal figures in the news. The children, having observed the marked emotional impact a text had made upon their teacher, were often interested to hear more or read the books themselves. This prompted informal waiting lists for books and fostered the development of more children's 'books in common' and new reader to reader networks. In this way RTs were inviting children to experience their passion for reading and for particular texts that had personal resonances for them as adults. Gannon and Davies (2007) argue that affect is relational and may even, in some contexts, be intersubjective. Certainly in the RTs' classrooms, many examples of shared passion and pleasure in texts were observed and these were seen to act as reading motivators. RTs noticed that their openness to sharing more of themselves with the children, and discussing their values, emotions and attitudes in casual yet serious conversations about texts, markedly influenced the young learners who began to see their teachers differently. As the RTs shared what certain texts made them think and feel, teachers perceived that children too came to talk more openly and spontaneously about their feelings and the issues arising from texts they were reading.

For instance: 'The children also became much more open in saying how a story made them feel – I suppose because I had modelled it' (Teacher, written reflection, Barking and Dagenham).

These responsive discussions offered the RTs rich opportunities to get to know the young people better and to understand the children's perspectives on their lives. They often explicitly sought to tap into the hearts (and minds) of the young readers and developed a kind of 'readerly empathy' (Gordon, 2012) with children, which involved increased awareness of their feelings and attitudes to particular texts and of the life-experiences upon which the children drew. This enhanced teachers' sensitivity to the ways in which the children experienced the act of reading. Discussing literature and other texts appeared to create new and personal bonds between teachers and children; these reshaped traditional relationship boundaries (see Chapter 8).

For example, at the start of the year Carrie acknowledged that pressured by the national assessment tasks, she felt she hadn't any time to read, rarely read aloud for pleasure to her class of 9–10 year olds and didn't discuss her own or the children's reading. Yet in term three she observed that before registration, at break and during independent reading time she frequently found herself engaged in informal and unprompted reader-to-reader conversations. In commenting on this 'new openness', she observed:

> They know me as me now and there's a new kind of relationship – we talk about everything together, and they're so much more forthcoming now that they know I read. They constantly share stuff they're reading with me, loan me books and magazines and there's masses more 'book talk' – well talk about all kinds of texts and issues – newspaper articles, stuff we see on TV – you know'.
>
> (Teacher, interview, Kent)

Positioning herself as an RT, who shared her reading practices and views, read aloud regularly and knew more about the children as readers and as young people, Carrie had enabled the architecture of a new community of practice to develop in her classroom and in the process had arguably altered the lived experience of reading both for herself and the children. This was exemplified one wet breaktime when a group of children were gathered in an apparently impromptu manner urgently discussing Malorie Blackman's *Cloud Busting*. When Carrie walked past, one of her previously disaffected boy readers, who knew she had read it, invited her into the conversation. In the heated discussion that followed, Carrie's contribution was 'but one voice among many' (Nystrand *et al.*, 2003: 187); she did not dominate or assert her view with authority, but agreed with one child, disagreed with another and demonstrated her desire to talk about the issues of friendship and betrayal in the book.

Voicing their perspectives on texts and sharing their identities as engaged interactive readers, both in the professional development sessions and in their classrooms, the RTs came to see reading as more of a social practice, both for themselves and for younger readers. They commented upon and valued the informal interaction and reciprocal reader recommendations and relationships which developed, and began to adopt a broader conception of reading in which talk was seen to be crucial and constitutive. It was no longer viewed as an optional extra to talk about texts *if* there was time, nor was such talk viewed as a 'speaking and listening activity' within the curriculum, but as endemic to reading and being a reader.

I see reading differently now – I'm not sure why I didn't recognise how social it is – I just thought of it as personal book reading … that's all changed.

(Teacher, interview, Medway)

I trained quite recently and just learnt about teaching reading – you know, sounding out and skills and such. This project has made me think about much more – about developing readers and what readers actually do – why they bother and the pleasure and real importance of talking about it.

(Teacher, interview, Medway)

Nor were the conversations confined to texts, the relationships that developed opened up new opportunities for dialogue:

[Such talk was] connected to anything and everything – you know, books, authors, reading, homes, families, sisters and brothers, relationships, politics – life.

(Teacher, interview, Kent)

I find that I am able to talk in detail about books with the children – in an informal way – without a set purpose in my mind of what I want them to be achieving and where I want this conversation to be going. Presenting myself as a reader to the children and discussing what I'm reading has opened up new sorts of conversations between us.

(Teacher, interview, Birmingham)

Being a Reading Teacher makes me feel more connected to the children, we seem to have more in common now. Through sharing my reading life, I share more of my own views and values with them and they've opened up too.

(Teacher, interview, Birmingham)

Readers' rights

At the start of the project the focus children clearly felt they had little control over what they could read in school. Some were limited to reading scheme books; others, classed as 'free readers', were required to select from a colour-coded box; few were offered anything other than class or school library books. Over time, however, the teachers began to recognise the agency evident in their own adult reading practices. They chose what to read for pleasure: recognised their favourite authors/newspaper/magazines/websites; acknowledged the influence of friends' recommendations and their own reading habits; and exercised their discrimination and rights as readers. As a consequence the RTs came to appreciate the need to offer increased agency to all readers, regardless of ability. As well as widening the breadth of reading material validated in school, they actively supported children in making choices. Interestingly, these professionals were not applying research evidence, which indicates the motivating power of choice (e.g. Clark and Phythian-Sence, 2008), rather they were extrapolating from their own experience of reading and the recognition that the right to read what you choose is crucial.

In seeking to demonstrate this, many RTs used Daniel Pennac's (1994, 2006) *The Rights of the Reader*. They purchased the Walker poster of these rights (illustrated by Quentin Blake) and organised activities that demonstrated readers' rights in school. For example, they sought to show that the children too had the right to give up on books, to remain silent, to read anything, to re-read a favourite and to be themselves as readers, just as their teachers did.

The Rights of the Reader

The right not to read

The right to skip pages

The right not to finish a book

The right to re-read

The right to read anything

The right to 'bovarysme' (a textually transmissible disease)

The right to browse

The right to read out loud

The right to remain silent

Pennac (1994: 145)

The majority of the teachers focused on the 'right to read anything' and widened the textual range which children were allowed to read in school. This motivated many young people, who found renewed pleasure in reading, began to see themselves as readers and read more widely as a consequence. Many RTs also focused on the 'right not to finish a book' and brought in adult books from home that they had abandoned. They talked about these and explained why they had given up on them, prompting extended discussions about books that children found they couldn't connect to or which failed to sustain their interest, despite the intriguing blurb or the author's reputation:

> If the children read something they don't like, they blame it on themselves as readers – their lack of competence. They don't see it as anything to do with the actual text. So I started sharing some books I had read and not finished or not really liked in the end and asked if they wanted to try them – to see if they liked them – if you think about it why would they know it's not them? Or that you can dislike something?
>
> (Teacher, interview, Birmingham)

Some RTs, in seeking to profile this right and communicate their message more widely, made corridor displays about this (Figure 6.1) in which children commented upon books they had not completed. For example:

> I didn't finish *Megastar Mysteries* because it got a bit boring because I could not understand some of the words in it and that made it hard to get a picture in my mind of what was happening in the story.

> I never finished reading *Midnight* by Jacqueline Wilson. I tried to several times but found it boring. It kept going on about her and her brother. Also it isn't my kind of book, it's all about fairies and magic creatures.

I'm giving up on *Harry Potter and the Prisoner of Azkaban* as it's taking too long and it's got a bit boring. The films are good and I do want to read it one day. I'm going to wait for a bit and come back to it when I'm older.

(Children, writing, Kent)

Exercising this right did not result in children constantly giving up on books and made a significant impact on many of the focus children, who talked more confidently about being able to choose as readers. It also influenced parents. For example, following a focus on the right not to finish a book, 9 year old Nathan, who had been very slowly ploughing through *Danny the Champion of the World* by Roald Dahl, gave up on it and moved on to the *Astrosaurs* series by Steve Cole. Nathan read several of these in quick succession and later, with his teachers' guidance, moved on again to pastures new. For Nathan, being given permission to move on to something more personally motivating, supported his development. As his teacher observed:

If I hadn't let him give up on Danny he'd probably still be reading it now! It made all the difference, he's really taken off, it's a joy to watch, he's rattling through these now, and his mum is delighted he's reading so much and with such enthusiasm − apparently he asked her to join the library and wanted books for his birthday.

(Teacher, interview, Kent)

Other parents, responding to their young readers, began to appreciate that energy, commitment and interest also counted, and this had consequences, as one RT noted: 'I think the parents are beginning to realise children need to choose and it's the children's interest and enthusiasm not long, thick, hard books that count!' (Teacher, interview, Kent).

The right to remain silent and not answer endless comprehension questions about a book or write a book review was also explored. Some classes created their own bills of readers' rights, including the right to: 'talk about it to who you want to'; 'have a view

Figure 6.1 Display of The Rights of the Reader

and voice it'; and 'keep it to yourself until you're ready'. Recognising the salience of reader volition in motivating young readers, RTs tried to help them make thoughtful and informed choices and the locus of control shifted. In the process, they were helping children develop new understandings about what it means to be a reader and, in line with Hall's (2012) research, were enhancing their agency and autonomy as readers. Many RTs commented on this, for example:

> Reading cannot be inflicted upon a person! They need to have choice in it!
> (Teacher, written reflection, Barking and Dagenham)

> We are more open about our reading habits now as well as what we are reading and I think this has an impact on the children. I think we are allowing them to be readers – readers for themselves, not readers for the school.
> (Teacher, written reflection, Medway)

> I feel like I've given them back ownership of their own reading.
> (Teacher, presentation, Birmingham)

Influencing children's perceptions and dispositions

At the start of the project the focus children were not sure their teachers were readers; 55 per cent voiced a degree of uncertainty, noting that their teacher only 'probably reads or probably doesn't read'. Their responses became increasingly positive as the RTs made time to share their reading practices. The children's comments in the spring and summer terms demonstrated that they were interested in their teachers as readers and that in many cases this had considerable salience for them. Many described their shared knowledge about their RTs' habits, interests and desire to read, and spoke about having witnessed their teachers' emotional responses. Their comments reveal aspects of their teachers' reading identities:

> She says sometimes she reads the last page, and it makes her feel guilty, but she just has to know. I know what she means – I do that sometimes too.
> (Child, interview, Suffolk)

> We read a book called *The Boy in Striped Pyjamas* and she cried because it had a sad ending because they got gassed.
> (Child, interview, Kent)

> Adventure books! Almost every book she chooses to read is an adventure book. She's got an obsession about Michael Morpurgo.
> (Child, interview, Birmingham)

> I saw her (teacher) reading um, it was *Hitler's Daughter* in school. But she's finished *Hitler's Canary*. She read a book called *Saffy's Angel* and then I read it after her. She reads a lot and brings her books in from home.
> (Child, interview, Kent)

> He showed us – he's got lots of information about Australia, he is going there soon.
> (Child, interview, Barking and Dagenham)

Figure 6.2 Gurjit's drawing of a reader

In the last interview when the focus children were invited to picture a reader in their mind's eye (either an imaginary reader or someone they knew) and draw them, several drew their RT, reinforcing a sense of this teacher as reader and role-model. Seven year old Gurjit drew her RT, Brenda, reading aloud (Figure 6.2).

Commenting on her drawing, Gurjit responded to the prompt questions as follows:

Who are you thinking of? 'Mrs Longing (Brenda)'.

Where is she reading? 'In the classroom in our armchair reading out loud'

What is she reading? '*A Sudden Glow of Gold* by Anne Fine' (current read-aloud book).

How is she feeling? 'Enjoying the story and reading to us'.

What is she saying and why might she be saying this about reading? 'If you read when you grow up you might be a poet or a writer – She wants to get us to think about stories and life'.

What's one word to describe her? 'Brilliant'.

Why did you choose this word? 'Because she loves it and is a really good reader'.

(Child, interview, Medway)

As with many of the children, Gurjit's drawing indicates a social conception of reading; she drew herself in as well as friends' faces, perhaps reflecting her sense of the community of readers of which she and Brenda are part. She appeared to see her teacher as someone who enjoys reading immensely and who finds sharing her pleasure in class an enjoyable experience. Additionally, Gurjit is becoming aware that stories connect to life. In order to show the complex interplay between this RT's increased awareness of herself as a reader, her knowledge expansion, shifting pedagogy and repositioning in the classroom, her development as an RT is now examined.

A case study of Brenda, a Reading Teacher

Brenda, Gurjit's teacher, was an Early Years professional with 31 years' experience. She referred to herself from the beginning of the project as an avid reader, though recalled this had not always been the case; she found learning to read a trial and received remedial help as a child. Brenda listed historical novels, texts about China (her new daughter-in-law was Chinese), newspapers and specialist scrapbook magazines as her current reading interests. She noted with enthusiasm that talking to colleagues on the project about books had reminded her of the pleasure she found in poetry and that through the Medway focus on this art form, she was widening her repertoire:

I feel like I've given myself permission to take my reading into school, and I'm finding again how much I love the old fashioned poets like Christina Rossetti and Robert Louis Stevenson. I'd forgotten how much music and pleasure there is in their work – I'm reading a biography of Rossetti at the moment.

(Written reflection)

I've set myself the challenge of getting to know – really know the work of two poets a term – the children love Gervase Phinn – I hadn't realised he wrote poetry and Sheree Fitch is my other new writer at the moment – she's Canadian – have you read much of her?

(Interview)

As Brenda read and talked to colleagues about her favourite poets, she took the step of sharing something of herself as a reader with the 6–7 year olds in her class. She told them about her early difficulties with reading, her experience of needing 'special help' at school and the 'fear and failure of words in tins to take home and learn'. Brenda sought to ensure the children had more positive experiences. She shared her passion for fiction and poetry and talked about her current reading practices outside school, demonstrating that reading is something she does daily, as part of her everyday life and that it offers her pleasure and satisfaction. She also started a reading journal, set up poetry boxes and began to read poetry aloud in class more frequently. This had consequences both for Brenda and the younger learners:

I told them that I'm trying to get to know new poets and three children brought in collections from home for me to read – so I've lent them some of my books too.

(Interview)

I feel I'm more free now to revisit texts that I'm more passionate about myself – and it's what you're interested in that the children take on board. The project's enabled me to be part of their reading lives and shape my own more consciously. It has allowed me into my teaching again – to share something of my own love of literature and particularly poetry.

(Interview)

In her journal, Brenda captured many of her reading habits and practices and through discussion and reflection began to develop an increased awareness of the strategies she employed when reading poetry. She noted, for example, that she often: re-read particular favourites; visualised poems; subvocalised lines; asked questions; paused to ponder, made connections, remembered or imagined; and listened to the poems' tunes and patterns in her head, comparing one poem with another (Cremin, 2013a). Occasionally, and dependent upon the poetry, she also found she became physically engaged in verse, tapping her fingers or feet to the rhythm. Many of these are crucial comprehension strategies, as identified by Pressley (1998), which Brenda observed she had been largely unaware of until she began to keep her own reading journal and consider the experience of reading poetry.

As a consequence this RT created opportunities for the children to employ such strategies and made explicit her own cognitive processes by, for example, sharing her own questions/connections and inviting the children to identify theirs, too. The children also engaged playfully in exploring the words, sounds and layers of meaning in poetry through dance and drama, and adding music to verse or turning poems into songs, and took part in many informal discussions and spontaneous small-group chanting of their favourites. As the class read, re-read, interpreted, performed, wrote and re-created poetry in different media, their aesthetic experience of reading poetry was considerably extended. As Brenda observed, re-reading became common practice, both her reading particular poems to the class and the children revisiting such 'texts in common' for themselves:

They love *Our Cat Cuddles* – It feels like I'm reading it nearly every day – "Again" they say – '*Cuddles* again!'

(Interview)

I had been repeatedly reading R.L. Stevenson's *From a Railway Carriage* and was delighted when I heard Harry during ERIC quietly reading it out loud, with the same rhythm and evident engrossed pleasure. It spurred me on.

(Interview)

Additionally, poetry was heard being spontaneously voiced and sung in the classroom, on the playground and on school trips. It was also experienced more formally in class, in assembly and at a local schools' poetry festival. An undersea role-play area based upon Claire Bevan's poetry collections was created and poetry displays, and a well-used poetry book box declared the popularity of this literary art form in the classroom. Her pleasure in reading poetry and other texts did not go unnoticed; in the spring interview the children talked about what Brenda was reading to them and again their responses reveal what they knew about her as a reader and that they were influenced by this:

JONAH: She says she goes to bed early when she's reading her book about that famous French man.
GURJIT: Bonaparte – It's three books actually – she's on number 2.
JOHN: Yeah and I do that sometimes – I like to read in bed.
GURJIT: So do I.
TROY: She hates books with loads of speech in them.
GURJIT: I don't, I like them, like that Anne Fine.
JONAH: She found a book with too much speech and she got cross and didn't read anymore.
GURJIT: If you don't like it when you're a free reader you can stop reading it.
TROY: She also reads poem books and her magazines to make her scrapbook.
JONAH: She likes magazines that help her do it – she gets three I think each month.
GURJIT: Delivered to her door!

(Interview)

It was clear from the comments of these 6–7 year olds that Brenda offered them a potent role-model as a reader, but, whilst conscious of her practices, they do not appear merely to emulate her and are developing their own views. Unlike her teacher, Gurjit likes books with speech in them, though she likes to read in bed as Brenda also does. By the end of the year, the class's repertoire of poets was extensive and remarkable, especially for such young learners, as this extract from the final interview with the three previously uninterested focus children indicates:

INTERVIEWER: Who are some of your favourite poets?
GURJIT: Eleanor Farjeon – 'Cats sleep anywhere, any table any chair' and Claire Bevan, she's popular – they're all about mermaids…
TOBY: and Mer kings…
GURJIT: and Robert Louis Stevenson – when he writes the 'Railway Carriage' it's like the rhythm of the train…
JONAH: and Wes Magee and Edward Lear, 'The Owl… *(Toby and Gurjit join in)*
JONAH, TOBY AND GURJIT: 'and the pussy cat went to sea in a beautiful pea green boat, They took some honey, and plenty of money, wrapped up in a five pound note'.
GURJIT: Richard Edwards.
TOBY: Tony Mitton and John Agard – 'I din do nuttin I din do nuttin, all I did was throw granny pin in rubbish bin, I din do nuttin'.
GURJIT: Christina Rossetti and Sheree Fitch – 'There is no land of perfect child– there is no land of…
TOBY: *(Overlaps)* Gervase Phinn – do you remember *Our Cat – Cuddles*?
TOBY, JONAH AND GURJIT: 'Dominic said "I'd like a fat cat, a fierce cat. A ferocious, catch-a-rat-cat." Mum said "I'd like a furry cat, a fluffy cat. A friendly, sit-on-your-lap cat."'

This conversation between Toby, Gurjit and Jonah represents an example of child-led 'inside-text talk'. Spontaneously, they chanted a section of *Our Cat Cuddles*, which Brenda had read aloud several times, though the children had not been expected to memorise it, the pattern and rhythm of the verse had enabled them to do so. Brenda expressed surprise in the children's capacity to engage with poetry, to remember and chant lines and verses, even from poems that had not been read particularly frequently by her. She recognised that in connecting to her own reading practices she was setting aside 'more time to ponder and wonder ... you know just read them, hear them and then *not* discuss them [poems]'. As Martin (2003: 16) acknowledges, 'a poem is worth reading for its own sake not simply in order to teach something about poetry'. Her work and the class's response raised her expectations of the children, as she noted: 'they're much more able than I realised to reflect upon poet's themes and so on – it's amazed me even after all these years'. Reflecting more widely on the project and her new positioning as an RT, Brenda was clear that this had made a significant difference to her teaching:

> The project has empowered me to expand my teaching of reading beyond the 'nuts and bolts' of literacy. Many more children have become real readers through my explicit teaching – modelling of techniques and reading strategies, e.g. how I will turn back a page to re-read a section because I don't understand that bit – how I might stop reading a book if I can't get on with it; it doesn't interest me, I can't identify with the main character etc.
>
> It is surprising how you think the children would obviously know you are a reader and enjoy reading – they don't necessarily – unless you explicitly tell them and give examples and show them the adult books you are reading. All this needs to be taught – I now teach from a reader's point of view.
>
> (Teacher, written reflection)

Whilst teachers are not solely responsible for defining reading for children, they do influence the perceptions children have of themselves as readers, and to a large degree they hold the reading reins in schools, potentially controlling textual access, reading contexts and the time available to read, and think about meaning. In addition, if they choose to consider their own experiences and possible consequences for classroom practice, and share their reading lives and strategies, as Brenda did as a RT, then their engagement as adults is potentially more personal and their influence more marked.

Data from the observations and interviews with children of the RTs indicate that the characteristics of these enhanced professionals – their openness, enthusiasm for reading texts of their own choosing, preparedness to share their reading preferences and talk extensively, authentically and with passion about what they were reading, and their experiences of reading – were mirrored by the children. This was the case regardless of the age of the young learners. In the classes of the RTs, more authentic reciprocal relationships between teachers and children became established around reading.

Developing as a Reading Teacher

Teachers who perceive there is value in this RT stance can make choices to share more of their reading lives and practices in the classroom as they seek to apprentice younger readers who also read for pleasure. Although as one RT observed:

It's no good just meaning to do it – it's all too incidental and unplanned – I mean, it needs to be spontaneous at times of course, but I think 'how can I show I am a reader?' – 'how can I share my reading life with them?' and then I plan something.

(Teacher, interview, Kent)

Most RTs in the project began to keep some personal reading in school, both to read during independent reading time and to enable them to articulate spontaneously emerging insights about their preferences, habits, emotional responses and so forth. They also planned class activities which prompted reflection upon the experience of reading, consideration of what readers do and feel and what reading in the twenty-first century involves. These activities, which were not prescribed, were as diverse as the teachers who generated them, and included for example, sharing:

- books, comics and magazines from childhood;
- reading histories, both the pleasure and the pain, the texts, contexts and people involved;
- the diverse forms of reading engaged in across a week/couple of days;
- responses to news items, with a news board and on-going articles;
- current reading and responses and connections – about life, prejudice, power, oppression, relationships and so on;
- re-reading practices;
- books that remain unfinished and why;
- what gets in the way of reading for pleasure/leisure;
- reading habits, e.g. skipping passages, reading the end before the end, adding post-it notes etc.

Each of these acted as triggers for children to share their thoughts, views and reading practices in a reciprocal manner. For instance, recalling childhood favourites, some teachers invited children to bring in favourites from home, and others arranged a trip to a class of younger readers in order to borrow from their collection for an afternoon of pleasure, revisiting, re-reading and related activities.

Conclusion

Developing as an RT represents a new challenge, particularly in accountability cultures where tests and targets dominate, yet as the project reveals this stance has potential. Through reflecting on themselves as readers, and documenting their practices as readers, teachers in Phase II began to appreciate more fully the diverse individual habits, strategies and practices in which they as readers engaged in response to different texts, contexts and purposes. They also came to recognise the significance of readers' identities. Those that positioned themselves as fellow readers and RTs, who talked about their own practices and explored the dynamic between the children's reading experiences and identities and their own, developed into RTs: teachers who read and readers who teach. In the process, the locus of control around reading shifted and more overtly reciprocal communities of engaged readers developed. These teachers made the most impact on the focus of children's attitudes to reading and their pleasure in reading.

Yet the project reveals that teachers need support if they are to understand the value and maximise the latent potential of this subtle role-shift as well as handle the consequences of repositioning themselves as readers in the classroom. In seeking to develop as RTs, practitioners can reflect upon their engagement as readers, set themselves personal and professional reading challenges and document their reading lives and practices. Capitalising upon any newly nuanced understandings about the experience of reading, emergent RTs are likely to offer tailored opportunities for children to consider their own reading lives and identities as readers, and to make changes to their classroom practice, transforming their conceptions of reading and what counts as reading in their classrooms. As RTs they are also likely to foster readers who can and do choose to read for pleasure and who, like their teachers, are motivated, socially engaged readers.

Chapter 7

A Reading for Pleasure Pedagogy

Kimberly Safford

> You can't teach pleasure: you have to share it.
>
> (Frank Cottrell Boyce, quoted in Weber, 2013)

This chapter examines the distinctive Reading for Pleasure Pedagogy developed by teachers in the Phase II project *Teachers as Readers: Building Communities of Readers*. Research findings concretise the statement above by Cottrell Boyce, a well-known children's author, and provide evidence of how 'sharing pleasure' can become part of a robust pedagogic strategy for supporting young readers. The Reading for Pleasure Pedagogy was seen to encompass four specific practices: reading aloud, social reading environments, book talk and recommendations, and independent reading. Combined in different patterns and made real through action and continual reflection on the part of the teachers, these practices contributed to the development of communities of readers in school. Many of the child members of these communities came to participate in spontaneous inside-text talk; child-initiated conversations about texts and reading were seen to count and contributed to the informal, yet supportive, reading environments which were documented.

The chapter explores each of these practices in turn. It notes the value of teachers becoming reflective readers who are not only knowledgeable about texts, but who take action in the classroom based on their knowledge and reflection, and offers a case study of the work of two teachers. It commences with an examination of the project teachers' previous pedagogic practice with regard to reading for pleasure and reader engagement.

Initial pedagogic practice

At the start of the project, no teacher explicitly planned to develop a Reading for Pleasure Pedagogy, or expressed awareness of the need to do so. This was not surprising, since reading for pleasure was not foregrounded at the time in England, nor was it even included in the original National Literacy Strategy (DfEE, 1998) which teachers were expected to follow. Research also suggests that in accountability cultures, teachers tend to side-line what they understand about pedagogy and the role of talk in learning (English *et al.*, 2002) and that they may allow the focus on curriculum coverage and pace to dominate their practice (Burns and Myhill, 2004).

The project teachers were aware that many children were not enthusiastic about reading. Many participated in the research in order to tackle underachievement in reading both at the school and classroom level. They did not, at the start, describe any specific strategies that they employed regularly in order to foster reading for pleasure. Some mentioned activities such as book swaps and book sales for parents and children, noting nonetheless that those children who came to the one-off book shop at school tended to be the eager readers, and that this may have affirmed their position and pleasure but did not afford support for those less interested in reading. At the outset too, the teachers did not connect personal dimensions of themselves as adult readers to their classroom practice. However, through professional development provided in national and local meetings, teachers widened their knowledge and use of children's literature (see Chapters 4 and 5). At the same time, as research participants, they were invited to reflect on their own experiences of reading, where they like to read, and to share what they enjoy reading. They considered the significance, for themselves, of space to read and were given time to think and talk about their histories and identities as readers. They also began to find out more about the children as readers. In meetings, they shared both child and adult texts, and began to respond more affectively and aesthetically to the former (see Chapter 6). With on-going engagement in this reading community with peers, teachers reported taking more pleasure in reading themselves.

Drawing on their enhanced subject knowledge and personal reflections on the experience of reading, the project teachers began to take new directions in classroom practice. The research supported them in planning, developing and sustaining four core practices, which aligned with their new understandings about readers and reading. These included:

- reading aloud to the class for pleasure (rather than for instrumental literacy teaching purposes);
- creating diverse, supportive and social reading environments;
- talking about books and making recommendations to individuals and the whole class;
- creating frequent opportunities for children to read independently for pleasure and giving them choices about what to read.

Teachers made gradual changes in their classrooms in relation to reading aloud, physical space, talk and socialising about books, and quiet reading. As they observed the impact of these changes on themselves and on the children, they began to identify the core features of fostering a love of reading and to articulate an informed and strategic rationale for selecting and using texts to support reading for pleasure. Across classrooms, where teachers implemented the four practices, there were common patterns of pedagogic development. These developments were neither equal nor consistent for every teacher, due to enabling and constraining factors within schools and local authorities, particularly where teachers were preparing children for end of primary school tests. Also, at the individual personal level, not every teacher was comfortable sharing their identities and practices as readers or exploring the affective nature of reading with children (see Chapter 6).

The observable pattern of pedagogic development was a progressive weaving of subject knowledge, personal reflection on the experience of reading, development of environments to foster reading for pleasure, and interaction. The starting point was the development of subject knowledge, self-reflection on the nature and experience of reading, and an understanding of conditions which make reading pleasurable. As teachers became familiar with a wider range of children's texts, and aware of children's everyday reading practices beyond school, they began to enhance classroom reading environments to make reading more visible, providing more resources of a diverse nature and making more space for reading. In these environments, teachers began to organise regular reading activities that involved increased interaction and more choice, as well as a focus on readers and their different practices and preferences. This improved their understanding of children's reading interests and development and prompted them to use their knowledge of texts to recommend books to children, and in this process extend their subject knowledge further and reflect again on the nature of reading. Some also developed as Reading Teachers (see Chapter 6). Whilst the classroom practices introduced – book talk, reading aloud and independent reading – were initially teacher framed, over time, teachers offered more scope for children to initiate and lead within the reading environment. This combination of pedagogic practices served to support the development of young readers, positively influencing their attitudes and attainment (see Chapter 9) and served to build richly reciprocal reading communities in the classroom.

Reading environments

> I like to read when I'm relaxed. I like to read something I can switch off to. How does this work in the classroom? I hadn't thought of those questions before.
>
> (Teacher, written reflection, Birmingham)

Reflecting on their own preferred environmental conditions for reading – what they like to read, when, where and how they like to read – teachers sought to make connections to pedagogic practice. First steps usually began with altering the look and feel of the classroom, improving resources and reconfiguring space for reading.

In this context, teachers thought explicitly about offering wider reading choices to children, to reflect the diversification of children's reading preferences and habits in the twenty-first century (Maynard *et al.*, 2007; Twist *et al.*, 2007; Clark and Douglas, 2011). They organised well-stocked and attractive book areas for browsing and reading, and in some cases were able to broaden school library provision. Classrooms featured author boxes, new texts and authors, picturebooks, joke books, comics, graphic novels and poetry. Knowledge of texts, in print and online, was a key factor in this changing practice. Acknowledgement of diversity was a parallel key factor, as teachers encouraged children to bring their personal reading preferences, such as comics, manuals, catalogues and magazines to school. Many classrooms, for the first time, began to regularly order these types of texts, subscribing for example to *Simpsons Comics*, *Shout!*, *Young Geographic*, *Shoot* and *First News*.

To enable children to access these resources, teachers radically altered their classrooms in order to create comfortable reading areas and took increasingly creative approaches to using these environments. Most just had a simple shelf of books at the start of the project and felt they did not have the room or resources to create engaging reading areas. But as they considered their own need for a relaxing space to read, the importance of accessibility and value of the physical environment, they found inventive ways forward. Several classrooms read Tim Hopgood's picturebook *The Big Blue Sofa* and purchased or found sofas and comfortable seating to enrich reading areas. Reading chairs and cushions, reading tents and reading 'cafés' were observed to draw children in, as teachers provided unstructured time to browse the resources and occupy the spaces. As one teacher noted: 'Now they can relax and move around to share reading with friends. If they choose to read comics or magazines they can (Teacher, interview, Birmingham).

Creative displays further enhanced reading environments in school corridors and entrance halls as well as in classrooms, particularly where teachers talked with children about their own reading beyond the classroom, for instance:

- *Readers in Disguise*, where school staff take photos of themselves reading but in disguise, and children guess who the readers are based on the text and their knowledge of staff interests;
- *Extreme Reading*, where staff, parents and children take photographs of people reading in unusual places: a mechanic under a car, a swimming-pool attendant, a child in a supermarket trolley;
- *24-Hour Reads*, where children and teachers record everything they read over 24 hours and make posters, scrapbooks and diary entries to demonstrate this (see Chapter 5);
- *Desert Island Texts*, where teachers and children discuss and display the books they would want if they were stranded on an island (see Chapter 6).

Such displays sparked talk about books. Some teachers shared with children photographs of themselves (Figure 7.1) and members of their family reading various texts at home, on holiday and elsewhere. Children were invited to take photos of their own families and friends reading, so that teachers could create displays and discussions about diversity and preferences. Displays that featured personal, home and community aspects of reading added much wider contexts to literacy-based displays that tended to focus on particular texts, genres and/or authors. They carried significant messages about readers and offered a sense of a collective identity in which all members of the classroom community – children, teachers, teaching assistants – were positioned as readers.

In most classrooms, these resource and environment changes were incremental. But even with small changes, teachers observed that applying their increasing knowledge of children's texts and their growing understanding of reading as a social process led to positive changes in classroom culture, so that reading became a more shared, sociable experience:

> Lots of things have developed together though the environment... The climate and culture of reading ... Like knowing that some of the children are excited by graphic novels – similar to their reading habits with comics I suppose ... and computers. Children relax – that creates an atmosphere too.
>
> (Teacher, interview, Birmingham)

Unstructured access to a range of reading materials in comfortable environments that reflected the diversity of reading prompted conversations about texts, about children's (and teachers') preferences and shared readings when several young learners would gather together around a comic or picturebook to share it. In weaving these elements as conscious pedagogic practices, teachers encouraged children 'to read anything, to read anywhere, and to dip in' (Pennac, 2006). Choice of reading and interest in reading are strongly related (Schraw *et al.*, 1998; Clark and Phythian-Sence, 2008), and it

Figure 7.1 Displays to profile reading as part of a supportive environment

was evident in the project classrooms that an important factor in developing children's reading for pleasure was choice. In these environments, teachers observed children making personal meaning from their reading choices and acting as readers in ways that were outside the more typically used classroom typologies of readers: fast, slow, fluent, struggling, distracted, uninterested.

With knowledge of texts and understanding of conditions that invite reading, teachers saw how they could create environments to promote more positive dispositions on the part of the young readers. These changes in resources and environments laid the groundwork for further key developments in pedagogy. The initial focus on subject knowledge, reflection and environments enabled teachers to make reading aloud, 'book talk' and recommendations, and independent reading time more regular, routine, interactive and open-ended classroom experiences. It was evident that where teachers were committed to engaging with these approaches in a sustained fashion, they observed and articulated a positive impact on their understanding of what constitutes the effective teaching of reading, on children's enthusiasm for reading and on sharing their perspectives as readers.

Reading aloud

> I would only read texts aloud in the literacy hour and never complete the book. If I was focusing on story openings, I'd only read the story openings and never get to the end. How awful was I?
>
> (Teacher, interview for *Times Educational Supplement*, Kent)

A quick look around the World Wide Web, a bookshop or a library reveals an abundance of advice, guidance, book lists, tips and videos on reading aloud – all aimed at parents. In early childhood, reading aloud is considered to be one of the most important things a parent can do to give a child a good start in school and even in life. There is much evidence that expressive reading aloud conditions a child's brain to associate reading with pleasure, creates background knowledge and provides a reading role-model; when children are read aloud to, they are 'enveloped' in a risk-free learning environment that 'removes the pressure of achievement and the fear of failure, allowing the freedom to wonder, question, and enjoy material beyond their reading abilities' (Wadsworth, 2008: 1; see also Fisher *et al.*, 2004; Childress, 2011; Trelease, 2013). Teachers in the research project were invited to consider and apply these understandings in the primary classroom context, and extend the practice of reading aloud beyond early childhood to older pupils.

At each national day and local session teachers were read to, aloud. They developed experiential knowledge of reading aloud as listeners, and considered the affective impact of reading to 'reassure, to entertain, to bond, to inform or explain, to arouse curiosity, to inspire' (Trelease, 2013: 4). As the research progressed, teachers developed a deeper understanding of the pedagogic principles involved in reading aloud: how it is an externalised model for silent, independent reading 'in your head' – modelling to children how a book should sound and feel, helping them to hear 'the tune on the page' (Barrs and Cork, 2000) and helping them develop expressive reading and the music of language in their own heads.

Whilst teachers found reading aloud an enjoyable experience for themselves and recognised its personal, social and cognitive benefits, it took time for them to find and make the space to read aloud regularly in the classroom and to identify this pleasurable practice as pedagogy. It is possible that the de-professionalisation of teaching in England (Burgess *et al.*, 2002) and recent stringent requirements to test small units of literacy such as synthetic phonics, spelling, punctuation and grammar, have deskilled teachers for reading aloud. It required a genuine shift in thinking for teachers to consider reading aloud as a key pedagogic and professional practice, although there is considerable evidence that reading aloud to children enables them to process challenging content, text features and vocabulary – even in subjects not normally associated with reading aloud such as science and technology (Heisey and Kucan, 2010). Furthermore, reading to 4–5 year olds more frequently has been shown to lead to higher reading, maths and cognitive skills at age 8–9 (Kalb and van Ours, 2013).

At the beginning of the research year, in classes of older children in particular, many teachers found it intensely challenging to initiate and sustain reading aloud. One teacher, who was relatively new to the profession, reported that due to time pressures she rarely read aloud to the class except when reading extracts to be studied in literacy lessons. Where teachers did read aloud to their classes, this was usually followed by literacy work focused on developing word, sentence or text level skills linked to the reading. This had consequences. For example in one primary school, at the first interview when three dis- affected 8 year old readers were asked whether their teacher read aloud, all pointed to the card 'Often' (there were three options: Often/Sometimes/Almost/Never). However, when they were invited to respond to the question, 'Do you like your teacher reading aloud? all three immediately pointed to the card 'No, I Don't Like It' (there were three options: Yes, I Like It/No, I Don't Like It/It's Okay). Discussing the reasons for their vehemently held negative views, it was established that as their teacher Gill never read aloud except as part of the literacy hour, the children associated reading aloud with written work. Gill had chosen these focus children as they were not keen readers (nor particularly assured learners), and it was clear they were not enthusiastic about her reading aloud or the resultant work. This was fed back to her. She was concerned to realise that she had unconsciously tethered reading aloud to literacy teaching; she offered no provision for hearing literature or other texts read aloud without attendant work. As she observed: 'I guess I only really read in order to kind of introduce the objectives, set the scene if you know what I mean (Teacher, interview, Medway).

As a consequence, Gill began to read picture fiction and poetry aloud independently of literacy lessons and commented in the spring term that she found this 'Very affirming, they're always asking me to read particular books again and again and I enjoy it, it's like our time'. The focus of children's views also altered dramatically. All three, when asked in the spring term, were clear that they loved Gill's reading aloud and they retained this view through into the summer term. As Nathan noted: 'She reads really funny stuff and we get to make suggestions and choose too! My favourite is *The Book Eating Boy* – there's a hole in the back of it that been eaten! (Child, interview, Medway).

Over the research year, reading aloud was an area of practice where teachers developed considerable confidence and sometimes, as with Gill, made dramatic changes. By the end of the year, all teachers reported reading aloud 4–5 times per week, every day and, for some, 'every chance we get'. These changes were accompanied and driven by a growing sense amongst teachers that reading aloud is intrinsically valuable, and that books should not be used solely as conduits for delivering curriculum literacy objectives.

> I now read to the class without thinking 'I could do this with it or I could do that with it' and I think the children sit back and think 'I can just enjoy this' … that had been a big struggle – thinking how many boxes can I tick, what objectives can I cover and you actually then lose the impact of … the book. You know, just enjoy it for a book and a good story and a good emotional journey.
>
> (Teacher, interview, Kent)

Reading aloud was encouraged and supported by book sharing and swapping within the reading community of teachers involved in the project. In interviews and written reflections, teachers observed how reading aloud creates a sense of community, offering texts in common and a shared reading history for the class. It was also noted that it gives children access to sophisticated themes and literary language which are beyond their independent reading capacities; it can be cognitively challenging without placing literacy demands on children. The teachers observed how reading aloud is an inclusive practice that involves children of all reading abilities. Through reading aloud, teachers realised that they could demonstrate the power and potential of literature and thereby influence children' perceptions of the pleasure to be found in reading. One school implemented 'Teacher's Choice', where once a week the staff chose a book to read to the whole school. Other schools involved teaching assistants in reading aloud to small groups and whole classes; several teachers began to read aloud in staff meetings as a way of demonstrating the potential of reading aloud, and the potential to share books with the rest of the staff.

Children expressed considerable enjoyment in listening to their teachers read and were eager to talk about the ways in which they made literature 'come to life like a movie', for example:

> *Charlie:* ...when she stops [reading aloud] she leaves us on a cliffhanger and it's really exciting...
> *Darren:* Yeah, because it's really expressive.
>
> (Children, interview, Barking and Dagenham)

> When she reads some poems she slows down and kind of does actions and descriptions with it – so when the people turned into stone she kind of did this *(he imitates her going into slow motion)* and made it slow and we could see them turning into stone and it was brilliant – I love her reading aloud.
>
> (Child, interview, Medway)

As teachers developed their reading-aloud skills, they took more pleasure in 'doing the voices' and inhabiting the text, and became more confident to pause in the reading, ask questions and invite responses. Reading aloud became an interactive experience, as teachers and children initiated in depth or brief conversations about what was being read and additional book recommendations were made. Teachers also seized informal, unplanned opportunities to read aloud at different times of the school day, reading aloud not just from novels but also from picturebooks, poetry and information books. Sometimes this involved reading brief passages of books, as 'tasters' and other book promotion activities that tempted children to read more widely. Variety and spontaneity enabled teachers to demonstrate, and children to experience, a rich model of reading aloud. The practice of reading aloud enabled classes to come together and share potential 'books in common', books that all members had experienced and could talk about. Reading aloud also appeared to influence children's perceptions of their teachers as readers (see Chapter 9 for more details).

Book talk, inside-text talk and recommendations

> If a child comes up and says 'I've finished this book' ... I actually feel much more able to say 'If you like that, what about trying one of these', whereas before it would be 'OK, well go and choose another book'.
>
> (Teacher, interview, Kent)

Book talk, conceptualised by Chambers in 1983, was extended in this research project to encompass a wide range of discourse about books and other texts as well as talk about reading. Such book talk features strongly in the research data: teachers created frequent opportunities for discussion with the whole class, small groups and individuals about different texts, authors, preferences and readers' responses. This talk flourished in response to the improved resources and environments initiated by teachers. Teacher involvement and interest in the talk were key to effective practice.

Children were encouraged to talk to one another about their current reading and over time spontaneous child-led text talk also emerged. This energetic practice was named 'inside-text talk' as the project team wanted to draw a distinction between this and book talk – Chambers' term – which tends to relate to explicit teaching contexts and is more often teacher led. Inside-text talk by contrast is more frequently child-initiated and undertaken in informal contexts. Teachers realised that their growing subject knowledge enabled them to join in such inside-text talk conversations with increased assurance and genuine engagement. Their knowledge also enabled them to make recommendations to children about where they might independently take their reading further: '… and even if I don't know the books – I talk to them about the blurb and I ask them to tell me about it – would they recommend it to me? So it's a two-way thing' (Teacher, interview, Birmingham).

In these discussions, teachers shared their own reading with children, found out what they were reading outside school and asked them for their opinions about books or other published texts. Teachers initially viewed these as interesting conversational encounters but, as with reading aloud, over time they began to observe the pedagogic purposes of such social interaction in children's development as readers:

> [T]hey need advice much more than I realised. Before the project our talk about books would be based on re-telling – say in guided reading they would have the book open as they were doing that … 'so this book's about …' and they would be looking back at it to remind themselves of the plot. Now, when we talk about reading it's different talk, it's about their enthusiasm for the book, what they have liked about it and why. It isn't forced. … I have just realised how important such talk is. It just wasn't part of my thinking before the project.
>
> (Teacher, interview, Birmingham)

Talking about texts also gave teachers useful insights into children' lives; knowing children better enabled teachers to be more effective in choosing and recommending texts:

> We know much more now about the children – their histories – where they are coming from. I can tell you what the children like – their tastes in reading – I can't believe that I didn't know these things. It's just been pushed out. There didn't seem any time for this sort of chat.
>
> (Teacher, interview, Birmingham)

> We spend loads of time now recommending books to one another. That just didn't happen before – I guess I made no space for it.
>
> (Teacher, interview, Medway)

As Maynard *et al.*, (2007) have shown, few children perceive that their teachers help them choose books; in their survey, only 13 per cent of 5–7 year olds and 9 per cent of 7–11 year olds noted that their teachers did so. This may be because teachers know too few contemporary texts to make specific recommendations or they may not see this as their role, perceiving perhaps a stronger role in relation to teaching reading in shared and guided reading contexts. In the Phase II project, teachers became able, many for the first time, to make personal recommendations to individual children, often suggesting two or three possibilities which they believed the child would value and find interesting, relevant and appealing. However, as this was a new departure, initially some children thought their comprehension would be tested after reading the recommended text:

> To start with the children thought I had a motive when I recommended texts – they thought I would ask them questions about it! Now they know we can just talk about it – and they ask me for recommendations, check out if I know the one they have chosen and recommend books to me too.
>
> (Teacher interview, Suffolk)

Recommendations began to be shared both ways, and more reciprocal reader relationships and networks of readers developed (see Chapter 8). The teachers' recommendations often had consequences, for example introducing children to authors new to them: 'Miss told me to read *My Mum's going to Explode* by Jeremy Strong because my Mum is having a baby. It was brilliant and now I have now read four of his books and lent one to her' (Child, interview, Kent).

Teachers observed that talk and dialogue about reading encouraged children to think in different ways and to make more extended exploratory contributions. They found children were asking more questions and they also perceived that the questions were more probing, demanding much more than simple recall of facts. Some teachers also commented that, over time, child-led questions were enhancing comprehension of texts, not through the explicit teaching of strategies alone (Parker and Hurry, 2007), but through fostering reader engagement and the emergence of inside-text talk which afforded children additional opportunities to discuss what they were reading. Teachers not only saw the value of book talk for the authentic assessment of reading, but also recognised that it facilitated meaning-making; in Littleton and Mercer's (2013) terms there was evidence of children engaged in 'interthinking', making collective meanings together.

Book talk involved close conversations, reader to reader (both teachers to children and children to children) about specific texts, characters and scenarios, or named authors or poets. Inside-text talk complemented book talk and arguably enriched it; this child-initiated talk about texts of the children's choosing began to be heard in classrooms and on the playground (see Chapter 8 for further discussion and examples). A key impact of the classroom book talk and inside-text talk was the shared understanding amongst children, between teachers and children, and amongst teachers, that reading is intrinsically worthy of discussion; everyone responding to reading and sharing responses was positioned to achieve success. In classrooms where teachers initiated and encouraged book talk in the context of diverse resources and sociable environments, aspects of 'competence pedagogy' were evident (Hall *et al.*, 2007: 613). This pedagogy, documented elsewhere in schools' collaborative work with artists, emphasises 'the present and the process', focusing on what children say and do, the co-construction of understanding, with no ranking, ability sets or achievement tables. It also highlights the value of children's out-of-school experiences which are seen as legitimate topics for discussion. Connections to such out-of-school life experiences were often triggered by 'books in common', books that several friends or peers read, and books that teachers read to the class, often several times. Such books also formed the basis of many children's inside-text talk conversations.

Independent reading/everyone reading

> Now there is ERIC [Everyone Reading in Class] own reading time … this has gone to 10 to 15 minutes every day at least. This has prompted more book talk and informal recommendations. The reading chat is constant then, and at other times when children just seize the moment and talk about what they are reading to me and to each other … I've gained so much knowledge through them.
>
> (Teacher, written reflection, Medway)

At the start of the project, most teachers did not allocate any time in the curriculum for independent reading. Such reading, widely known in the USA as free/voluntary/independent reading, is led by children's choices as choice is critical to reader development (Gambrel, 2011). One relatively newly qualified teacher, working with 9–10 year olds, even commented she had never seen such practice and had thus never established it. She expected the children to read at home each night, either from their scheme book if they had one, or from their free choice or library book, although she reported that many of them did not. Most teachers acknowledged that any time that was set aside for independent reading was often sandwiched into registration periods and frequently interrupted or shelved. There were differences in classes of younger and older children in relation to what teachers believed they could take on and achieve, given the perceived timetabling restrictions and pressure from the statutory testing regime.

In the research year, teachers across all age phases established more frequent and sustained independent reading sessions. Children were not expected to read alone or in silence, although they could choose to do so; many socialised and shared their reading with each other and with their teachers. Teachers began to see talk as part of their independent reading routines, as children made selections and recommendations to one another, sharing the reading of a single comic or swapping chosen picturebooks part way through the time. Teachers also recognised that the wider range of choices and informal environment engaged children as readers.

This pedagogic practice, embedded in relaxed reading environments with diverse resources, enabled children to develop stamina for reading through choice, where they could develop 'the will' to read as well as 'the skill' (OECD, 2002). Teachers reported renewed understanding of the value of independent reading as a planned pedagogic routine rather than something children could do when all other work was completed. Many teachers took more active roles, recognising the significance of their participation, and some regularly took time to read themselves in these sessions. Teachers making time for their own independent reading in the classroom marked a significant change in practice. Before the research project, teachers did everything except read during independent reading time – it was normally a time to get other jobs done. They came to recognise how reading themselves in the classroom, like reading aloud, is a pedagogical approach that affords children a positive model of being a reader and sharing reading. It also forged positive relationships around reading between teachers and children.

> I think the children seeing me read *Saffy's Angel* by Hilary MacKay encouraged some of them to read it and then we started chatting about it and it made some others interested, one of the girls had read another in the series so she brought that in and we have the set now and there's a real Saffy group who are passing them all round and talking about them.
>
> (Teacher, written reflection, Kent)

> A lot of them are choosing to read in free choice time, like Abdul, he asked me if he could talk to me about the book he was reading. I think a lot of that is just because they know now that I'm interested … I definitely know more now about their reading ….
>
> (Teacher, interview, Birmingham)

The shared experiences of reading aloud and book talk influenced the ways in which teachers organised children's independent reading in the classroom. Teachers began to perceive independent reading as an active opportunity for learning and teaching, rather than a passive 'holding' strategy whilst they were focused on – and therefore implicitly privileging – other types of literacy instruction.

> I don't think we'd thought before about planning to support them as readers, like for their own reading, we'd just expected them to get on with that whilst we did guided reading or comprehension or whatever. But now with more reading aloud and lots of book talk we are encouraging them as readers, helping them make good choices, accepting much more reading material and giving them a chance to be readers really.
>
> (Teacher, interview, Suffolk)

Teachers reported that a Reading for Pleasure Pedagogy prompted a more inclusive approach to reading and observed that children who had been 'switched-off' and were previously reluctant or disaffected readers, both their focus children and other members of their classes, become drawn in, increasingly motivated and keen to read and talk about texts. Authentic independent reading involves thoughtful engagement with the text Ben-Yosef (2010) argues, and the impact of sustained time to read and to talk about texts more freely was evident in children's responses:

> I never liked reading before – now we have time to get into books, before we just had five minutes here and there and it was never enough.

> Teachers should give us time and tell us about good books, my teacher does and she has made me a bookworm!

> In Year 5 I hated to read but I've got really into books now because I have found books and magazines that I really enjoy and we have time to get into our reading and sometimes I just can't bear to stop.

Before this year I didn't read because I wanted to, I read because I had to. But now we get time to talk about books and I've found out what I like, so now I enjoy reading – in fact I LOVE it!

(Children, written reflections, Medway)

Other research has shown that just 15 minutes a day of independent recreational reading significantly improves children's reading abilities (Block and Mangieri, 2002). Quantity of reading and reading achievement are related: as the amount of reading increases, reading achievement increases, which in turn increases reading quantity (Cunningham and Stanovich, 1998, cited in Clark and Rumbold, 2006). Across classrooms and schools, diverse activities arose which extended independent reading into more recreational routines, such as:

- *Reading Prefects*, where children profile and popularise reading, making reading a high-status activity;
- *Book Swaps* across the whole school, where children bring a book, swap it for a token and choose a 'new' book;
- *Boys' Library*, established by boys for boys with the help of the teacher, where boys become role-model readers for other boys;
- *Reading Buddies* across age groups, and with secondary-school children.

Such peer-led sessions position reading as a creative activity and an active process (Holden, 2004; Pullman, 2004) and also, particularly for older children, act as a form of imaginative play where they can experience other worlds and roles and learn from temporarily dwelling within them (Nell, 1988).

Ben-Yosef asks rhetorically, 'Who tests us adults about our independent reading? To whom do we owe an explanation if we give up on the book after the first chapter?' (2010: 47). These questions were salient as project teachers observed the impact of new environments, resources and routines for independent reading on children's motivation to read. Teachers learned that in the classroom they could create a more 'real world' experience of reading, where children could control what, when, where and how they read and could exercise their rights as readers (see Chapter 6). Teachers and children were observed to experience routines such as the ones described above as 'pedagogical equalisers' (Ben-Yosef, 2010) where it makes no difference if a book is being re-read, or skimmed, or what level the book might be; the success criteria are that children participate and respond according to their interests and enthusiasms.

A case study of Steph and Eleanor

This chapter now turns to a case study of two teachers, Steph and Eleanor, who worked together in their school to develop a Reading for Pleasure Pedagogy. Woodlands School is a three-form entry primary school in England, in a mixed social and economic area. Steph and Eleanor participated in the action research because they were concerned about problems in the school and in their classrooms, they reported that many children read 'only when they had to' and in particular that 'Children had low self-esteem as readers. [There was] a general lack of interest in reading, particularly in Year 5 boys'. They also reported that 'very little reading took place in our classrooms outside of the Literacy Hour, there was no time [to read] a class book, no ERIC [Everyone Reading in Class] time' and that reading aloud was 'rare'. They did not, at the start of the project, comment upon the relationship between the children's less than positive dispositions towards reading and their classroom reading practices or the school reading environment or ethos.

In the two classrooms (with 7–8 year olds and 9–10 year olds) children's questionnaires revealed very limited knowledge of authors. A large proportion of children described themselves as 'only OK' readers, and boys listed football biographies and non-fiction as preferences. Faced with these data, and her self-reported lack of knowledge about children's literature, Eleanor, whilst recognising she was an avid reader as an adult, admitted a feeling of failure with regard to supporting children as readers, commenting for example, 'I am a big reader myself, but I wasn't putting it across to children' and 'We just don't do enough here, it hasn't been a priority for years'.

The teachers decided to make raising interest in reading itself their first priority. Their longer-term goals were to develop children's interest in reading independently for pleasure, and to reach reluctant readers, particularly those boys who reported only reading non-fiction. The plans Steph and Eleanor made and the steps they took, with support, illustrate the process of teachers taking deliberate, thoughtful and collaborative actions to improve the climate of reading in their classrooms and the school. Their actions clustered around the four strands of a Reading for Pleasure Pedagogy and made a marked impact upon the children as readers.

Conscious that the questionnaire had revealed a gap in their knowledge of children's authors, poets and picture fiction creators, the two teachers read children's literature more widely and increased their repertoires. They set themselves reading targets, swapped books with one another and with their project colleagues in the local authority and read more widely, determined to get to know more contemporary writers suitable for their classes. Their first action was to introduce children to the concept of 'Reading Rivers' (see Chapter 5), to illustrate and discuss the importance of reading and 'how it is all around us'. They made their own rivers to demonstrate the diversity of their own reading practices and felt they learnt a great deal from discussing the children's own Reading Rivers with them. This was followed by increasing the visibility and variety of books and other texts, and building-in time for children to read independently and to share their responses to reading in school. The changes were incremental and cumulative, and were observed to develop organically, as Steph and Eleanor gained confidence to access new resources and develop different routines. They moved from a position of shared wider subject knowledge to collaborative action, introducing new texts, organising diverse reading environments, reading aloud more regularly from a wider range of texts (not just material being used for literacy instruction), promoting book talk and making time for independent free-choice reading. Over a school year, their actions included:

- purchasing new and current titles, introducing new authors 'to create a buzz', updating class libraries, labelling book areas and creating author boxes;
- subscribing to comics and magazines (one boy commented 'I didn't know we were allowed to read these in school – brilliant!');
- displaying weekly and holiday book reviews written by children and teachers around the school;

- displaying posters by children of their favourite book with a brief quote;
- inviting children to select and research an Author of the Month and display information around the school;
- setting aside time every day to read a class novel aloud, giving children a choice of three in order to foster enjoyment of 'hearing a whole story';
- inviting children to take the teacher role and read aloud to the class;
- scheduling quiet reading time daily and encouraging pair and small group talk about texts after this;
- giving children reading diaries to record all books read at home and in school, to help monitor the impact of their changes;
- encouraging staff to read new books for themselves and then recommend these;
- scheduling reading assemblies to involve parents and encourage children;
- inviting teachers and children to bring favourite books from home for World Book Day;
- visiting a secondary school library;
- developing cross-curricular work that connected to literature, e.g. pictograms of favourite genres, creating artwork and playscripts from Greek myths.

Steph and Eleanor can be seen to have developed a Reading for Pleasure Pedagogy although, when they talked about what they were doing, they never explicitly identified the changes as a distinctive, holistic pedagogy. They did, however, express greater consciousness of their role in promoting reading for pleasure and the importance of planning reading for pleasure. At the end of the research year, they reported that children were:

> reading more and choosing books independently without being told they have to. They are spontaneously talking about books with each other and with us. They want to get to the next book, complete a series, share the best bits. They want to be the next to read a favourite book aloud to the class and review it for their friends.

Children reflected the impact of their teachers' reading aloud, e.g. one boy, Will, noted: 'Miss read *Beaver Towers* in class and now I got the second one for my birthday'. The two teachers were particularly struck by how the social dimensions of reading could inspire children to join the classroom community of readers. They believed, based on their experiences, that the best way to encourage reading was for children to recommend books to each other, noting that children 'love recommending books and poems and consistently ask to do this. ... There is a group of boys all swapping Robert Muchamore books'. They also noted the importance of their own enhanced subject knowledge in enabling children's talk about books and in making recommendations.

Steph and Eleanor, like all the project teachers, kept observational notes on their focus children, three readers who, whilst they could read, were not motivated or sufficiently interested to do so. Extracts from these teachers' reflections and descriptions illustrate their growing knowledge and understanding of what makes children 'tick' when it comes to reading, and the role of parents and librarians in supporting children's reading development:

Alongside their observational notes, Steph and Eleanor tracked the reading scores of their focus children and of their whole classes, testing all children at the start and at the end of the project year using England's statutory assessment framework and levels for primary-school reading.

George, aged 7 years, moved from a level 2a to 4c in the year. As Steph noted, he was from the outset:

> a confident reader who changed his reading book fairly regularly. He had an average reading score for his age. He had a positive attitude to reading as a skill but not as a pleasure. He saw fiction as something he had to read, not his first choice and he did not want to talk about his reading. Before the project George enjoyed reading non-fiction particularly books about snakes and insects. Working from his interests, I gave him *Dinotopia* by James Gurney and he took off from there really. George now enjoys a range of stories. He has discovered Jeremy Strong and is keen to share his reading in our weekly book reviews and chats to his friends (and me). He has also become a member of the local library.

Charlie, aged 9 years, moved from a 2b to a 3b in the year. As Eleanor noted:

> Before the project Charlie was a very reluctant reader. He rarely changed his reading book and his Mum said she had to force him to read in the evenings. He mainly read football books, particularly autobiographies about Chelsea football stars. He had a below average reading score for his age. Now two terms later, Charlie needs no encouragement to read and often asks me if we can have quiet reading time in class. Authors such as Anthony Horowitz and Robert Muchamore have captured Charlie's attention. There are many books by these authors and Charlie is desperate to read them all. He regularly asks his Mum to buy them for him or to visit the library. His Mum has commented that he is reading without being asked to and preferring it to playing on his Play Station.

Improvements in reading scores were seen across both classes and for the focus children. George in particular made significant progress.

It is notable that in a single academic year every child in the two classes showed improvement and some children made substantive progress. Whilst recognising that children's reading abilities generally get better as they mature, higher reading test scores for every child in each was unexpected. Children' reading scores within England are expected to increase by two sub-levels over a school year, but in Eleanor's class 50 per cent rose by three sub-levels or more and in Steph's class 45 per cent rose by three sub-levels or more. This is unusual. The teachers attributed these improvements to children reading more actively and more widely, reading more frequently and for more sustained periods of time in school and at home. For children like George and Charlie, widening reading repertoires and their teachers changed pedagogic practice appeared to have a significant impact on attainment.

Steph and Eleanor voiced the view that they had come to understand the affective nature of reading for themselves and for children and 'the difference passion makes'. They were not subject experts in English or Literacy in their school, but felt, as Steph expressed on behalf of both of them, that they had developed

[k]nowledge and understanding of what reading really involves – making meaning and finding pleasure in the process .... We're not Literacy Coordinators, and the changes may seem small, but we started with where we were and where the children were.

By the end of the research year they were aware that reading for pleasure needed to be continually planned and resourced – and that reading for pleasure could not be embedded or sustained without teachers' personal and professional commitment to practice it daily. The changes Steph and Eleanor implemented enhanced relationships both within and outside the school. They reflected together on the new enjoyment of reading for teachers, children and families:

> Reading is actually more fun for us, and the changes are not time consuming. ... [The children] ask me 'Miss when is it quiet reading time?' ... At Parents Evening, parents tell us that children are more willing to read and don't see it as a chore now .... Other teachers are asking us for recommendations – and we can make recommendations now.

Steph and Eleanor shared their subject knowledge and pedagogic practices across the school, giving training to staff on reading aloud, book talk and classroom environments that inspire reading. They led the school in writing an explicit reading for pleasure strand of the policy for English and Literacy and they continued to extend reading links with parents and the community, liaising with the local library and the secondary school. They involved parents as reading volunteers, and regularly schedule special days for an author focus. Steph also reported anecdotal evidence of a sustained impact on children as they moved up to their next classes: 'Teachers have commented on how much they (her previous class) change books without prompting', also noting, 'My old class still comes rushing in to tell me what they're reading'.

A Reading for Pleasure Pedagogy was evident in Steph and Eleanor's classrooms, although they never articulated their actions as such. They were motivated to continue because reading had become more fun, children were engaged in reading, and reading attainment was increasing. Their example shows how teachers, with subject knowledge and reflection, and starting from children' interests, can create classrooms where reading for pleasure flourishes.

Reading and becoming conscious

> There is nothing to measure enthusiasm, but attitudes to reading have changed dramatically. Small changes have a big impact. All children, regardless of ability can find pleasure in reading.
>
> (Teacher, presentation, Barking and Dagenham)

Project teachers overall became more autonomous and flexible in applying their subject knowledge, and many recognised their professional responsibility to sustain their knowledge and its application. They reported that the collective impact of broader choices, informal reading spaces, reading aloud, text talk and independent reading changed the ways in which they conceptualised children's reading development. Teachers felt increasingly confident to promote holistic approaches aimed at encouraging children to develop interests, tastes, preferences and views as readers and to develop positive reader identities. In this research there is compelling evidence of how improvements in teachers' reflective subject knowledge can trigger their agency to change pedagogical environments and practices, with resulting positive outcomes for children (see Chapter 8 for details). Furthermore, the coming-together of these strands of reading pedagogy had a positive impact on wider aspects of classroom life, as Chapters 8 and 10 reveal.

The act of reading has been defined as a process of 'becoming conscious' which 'enables us to formulate ourselves and thus discover an inner world of which we had hitherto not been conscious' (Iser 1978: 58). This research illustrates the process and impact of teachers becoming conscious by becoming reflective readers who are knowledgeable about texts and who take actions in the classroom based on their knowledge and reflection. Some also developed as Reading Teachers, becoming more conscious of their own experiences and identities as readers and taking additional actions as a consequence (see Chapter 6).

The research illustrates that a Reading for Pleasure Pedagogy must be explicitly planned for and underpinned by a thoughtful rationale. Awareness of time and space was a theme consistently raised in interviews and written reflections, as teachers began to understand how these intangible elements provide the pedagogic background to reading resources and activities. Teachers articulated the need to make time and space for reading so that children could explore texts in greater depth, share favourites and talk spontaneously about their reading. In the research classrooms, each teacher had a different starting point and undertook a mix of activities. The effectiveness, integration and coherence of the four core practices depended to a great extent on teachers' personal commitment to reading for themselves and for children, and on their preparedness to commit time and take responsibility for developing a Reading for Pleasure Pedagogy.

Conclusion

A Reading for Pleasure Pedagogy contains four core practices: reading aloud; social reading environments; book talk and recommendations; and independent reading. These practices are realised and made authentic by teachers' commitment to extend their subject knowledge of children's literature and other texts and continually reflect on what it means to be a reader, for themselves and for children. It would be difficult for a teacher to just 'do' the core practices without secure subject knowledge and thoughtful appreciation of reading and being a reader. The data strongly suggest that if teachers are to take responsibility for engendering lifelong reading habits amongst children, they must also develop their own dispositions for reading and a commitment to reading engagement and reading for pleasure.

In an accountability culture, a Reading for Pleasure Pedagogy is not without anxieties. As one teacher observed, there is nothing to measure enthusiasm. Whilst pleasure and enjoyment may be seen as desirable outcomes of teaching and learning, their sustained promotion is not normally articulated as an essential pedagogy that must be explicitly planned for. This is particularly the case where teachers and children must keep up with a demanding curriculum, target-setting and high stakes testing. In such contexts a Reading for Pleasure Pedagogy may be viewed as a pedagogic option not an essential reader-focused requirement. But all primary teachers are responsible for developing children as readers who can and do choose to read. Where statutory curricula foreground pleasure and enjoyment, teachers are legally required to take action. In England, for example, the new National Curriculum calls for children to 'develop pleasure in reading and motivation to read by listening to and discussing a wide range of poems and stories at a level beyond that which they can read independently (DfE, 2013: 7). These descriptors – widespread reading for enjoyment, motivation to read, listening to and discussing texts beyond independent reading capabilities – are observable practices and outcomes of a Reading for Pleasure Pedagogy. It is evident from this research that a Reading for Pleasure Pedagogy can enable teachers and children to achieve specific curriculum aims.

Many teachers will be enacting a Reading for Pleasure Pedagogy without explicitly identifying it to themselves or others. Others will retain a Reading for Pleasure Pedagogy in their classrooms, not impacting across the school. Still others may simply 'do' reading for pleasure occasionally, or partially. A continuum of practice is likely to exist, reflecting teachers' understanding of the importance of pleasurable reading engagement. Across project classrooms, practitioners enacted a Reading for Pleasure Pedagogy in different ways, implementing some practices more frequently, consistently and confidently than others. As this research demonstrates, when teachers take planned, deliberate and sustained actions, reading achievement and attainment improve (see Chapter 9). The data strongly indicate that where teachers develop these core practices coherently, consistently and collaboratively, based on sound subject knowledge and reflection, they experience tangible positive outcomes for children and for themselves, professionally and personally.

Chapter 8

Reader relationships within and beyond school

Marilyn Mottram

> Open book time is the best thing we've ever done in school. You get to talk to each other about what everyone is reading – any sort of reading at all …. It just makes you want to read something that someone else has talked to you about.
>
> (Kasif, aged 10)

The Phase II project, *Teachers as Readers: Building Communities of Readers*, sought to broaden opportunities for all children to talk to each other about what they were reading, to share their reading for pleasure choices and to value themselves, and others, as readers. In part the project aimed to do this by drawing different groups of people together to share their self-chosen reading and to talk about it, thus building new communities of readers. The multiple combinations for such relationships included:

- children sharing reading with children;
- children sharing reading with teachers;
- teachers sharing reading with teachers;
- families sharing reading with children;
- families sharing reading with children and teachers;
- librarians sharing reading with teachers, parents and children.

This chapter commences by setting out some of the challenges that the teachers faced as they began to reflect on the current relationships around reading in their class-rooms. Many started by conducting an audit to determine the extent of opportunities currently on offer for children to read for pleasure and talk about their choices with one another and with teachers. Most of the teachers found that *they* were the ones controlling the reading on offer to children. The chapter continues by sharing some of the findings that emerged as teachers sought to establish more equitable relationships around reading. One of the most significant themes to emerge from the changes in reader relationships was the notion of 'reciprocity': a sense of complementarity and a degree of giving and receiving as readers. As children were invited to bring something of their reading selves to school, the boundaries between reading in school and beyond began to blur. Additionally, the nature of discussions around reading became more shared. A new sort of reader relationship emerged as a result: one with reciprocity at the heart.

The important role played by libraries and librarians in the project is also explored and the potential for them to play even more of a central role in building communities of readers is noted. A case study of the reader relationships which developed in one school demonstrates the value of exploring the social space between children, teachers, families and communities in order to maximise opportunities for them to come together as readers. It also highlights the transformative potential of building trusting reader relationships.

Reader relationships at the outset

At the outset there was an assumption that opportunities for children to share reading for pleasure with classmates and teachers would already be established practice in classrooms. It was anticipated that the teachers would be strengthening and broadening these opportunities by drawing different people together from within and beyond school, including families, communities and local libraries. However, it soon became apparent that this was not the case. Data show that the sorts of relationships around reading, between children and between children and teachers, were limited and were overwhelmingly founded on more formal exchanges around school-based texts, those that were being studied for literacy learning. Opportunities to read for pleasure and discuss free-choice reading in class time were almost entirely absent. Furthermore, teachers and headteachers recognised that a significant cultural shift was necessary in order for this situation to change.

Almost every teacher in the project voiced the view that it was difficult to establish engaged reader relationships with the young people, the sort of reader relationships where all sorts of reading experiences are valued, where everyone feels that they have something to offer as a reader and no one person is in control of asking questions and judging answers. Two particular challenges almost immediately emerged. One concerned the nature of the 'talk' around reading for pleasure and the time and space for this to happen in classrooms. The second concerned the whole notion of 'what reading is' – what counts as reading. These two elements were interrelated and very closely linked to the sort of texts on offer in school and the sort of texts that children experienced beyond school.

In most classrooms at the start of the work, 'talk' about reading was confined to the 'taught' reading curriculum and to highly focused learning outcomes. Headteachers and teachers recognised this early on and wrestled with this tension in different ways:

> The sessions that we have for reading at the moment are all teacher directed and this project is encouraging us to think about having sessions that – although they are structured – are not so teacher directed and teacher-led. Now this is a dramatic move for us.
>
> (Headteacher, interview, Birmingham)

The project was not seeking to criticise the focused teaching of reading. The research team recognised that teachers must teach reading skills and strategies effectively and in context. However, questions about the whole reading curriculum needed to be raised, in particular about the balance across the spectrum of different reading activities and the experiences on offer to children. Was the curriculum effectively developing readers who read widely? Were children becoming discerning, critically reflective and engaged readers who can and do choose to read for pleasure? Concerns expressed by schools and teachers suggested this was not the case.

This led to the second challenge. In most classrooms, children's reading choices were limited to texts offered by school. Teachers quickly recognised that encouraging children to share their reading preferences and choices meant finding new spaces to allow different sorts of reading into the classroom. Although it is widely recognised that children come to school with a wide variety of reading experiences, including multi-modal texts (Bearne, 2005; Marsh, 2003b; Pahl, 2002), little was known about the everyday reading habits and practices in the children's lives. In all of the project schools, it was clear that reading materials moved in one direction: from school to home (Marsh 2003c). Changing this was a significant challenge for the teachers; it was not simply a case of bringing different texts into classrooms. Teachers needed to re-examine their perceptions and consider the nature of reading and how it was viewed by schools, by families and by children. Even where schools recognised the need for change, a complex set of interrelated factors and locally held assumptions created challenges. Many headteachers recognised a tension between the concept of reading 'in school' and reading 'in life', for example:

> If you look at the community around here, they are very cautious about school. Historically, the ethos of education around here is not positive. Parents often haven't had good school experiences themselves and certainly don't have good memories of reading at school – more of being 'made to read'. Reading is something you do in school and for school. It won't be easy to gain trust and change their views of what reading is ... or to encourage families to share their reading with us ...
>
> (Headteacher, interview, Birmingham)

These comments capture how closely reading is linked to one's history and identity and how critical it is for teachers to build trusting relationships around reading. Sharing reading choices requires confidence and a belief that all views and voices, expressing particular individuals' preferences, are worth listening to. Different contexts brought different challenges. Project teachers were aware of the fact that building good relationships around reading was different for each school and for each and every situation. For example, in some schools parents' perceptions of reading were firmly framed by the need for their child to move through the various levels or 'colour bands' of reading scheme books:

> Our parents are very competitive and the children's attainment in reading is the greatest driving force for them.
>
> (Teacher, interview Kent)

> Our parents want their children to attain high levels – above all else. Many of our families came to this country to give their children a better education and they want to see them passing tests and getting on. Reading is about levels and test scores.
>
> (Teacher, interview, Birmingham)

These quotes highlight some of the complex tensions that exist around the reading curriculum. Naturally, parents want their children to succeed. It is vital that children and young people become competent readers and achieve well. Yet in schools where this was the overriding perception of reading, by some parents and some families, arguably, reading was seen as a school-based practice undertaken primarily for the purpose of achievement. Reading in everyday life and reading for pleasure were not necessarily seen as important. This perception of school reading as reified within a hierarchy was held to various degrees by parents, schools and teachers. This influenced the relationships around reading. In a few cases, 'reading' the school-assigned book, often from a scheme, was confined to a particular time and space in children's lives. It was seen as a means to an end. Recently, a perceived lack of recognition by parents of the value of reading for pleasure has been noted (Clark, 2013), perhaps framed by the lack of professional attention afforded to this agenda in schools.

At the beginning of the project, this dichotomy between reading for pleasure and reading to pass tests existed in many of the project schools. The former was side-lined at the expense of the latter. As Ellis and Coddington (2013: 235) observe, 'current monitoring systems may encourage teachers in many countries to attend … to measuring, telling, delivering, and controlling'. By the end of the year, teachers recognised there had been considerable shifts in perceptions:

> We used to only discuss reading levels with parents at parents' evening. Now we talk about the children's reading preferences and that includes less formal types of reading.
>
> (Teacher, interview, Birmingham)

> The discussions about reading now are totally different. Parents notice more about the children's reading because we have been talking so much about the different sorts of reading out there in their lives.
>
> (Teacher, written reflection, Barking and Dagenham)

The following sections explore some of the ways in which teachers made the changes necessary to enable them to reach this position.

Finding space for reader relationships in school

Initially, as noted above, in many schools there was no space for free-choice reading or conversations between readers. The evidence indicates that where such opportunities existed, it was more often in the younger age-groups. As one teacher typically noted, 'When we did our audit we found that, as children moved up the school, the chances for free-choice reading and talking and reading to each other became less and less' (Teacher, interview, Medway).

The reading curriculum in most of the schools consisted of guided reading sessions. Although reading was also 'taught' during literacy time, this was framed around teacher chosen texts and frequently involved teacher-led comprehension activities which led to written work. It was commonly felt that 'there is just no space for anything else, everything is so tightly timetabled'. Teachers were faced with finding ways of introducing other reading approaches into the classroom, approaches that profiled pleasure, choice and conversations about reading which were not so focused, directed or assessed. This meant carving out time and space for this and in many cases adapting more established ways of working. Schools met this challenge in various ways:

> We have asked colleagues to join us by finding a dedicated time for reading for pleasure – maybe even inviting parents in – but with tight timetables it is very difficult.
>
> (Teacher, interview, Suffolk)

> We are introducing more flexibility as part of our work on the curriculum, we already have half an hour a day for reading and that needs to be focused teaching time.
>
> (Teacher, interview, Barking and Dagenham)

There was also a geographical dimension to the notion of 'space' as many teachers made changes to the classroom – and even school – environment (see Chapter 7). In one school, sheltered outdoor spaces around the school were used to create 'reading and communication' spaces. Reading tents were erected on the field and reading cafes created in outdoor areas. These spaces were stocked with all sorts of reading materials including cards, books, newspapers, magazines and comics chosen by children and families. These areas were owned and cared for by children who were 'outside library monitors'. The areas quickly became established as places for older and younger children to share, to read to each other, to talk about their reading. The tents and cafes were full at lunchtimes and breaktimes and often before school too, older children were seen reading to younger children. Teachers noticed that there was a link between these geographical spaces and the more social kind of talk around texts. One consequence of this was that children and teachers started to know each other as 'readers' and to pass on and recommend reading materials, as this extract from an interview with three 9 year old boys shows:

SEAN: Well, I've got *Spy Dog Unleashed* here … it's good … it's about this man, called Mr Big, who escaped from prison and he wanted to steal a jewel. But Callum hasn't read this one yet have you? [*Callum shakes his head*] Well, no he hasn't because I've still got it … because I haven't finished it yet, he's got to wait.

Sean and Callum then talk together about a book they had both read and enjoyed called *The One Hundred Mile an Hour Dog* by Jeremy Strong. They interrupt each other and add bits on to the story. Then Sean, clearly keen to know, asks Callum where he got his book from. When Callum replies that it was Amy, Guy corrects him, 'No, it was Louie'. Such peer-to-peer recommendations became commonplace in project classrooms, affirming other research which has shown the significant role that peers play in each other's recreational reading (e.g. Moje *et al.*, 2008; Moss and McDonald, 2004; Edmunds and Bauserman, 2006). 'Book tracking' also developed, with children making sure they were tracking where significant books were and seeking to ensure they were on the list for receiving these after their friends. These practices fostered informal conversations about these 'books in common' and built 'reader networks' (Moss and McDonald, 2004), in which friends choose to read the same book, either simultaneously or in quick succession.

The new social spaces, in classrooms and in schools, shared one underlying component: the centrality of affect. The spaces began to nurture children's personal encounters with reading and, gradually, even children who were seen as low achievers began to show an intrinsic motivation, a desire to read and to talk about their reading with their friends. Teachers' observational journals show that children, who at the outset were frequently disaffected and disengaged readers, started to exhibit new more positive attitudes and behaviours towards reading.

Reciprocity in teacher–child reader relationships

Through hearing more books read aloud, opportunities for book talk increased (see Chapter 7). Significantly, through the new and different kinds of exchanges around reading which emerged, relationships between children and teachers began to alter. Teachers became conscious of this. They commented that gradually they 'felt' differently when they talked to children about reading. This was an insightful moment of realisation for many teachers.

The act of creating new reading areas also encouraged teachers to think differently about the relationship between formal and informal spaces and teaching and learning. Although it is difficult to identify direct cause and effect, it appears likely that the social space for reading which developed in many classes, contributed to more informal spoken interactions around texts. Transcripts reveal that over time the relations between teachers and children around reading changed significantly. Teachers were sharing more of themselves as readers and through the informal book conversations more of their lives outside school, as were the children. New positions were adopted and new identities enacted:

> I'm in a different position in the classroom now. I'm one of them. I just know them now – as people – as readers – not as average point scores or sub-levels.
>
> (Teacher, interview, Barking and Dagenham)

> We have conversations about what we are ALL reading – not just the children – me too. It's so easy to do this but it's something we just didn't do before the project. Having done it, I can see how such a small thing can be so effective in lots of different ways.
>
> (Teacher, interview, Birmingham)

The evidence clearly shows that, in turn, many children began to 'see' their teachers differently: as people who have reading lives. This was most apparent in schools where teachers developed more fully as Reading Teachers – teachers who read and readers who teach (see Chapter 6) and in schools where the project caught on in the staff room. In the latter cases, staff became engaged in book swapping and making recommendations to each other. Some schools set up book boxes and teaching staff, administrators, parent helpers and student teachers on placement added their books and magazines and borrowed texts, occasionally adding post-it notes comments to these. The boxes prompted considerable discussion and additional recommendations, too. The emerging reader relationships amongst the staff and others did not go unnoticed by children, as seen in this exchange between two 8 year olds:

Yea, she (the teacher) was talking to someone else the other day about a book she had read.

Did you know she's been borrowing books from Miss Jones too?

I heard her talking to Miss Jones about reading – they've been reading the same books you know.

Oh, yeah, I know, they were talking about that Philippa Gregory one.

Yeah, that the one that she's reading at the moment.

Yea, I know, it's on the side now, by her laptop.

(Children, interview, Birmingham)

Arguably, relationships were changing because the teachers were taking the learners into account more than they had previously and were enabling children to bring more from their homes, cultures and histories into school. The children became empowered to offer more of their everyday reading lives. As one teacher observed, 'It all became part of the way the classroom worked – just part of the day really – just taking more notice of them of their reading – well of their lives outside' (Teacher, interview, Barking and Dagenham).

New reader relationships became a significant finding across the project. Teachers identified changes in the discourse patterns between themselves and the children. They noted that conversations not only became more spontaneous, but were arguably less hierarchical and more reciprocal. As children arrived in the morning, during registration, independent reading time, in guided reading, breaktime and on many other occasions, children began to seize opportunities to initiate conversations about reading with their teachers. Reading became part of the fabric of the classroom and a culture and ethos around reading began to build.

As teachers reflected on why this had happened, a recurring theme emerged: many teachers felt that the project had revitalised their teaching. They perceived it had given them permission to focus on the rounded nature of the whole child as a young reader: a reader who belongs to a wider reading world than the world of school. For example, one noted: 'It's taken me back to the whole reason why I came into the job in the first place. It's reminded me what it's all about'. Whilst it is likely that this resulted from a complex interplay of project elements, it was clear that the shared talk about wider reading lives kindled interest, excitement and a new level of personal involvement for teachers, and that this was reciprocated by the children.

Reciprocity in child–child reader relationships and inside-text talk

Teachers also began to identify and comment on a change in the patterns of talk around reading between groups and pairs of children. The research team's observational records and interviews undertaken with children in groups confirmed this. Teachers noted, in particular, marked differences in the amount of self-generated, incidental talk about reading, and commented that they overheard children discussing reading around school and in the playground. They expressed surprise that children were talking together about reading in ways that were seen to be both unprompted and unexpected:

The big change for us is in the amount of talk about reading that goes on now in the classroom ... but also in the playground and around the school. We hear them talking about reading – freely – incidentally!

(Teacher, interview, Birmingham)

Particularly powerful models of the strength of pupil relationships and dialogue about reading were found in schools in Barking and Dagenham and Birmingham where children were invited to become researchers themselves. In one school the young researchers sought to find out what children like to read and later became reading ambassadors, promoting reading in various ways, including class presentations and assemblies. In another, the 10–11 year old researchers recruited representatives from each year group in order to find out what they liked to read, and what they thought about the reading materials on offer in school. Their findings included:

Kids really like to read all different kinds of stuff, not only books. We should do the survey to find out what sort of things they would want in their classrooms.

(8 year old)

I found that some books in our class library and in the home reader corner never get read.

(10 year old reading rep.)

Books we would like more of: Joke books, Dr Who books and cards, Bratz, High School Musical, Polly Pocket, Hannah Montana, Kid Wonder, That's So Raven, Tracy Beaker and Tiara Princess, Cheat Magazines, Simpsons comics and football programmes.

(9 year old reading reps)

The pupil research team set up a Blogbug school chat site to encourage discussions about reading, including book recommendations. Children from across the school established their own reading groups that were driven by their shared interests and relationships with each other. As they built on each other's conversations and views about reading, they expanded their repertoires, became acquainted with different writers and grew as readers. Seventy children became involved in one particularly popular book-swapping circle. Children who would not normally have chosen to read or talk about texts were part of the circle. Teachers in this Birmingham school observed a marked change in the children's attitudes and behaviours towards reading, towards learning and towards each other: 'They seem more motivated now in lessons. They stay on task longer and talk to each other more purposefully' (Teacher, written reflection, Birmingham).

Transcripts across the project support this and show that in addition to the quantitative changes, in reading attainment (see Chapter 9) there were qualitative differences. The nature of children's exchanges about reading altered radically as the year unfolded. Again, teachers frequently commented on this:

The biggest impact of this work has been on our book talk which is now much richer than it used to be – well, it's completely different – more thoughtful, more extended – more free.

(Teacher, interview, Suffolk)

I mean …we have freed up the sort of conversations we have about reading.

(Teacher, interview, Medway)

At the beginning of the project, when the focus children were asked to share what they were currently reading, the majority immediately talked about their current school reading book. A few were unable to remember what they were reading, and some simply shared the name of the book and had no idea of the author. The majority highlighted the number of pages or chapters the book possessed, as if length or layout was a marker of them as readers. For example, 'I'm reading *Bertie's Uncle*, it's a play and it's got 62 pages'; 'I've got a really long book it's taking me ages, it's got 10 chapters'; and 'I'm reading an information book about badgers. It's got a lot of chapters in and a glossary and an index'. By the end of the project, the same question produced a completely different response. Children drew on the reading experiences they had shared with each other and their teachers with considerable eagerness and excitement. The transcripts show how they sparked off each other's thinking and offered each other ideas that grew and changed direction, moving from one child to another, so that cumulatively and collaboratively, their pleasure in reading was demonstrated. For example:

OMAR: Basically Miss, there was a story of Red Riding Hood in the city, and the wolf is good, and when a robber is trying to steal a purse from this little girl, the wolf bites the robber's hand and the robber runs away.

SHAREEF: Yeah, and the people, they all say, 'Shame on him trying to rob a poor little girl?'

OMAR: … Yeah, and they say to the girl, 'You've got a nice little dog here'. And the wolf says, 'No I must go back'.

OMAR AND SHAREEF: *(Chorus)* For I am the *last wolf in Britain* and I must be protected so I am going back to shelter.

(Children, interview, Birmingham)

There was evidence in the children's talk of a new energy and enthusiasm rooted in shared interests, pleasure in reading and mutual trust. This was described by the project team as 'inside-text talk'; such informal talk was based on common text knowledge and interest in reading, and demonstrated that the children knew each other as readers. In many of the rich examples of inside-text talk collected, the young readers inhabit the text and frequently voice extracts from it, often in unison. This child-initiated talk was undertaken in a mobile and fluid manner and drew on common intertextual references. It was self-perpetuating due to its motivating and engaging nature.

The spontaneous presence of inside-text talk is in marked contrast to recent research by Janet Maybin which shows a complete lack of informal conversations about reading and about books in primary schools (Maybin, 2013). The difference may be that in the Phase II project schools, reading for pleasure and reading engagement was highly profiled and teachers developed a pedagogy that both explicitly supported book talk and facilitated the emergence of such inside-text talk.

The many spontaneous inside-text talk conversations noted by teachers and the research team in corridors, classrooms and on the playground were mirrored by adult readers in staffrooms, as well as in local meetings and the national day towards the end of the project. It was notable that children and teachers talked about texts from the perspective of participants, not spectators in the meaning making, and did so with commitment, focus and energy. The diverse examples of inside-text talk collected were reader-initiated and reader-directed and often encompassed making connections and reciting sections together or quoting extracts. As such they had an affective impact, as children and teachers talked about their lives and experiences. In one class of 4 and 5 year olds, for example, the pigeon books by Mo Willems: *Don't Let the Pigeon Drive the Bus*, *The Pigeon Finds a Hot Dog* and *The Pigeon has Feelings Too!* had become firm favourites, having been repeatedly read aloud by their teacher. Children often re-read them to themselves in the reading corner. During the spring interview, the teacher recounted the following event, which reflects both the children's shared knowledge of the narrative and the spontaneity of their inside-text talk:

> When we found a dead pigeon in the playground, we went outside to have a look and Fahad looked at the dead pigeon and then looked at me and said 'Well that pigeon won't be driving a bus!' and then another child said 'And he won't be able to find a hot dog' and the children spent ages having a joke together.
>
> (Teacher, interview, Barking and Dagenham)

In this inside-text talk conversation the children drew on their history of shared experiences and common knowledge of texts and sparked ideas off each other to generate new thinking about the position of the pigeon. There are some similarities between the spoken exchanges in the transcripts from classrooms and the characteristics of a 'discourse community' (Mercer, 2000) in which every member of the community has responsibilities towards each other and so 'can expect to have access to each other's intellectual resources'. This is seen in the way Omar and Shareef draw on each other's thinking about the *Last Wolf in Britain* and in the cumulative jokes and connections that followed the discovery of the dead pidgeon. As teachers themselves noted, this sort of discourse was not typical of classroom practice and pedagogy. Another example reveals the element of collaboration, sharing and performance which emerged as characteristic of much inside-text talk. In this instance three readers respond to a question about what they like reading most in the final interview.

GURJIT: I still love poetry best, though I like Anne Fine too.

JONAH: My favourite reading is poetry too.

INTERVIEWER: Why do you think that is?

JONAH: Well it's kind of short – though not all poems are short and it's enjoyable. You can choose what you like in a poetry book you don't have to read it all – you just read the ones that interest you – like *My Cat Jack* and the *Boneyard Rap* – who's that one – you remember?

TOBY: Wes Magee I think.

GURJIT: Yeah it is.

GURJIT, JONAH AND TOBY: *(Together)*

> It's a boneyard rap and it's a scare
> Give your bones a shake up if you dare
> Rattle your teeth and waggle your jaw
> And let's do the boneyard rap once more.

(Children, interview, Medway)

This conversation held between the three readers, which was fluid and responsive, was a noticeable change from the early autumn interview, when in a half-hearted manner they had taken turns to name the books they were reading; Gurjit had listed an Oxford Reading Tree book, Toby could not remember his school reader and Jonah had described his as 'very boring'. Three terms later, drawing on many 'texts in common' read aloud by their teacher, their inside-text talk had a performative element about it which reflected the children's newly found pleasure in word play and poetry. Spontaneously they began to chant the beginning of the *Boneyard Rap*, demonstrating evident knowledge of the poem and considerable pleasure in 'revoicing' it (Bakhtin, 1981). Inside-text talk appears to draw upon a desire to share knowledge and enthusiasm about particular texts and appears to foster positive attitudes towards reading. Driven by the readers themselves, it often involved collaboration, reader 'performance' and quoting from texts in common. Such talk for sharing a reader's engaged perspective was associated with relaxation, friendship and affect.

The evidence suggests that this talk, driven by the language of affect, is different from book talk (Chambers, 1985), which is more often triggered and mediated by teachers in teacher-led contexts. Inside-text talk appears to be more child-initiated and directed, although teachers, too, took part in some of these communal insider conversations which occurred in informal contexts. It appears to be linked to literature and is arguably based on some degree of common knowledge and understanding about the story or poem, and on a genuine acceptance of the others involved, who are also perceived as interested readers. It is suggested that the presence of informal, spontaneous and child initiated inside-text talk is a core element of a reading community.

Reciprocity: families–parents–schools reader relationships

The degree to which teachers were able to develop shared understandings of reading with families and communities was variable across the project. In concentrating on developing classroom communities of readers, teachers had less time to devote to building new relationships beyond school. However, some schools did begin to develop new shared understandings and the teachers supported parents by broadening the notion of 'what reading is', as reflected in the following parent's comment:

> She does enjoy magazines but I didn't really used to think about that as reading. I just hadn't made the connection. I do now sit with her and we have a chat about what she's reading – and I enjoy it really – well I enjoy reading magazines too.
>
> (Parent comment, Suffolk)

This mother had come to recognise that reading does not refer to books alone. Her daughter, Sally, one of the focus children, had been a very reluctant reader who lacked confidence, did not enjoy reading and would often 'forget' her home–school reader. At the outset, both Sally and her mum viewed reading through the school's lens and did not recognise everyday reading practices as 'reading'. When these were validated and what counts as reading broadened, mother and daughter were able to enjoy reading together. As Meek noted, 'we relinquish whatever hold we have on children's reading progress if we disparage what and how they choose to read' (Meek, 1998: 121).

Some schools focused on more traditional approaches to home–school reading partnerships, for example by running parent workshops to show parents how reading is taught in school. Though the project did not seek to promote particular approaches to working with parents, the project team were conscious that the schools needed to avoid privileging teachers' knowledge about reading instruction, and inadvertently positioning parents as 'non-knowing'. Many attempts at parent partnerships have been based on school-centric models that diminish the value of children's learning in other contexts (Lawson, 2003). Furthermore, if schools only profile a school book-based approach, they may fail to recognise ways into reading via other routes, such as through relevant popular culture materials for example. As one father on the project commented:

> It was my mum that got me into reading. She knew I'd got a problem and I was drifting along and she started to read the football programmes with me on a Saturday – it's only because of her that I can read now. Before that I was totally switched off!
>
> (Parent comment, Birmingham)

Nonetheless, many parents are supported by additional information and a widening understanding of how reading is taught in school. Where this was introduced in project schools, this proved to be helpful. Whilst not new nationally, such approaches were new in some schools and had very positive outcomes. One Barking and Dagenham school for example, ran a series of parents' practical workshops with their family learning coordinator, and unusually over 60 parents attended the three linked sessions. This raised the profile of reading. However, in schools where only traditional approaches were used there was little evidence of change in the shared understandings about the nature of reading in contemporary children's lives.

A few project teachers, many of whom developed as Reading Teachers, focused on creating more overtly reciprocal relations between parents, families and schools. They found that connecting to reading lives beyond school offered new ways to forge relationships with families, whilst also building new, shared knowledge and understanding about reading in the twenty-first century. Children in these schools engaged in a range of activities with families, all of which were designed to recognise diversity and give voice to different generations of readers. For instance in Kent and Medway schools, some children interviewed and filmed members of their family and others in the school community (including administrators, kitchen staff, teaching assistants and teachers) about their reading memories and practices. In Birmingham, some children interviewed parents, grandparents, aunties and uncles at home; this introduced the notion of personal and family reading histories and current reading habits and choices. A myriad of new information was collected, including:

- 'When I was younger, if I ever had any spare time, I would love to read any Islamic books and the history of many things' (Grandparent).
- 'I remember my dad reading Treasure Island to me when I was your age' (Father).
- 'My parents read Bengali and religious books' (11 year old boy).
- 'My dad reads English newspapers, Bengali novels, procedures and guidelines' (10 year old boy).
- 'On Saturday my dad reads the Sports reports, the football programme, his betting slips and he usually reads a book to my baby sister' (9 year old girl).

- 'This Saturday night my aunty came round and drew her reading river and she had read: the Quran aloud, her emails, websites and a novel called *Bindi Babes*' (8 year old boy).

(Children, family interviews, Birmingham)

Parents, grandparents and others in various schools were also invited to bring part of themselves and their lives into the classroom through sharing their particular interests and related personal reading with children in small groups. Examples from a Suffolk school included adults talking about their passion for: gardening (and sharing any related magazines, catalogues and books); cooking (and bringing in favourite recipe books and showing related websites), travel, biking, knitting and belly dancing. This talk around texts, linked to people's lives, personal interests and work outside school, signified a marked change in the perception of reading and expanded the notion of reciprocity beyond that established between children and their Reading Teachers. In these schools, genuinely reciprocal reading communities began to be established such that there was an emergent recognition on the part of children, teachers and parents of the diverse reading lives and practices of others. This had impact in many different ways:

- It helped to develop a broader, shared understanding between teachers, children, parents and families about 'what reading is'.
- It highlighted diversity, relevance and reading activities and habits more equally.
- It helped many more children to 'see the point' of reading in life outside school.

Reading Teachers who had shared their reading lives saw this move towards a wider awareness and celebration of parents' and families' reading as a natural and potentially powerful extension of their previous work. Reading materials started to travel for real reasons in two directions: from home to school as well as from school to home. It was not easy to establish this. Teachers commented on the challenges:

It took a long time to build trust and still it is very slow – parents are used to the school providing reading material – but gradually word is getting around and parents are beginning to be interested. Establishing trust is hard. Last week a child brought his Nan into school first thing in the morning and she asked me 'What's this all about then?'

(Teacher, presentation, Kent)

There was evidence of teachers gaining a much broader understanding of the children's reading habits, tastes and choices and of them acknowledging this in their practice. 'We were amazed to see how much reading actually went on in children's lives: a whole range of things linked to television and DVD and computers and books too' (Teacher, interview, Birmingham).

Whilst teachers were broadening their understandings of children's reading lives beyond school, it should be acknowledged that children themselves seemed to be well aware, all along, of the notion of 'school reading': 'We didn't think we'd be allowed to read these [football programmes] in school – yeah, it's great!' (Child, interview, Suffolk).

Research evidence suggests that many children become aware, very early on, that school reading is set within a particular framework and this framework doesn't really reflect the world outside. As Levy argues, 'children forsake their own constructions of reading in favour of, what they regard as, more in keeping with the school's definition' (Levy, 2009: 81).

There were signs that in some schools the boundaries between home and school reading lives overlapped and became less demarcated. Yet, across the whole project, teachers indicated that much more work needed to be done in this area; schools and communities face different challenges depending on their contexts, historical practices and people's perceptions. Shifting the locus of control from a schooled view of reading into a more shared understanding promises a new discourse about reading; one that includes popular cultural and digital texts, makes links to children's lives and local community contexts and creates new understandings and relationships of reciprocity. Such relationships have the potential to significantly influence children's reading and learning, although positioning the 'formal' literacy of school with the 'informal' literacy practices that take place outside it, is no simple task. This became a key focus of the Phase III research, *Building Communities: Researching Literacy Lives*, in 2009–10 (Cremin et al., 2012; Cremin et al., forthcoming).

Building relationships with libraries

As the Phase I research had shown, teachers' links with libraries were not strong (Cremin et al., 2008a, b). The Phase II work sought to establish such links both with the School Library Service (SLS) and through schools linking with local libraries. Additionally, other research suggests a worrying proportion of young people are not library members (e.g. in the UK, 48 per cent, Clark and Hawkins, 2011) and have strongly negative perceptions of libraries (e.g. in the USA, Meyers, 1999). Most of the schools in the Phase II project had existing relationships with the SLS; they regularly purchased book loan boxes from the SLS and there was some communication about the book selections. However, very few project teachers had actually visited the SLS or had ever met with their staff, perhaps due to the fact that the majority of the project teachers were not literacy leaders in their schools.

The biggest impact was not on the number of schools using the SLS, but on the new relationships that were established between SLS staff and project teachers. SLS staff in all of the five local authorities (LAs) supported the project in different ways. For example, some teacher sessions were held at SLS premises where teachers were able to meet staff and examine the wealth of resources available. Some LA project teams were provided with sets of books for the duration of the project linked to their particular literary focus. Some SLS staff also visited their local project schools to offer in-house support and some SLS staff set up new loan systems in order to supplement the overall book stock in classrooms. These activities established or renewed relationships between the SLS staff, LA consultants and project teachers and resulted in rich professional dialogue. Some schools also visited the SLS as a whole staff and planned to take children with them next time. Many teachers commented positively on the value of this:

> I saw so many different resources there and the staff were so interested in the issues we have. It really gave me new ideas about ways to get my boys into reading. The staff are so knowledgeable and we just haven't used their expertise before. I'd like us, as a staff, to be able to go there.
>
> (Teacher, written reflection, Birmingham)

Apart from the indirect impact this had on the reading choices offered to children, these new professional circles offered teachers more opportunities for professional learning and growth. The teachers overwhelmingly described the SLS support positively, as 'encouraging' and enabling'. Alongside the support offered in local groups, this collaboration with SLS staff helped widen teachers' knowledge of children's literature and enabled them to integrate the use of SLS resources into their pedagogical work, which in turn no doubt contributed to the improved attitudes to reading for pleasure documented in the project (see Chapter 9). In a not dissimilar manner, Norwegian researchers Tonne and Pihl (2012), in a project focusing on second-language learners and students with low socioeconomic status, claim that 'Literature-based literacy education, based on collaboration between teachers and librarians, had a positive effect on the development of reading engagement, measured in terms of attitudes to reading, frequency, and amount of voluntary reading and library use' (p. 191).

With regard to local libraries, none of the 27 schools had established links with their local library at the beginning of the project, although two schools encouraged children to take part in the Reading Agency's Summer Reading Challenge based at the library. Wanting to build local community links, some teachers set about organising trips to their local library, though they did not all find this particularly easy. For example, a minority of parents were not keen for their children to have library membership, as they were worried about having to return books on time and paying fines. This reflects some of the contextual challenges teachers faced and the need to be mindful that nothing can be taken as 'given'. If positive relationships of mutual respect are to be built, others' perspectives need to be heard and understood. Whilst teachers were able to reassure parents, this demonstrates the complex factors involved. In other cases, there was simply no local library within a reasonable distance. Many teachers found building reading communities in their classrooms took most of their time, and almost half of the schools did not establish regular class visits to the local library, nonetheless several made valuable library links in other ways. For example:

- Displays of children's work in the local library encouraged parents, grandparents and families to visit.
- Poetry readings and author visits held in the local library after school and at weekends provided shared experiences for parents, families, teachers and children.
- Teachers and local library staff met termly to discuss the project and possible partnership activities.
- Teachers introduced the Summer Reading Challenge to children and families in school, inviting library staff to school to award the children's certificates in the autumn term.

By the end of the project significant changes had been made in some schools, and connections had been forged between parents, families and schools with the local library acting as the fulcrum and a lever for bringing schools and families together. Teachers agreed, however, that this was an area ripe for further development. As Pihl (2011) has shown, when practitioners exercise professional autonomy and engage in interprofessional collaboration with librarians, there is considerable potential for professional growth, even without encouragement from schools or governments.

A case study of Victoria School

Victoria School is a very large inner-city primary school with over 700 pupils. Almost all children are of Pakistani or Bangladeshi heritage and speak English as an additional language. For most children, their families have lived in this area of the city for two or three generations. There is a strong recognition among the staff that learning happens inside and outside school. This drives their commitment towards developing a curriculum that is meaningful and connected to children's lives, whilst also supporting and challenging them as learners.

The school's hopes for the project

Developing reading is a central part of the school's priorities and they were keen to join the project for a number of reasons. They wanted to explore the increasingly diverse range of reading experiences that children engaged with outside school, both on paper and on screen:

> We know that we can't just tackle reading from an educational side of things. We do want to draw people together and develop better understandings about reading with school and families. But there is a certain view of reading, a certain amount of snobbery around reading. What should we have read? What shouldn't we read? We need to change all of that if we want people to share their reading freely. We need to change the whole culture – be more accepting and open about what reading might be today for all sorts of different people – and in languages other than English – in the here and now. That's why we want to be part of this project – we need some help to do it!
>
> (Headteacher, interview, Birmingham)

They also wanted to see teachers as readers who shared their reading with children and foster a love of books in the classroom:

> We have teachers here who are avid readers, and they are not getting reading for pleasure in their classrooms, so, how do we hope to get the teachers who are not themselves readers to encourage, support and develop young readers?
>
> (Assistant headteacher, interview, autumn)

Two teachers, teaching children aged 8–9 and 10–11, joined the project. Neither were on the senior management team, both were quite new to teaching, neither were responsible for literacy within the school. The assistant headteacher spoke highly of the action research model describing it as 'infectious' and a powerful way for the school to value its younger staff, allow them to flourish and bring new knowledge and energy into the school:

> It allows them to take a step back and link new ideas to what they already do in the classroom. Just being able to take a step back, have a look at the research without to pressure of having to implement something, is so important.
>
> (Assistant headteacher, interview, autumn)

Senior leaders in the school recognised that a barrier to this work for the whole school would be the issue of 'time'. They spoke explicitly about the 'battle' between objective-driven lessons and close tracking of targets and more open sessions that support reading for pleasure, but are still part of quality, purposeful learning environments. They were very clear about wanting to support the project teachers and learn from their experiences, for example:

> The fact that our teachers have selected three focus pupils each to look at more closely will help us to see how individual and unique children as readers are – we are hoping that we can learn from this – especially as these pupils are our lower achievers and quite disaffected. They do not choose to read. Reading is something that they 'do' for school and parents are very keen for them to achieve well and pass reading tests. We want to try to switch them onto reading. We want then to use the knowledge to hit a wider audience across the school.
>
> (Headteacher, interview, autumn)

It appeared, at least on the part of some of the parents, that they saw reading as something which their children needed to undertake 'for' school.

The school's journey

Both teachers identified three reluctant readers as focus children. All those chosen were boys. The teachers gathered data in their portfolios and kept detailed research journals, recording their close observations of these children's reading behaviours and competencies. They also logged their own professional learning journeys and kept reading diaries. By the spring term, senior management were starting to notice a change in the project teachers' subject knowledge and approaches to teaching reading:

> They are very enthusiastic and they are developing their knowledge around literature and reading … and increasing their own subject knowledge and confidence. They are discussing the project with staff informally around school … and they have given some more formal feedback in a staff meeting. There are good things going on in their classrooms and we can see the power of what it might be – we need to get it out now into the school more.
>
> (Assistant headteacher, interview, spring)

There were also signs of changes in children from the project classes. The headteacher spoke of one of the younger focus children as he carried a huge bag of books into the classroom. He told her excitedly that his mother had been buying books from the newspaper for him and now he had 17 and was going to share them at reading time. The introduction of reading buddies was having an impact too and other staff were noticing changes in the reading behaviours of the 10–11 year olds in the school library:

> Staff really like the idea that she [the teacher of the 10–11 year olds] has set up this paired reading at times in the library when others can see it working. It isn't too difficult to set up and she can show them that it has an impact on attainment in many

ways including attitude and motivation. People like to see that. So – it's just common sense really. If the children are reading more and choosing to read and talk to each other about reading, then they become better readers. One of our aims was to get staff thinking – and that's definitely happening.

(Assistant headteacher, interview, spring)

By the end of the spring term the project was sending ripples around the whole school and interest was gathering. Senior managers were beginning to talk about developing the project across the whole school and how the rationale and philosophy underpinning it linked to their drive for a more child-centred view of teaching and learning and more personalised approaches. The boys were choosing to read more beyond school too. During one of the final interviews, they described how they were choosing to read at home and had set up a 'reading party':

BIMAL: Well, we've started this thing now Miss where we have a reading party at one of our houses ... we just take all the books we have and we just look at them and talk about them.

JO: My sister comes.

MAHIR: Like, tonight it's going to be at my house so ... I've got this book from the book fayre ... you know the one?

JO: The one ... you got from the book fayre ... the joke one?

MAHIR: Yes, the one with the skeleton in. Miss, this skeleton wants to go to a party but he had no BODY to go with!

BIMAL: Are we going to go upstairs again?

MAHIR: Yeah, yeah, we're going to have it in my bedroom.

Parents spoke about noticing the changes in their children's attitudes to reading and this contributed to the richer conversations about reading materials and children's choices. As one of the teachers commented in the final interview:

I have very different conversations with parents now about how the children are developing as readers. It used to be very focused on levels and reading tests results. Now, it's more about what children choose to read and there is more of an understanding about what reading 'is'. I mean, many parents have loved the Reading Rivers and they *loved* being asked about their own reading. It's made a difference but I still feel that we have a long way to go.

(Teacher, interview, summer)

In their final reflections, the two project teachers from Victoria school considered what they had learnt, both about themselves and the children:

One of the most valuable parts of the project has been the chance to intensively observe my children and talk to them about reading in a different way. I mean one of my blue group readers, one of my focus children, told me in a guided reading session – Miss, you've just spoilt it for me! He told me I'd spoilt the book for him by doing the book-walk, you know this book is about ... he said 'you've spoilt it now, I like to do that myself.' And I thought, yes I did – I did spoil it – how many times have I done that? I am sure that he wouldn't have said that to me before this project. We just didn't have that sort of openness really. And also, I wouldn't have taken his comment seriously before. I used to just move through the formula of the guided reading sessions. It's generally part of the guided session – introduce the book and do the book walk – and do we ever think about whether the children want to always have that structure? Is it the best structure? I'm not certain now. I would never have questioned it before. The project has just opened my eyes.

(Teacher, interview, summer)

We hear far more conversations about reading amongst the children now. The change has really been quite dramatic. We overhear the children talking in the playground and they are passing books between each other in ways that we certainly didn't see before.

(Teacher, interview, summer)

By the end of the project the focus children in both year groups had all achieved or exceeded their reading targets, but for the school, the real impact had been about the development of the children's desire to read and to share their reading with others, often spontaneously and with enthusiasm, both in class-reading-related sessions and on the cloakroom and playground. The senior management recognised, however, that they still needed to do more to widen parents' perceptions of reading:

Working with parents on something like the Reading Rivers and extending that sort of activity will help us next year to develop a closer relationship with families from the beginning so that they also know that reading is more than just attainment targets and levels. It will really help us to value the wider range of reading experiences that our children have.

(Assistant headteacher, interview, summer)

Conclusion

Initially absent, reader relationships developed in all project classrooms, and a key feature of these was their reciprocity. The teachers, whose journeys began at different starting points, began to position themselves differently; some developed as Reading Teachers and opened up their reading lives and practices more fully than their peers, but all the project teachers made new more reciprocal relationships around reading with children. They talked about texts and about reading, as reader to reader, rather than teacher to pupil. This enabled a cultural shift in the classroom where shared pleasure in reading, freedom, choice and spontaneous talk could emanate from the new physical and temporal spaces that were created. Additionally, through more informal child-initiated talk about texts – inside-text talk – which was rooted in friendship and affect, children shared their newly found enthusiasm for reading with one another. In terms of policy and practice, the project showed that this deserves closer examination.

The blurred boundaries that developed between home and school reading allowed for recognition of the rich diversity of children's reading lives and the vast array of reading and reader possibilities. As this diversity became more widely recognised and legitimised, it led to a more inclusive and less competitive reading culture in some classrooms and supported the development of communities of engaged readers. Some schools brokered new relationships with the SLS and local libraries, and where these were developed they were professionally enriching. Although the majority of teachers were less successful at building relationships external to school than those they built within it, by the end of the project many had laid the foundations for moving onwards and outwards.

Chapter 9

Influencing children's attitudes, motivation and achievements as readers

Sacha Powell

In the Phase II project *Teachers as Readers: Building Communities of Readers*, as teachers read more widely, considered their own experience of reading, effected pedagogical changes and explored and shared their own and the children's reading lives within and beyond schools, differences in the children's attitudes, behaviours and achievements in reading began to be evidenced. Some changes and their perceived consequences were gradual and subtle, others more immediate and obvious, but all were positively linked to the aim of foregrounding reading for pleasure in classroom contexts. These changes could be traced to newly emerging and evolving reader identities and relationships, which simultaneously reflected the shifting dynamics in their classrooms and subtle changes in the locus of control over reading repertoires and behaviours. As noted in earlier chapters, conscious attempts to move away from framing reading within narrow school-centric definitions not only enriched the curriculum, as teachers learned of children's hitherto unrecognised interests, but also legitimised a wider spectrum of texts (some oral and pictorial). It also fostered rich connections between children's reading practices in classrooms and the world beyond school.

This chapter traces examples of classroom-based activities and conversations, which reflect the impact on focus children of teachers exploring and sharing their own reading identities, opening up to new ideas, offering space for children to participate differently, to experience different reading lives within school and make connections. This enhanced their reading for pleasure and pleasure in reading across communities of learners. It should be noted that the focus children did not experience any additional or special activities or intervention, they experienced exactly the same as their classmates; they were only focus children in terms of extra data gathered about them. The chapter explores some of the many examples of the children's increasingly joyful engagement in reading at school and their reading lives outside, bringing stories of independent and shared pleasure in the classroom and at home. This is illustrated through the story of Kasif who uniquely, yet typically amongst the project focus children, made the journey from being a reader who could but did not choose to read, to one who found immense pleasure and satisfaction from reading and was motivated to read, alone and with others in the classroom community of engaged young readers.

Connecting reading and pleasure

In a study conducted almost simultaneously to Phase II, positive attitudes to reading were seen to encompass the following elements: positive self-concepts as readers, tendencies to read, reported enjoyment of reading, and emotional involvement in reading (Sainsbury and Clarkson, 2008). A similar construct of positive attitudes to reading was formed at the outset of the project. But analysis of the data led to a distinction between evidence of children's independent reading for pleasure – a purposeful volitional act with a large measure of choice and free-will; and pleasure in reading – enjoyment of reading regardless of whether or not the act was self-chosen and whether intended for a particular (curriculum-based) purpose or not. Both were important in the context of English school classrooms where rhythms and routines are influenced by curriculum objectives, often leading to a dominance of teacher-directed and chosen activities, which have been seen to minimise opportunities for children to exert choice and preferences. Giroux (1987: 14), for example, observed that:

> Schooling is about the regulation of time, space, textuality, experience, knowledge and power amidst conflicting interests and histories that simply cannot be pinned down in simple theories of reproductions and resistance.... As institutions they exhibit contradictory positions in the wider culture and also represent a terrain of complex struggle regarding what it means to be literate and empowered.

Thus reading for pleasure in schools can be counter-cultural. As noted in earlier chapters, faced with an accountability regime that prizes attainment, teachers may be hard pressed to justify an emphasis on reading for pleasure in their classrooms, despite international evidence that links attitudes and motivation to achievement (Mullis *et al.*, 2007, 2012). Studies of children's learning behaviours recognise the vital role played by self-esteem, confidence and feeling a connection to the subject matter, and teachers' pivotal influence in determining classroom relationships which underpin children's attitudes about themselves as learners and their engagement with the curriculum (Powell and Tod, 2004).

Rosenblatt's (1978) transactional theory of the participatory experience of reading comprising efferent and aesthetic modes was also salient to this research. Analysis of data gathered from the children enabled the identification of language that corresponded with an aesthetic mode. This was taken as evidence of children's emotional responses to reading. Further analysis then allowed for an assessment of whether this represented pleasure in reading or reading for pleasure, or both, and when linked to the associated activity, further analysis allowed for distinctions to be made between pleasure in reading as a self-selected activity or one dictated by another (principally the teacher). By contextualising examples of aesthetic modes in reading and gathering data from teachers to triangulate the children's evidence, efforts were made to address Hunt and Vipond's (1987) cautions that responses to reading are situational and the results can be equivocal.

The focus children at the outset: Learning about them

Although entire classes of children were involved and affected by the project (indeed the influence spread beyond these discrete groups), more in-depth data were gathered from and about a sample of children who were chosen by their project teachers. They were described as the focus children. This chapter draws from the data collected about all the 129 focus children across the project, but in particular draws on the sub-sample of the 49 focus children who were in the classrooms of the 16 case study teachers (see Chapter 3).

The teachers were given a brief to select children who could but did not choose to read (Moss, 2000), they selected those whom they believed regularly chose not to read, regardless of their reading ability and who seemed to experience little or no pleasure in reading; they were seen to be uninterested and disengaged readers. Furthermore, in most cases, the teachers reported that these children represented the majority of their peer group in terms of a perceived lack of interest in reading for pleasure, preferring instead to engage in a range of other activities when afforded the freedom to choose, which seemingly corresponded with findings from PIRLS (Twist et al., 2003, 2007).

However, it should be noted that the teachers based their selection and made these assertions at the start of a new school year, using discussions and records from the children's class teacher from the previous year and reflections on the first few weeks of teaching them. As was demonstrated through project data, some children's attitudes to reading diverged from the teachers' perceptions and varied from one context to another, although school was seen to influence home and vice versa. Nevertheless, the teachers based their selections on relatively limited information, reflecting a general tendency within the schools at that time to make assumptions about children's attitudes to reading without knowledge of their lives beyond the school or efforts to learn through exploratory conversations with the children. This finding supports Hunt and Vipond's (1987) assertion that responses to reading are situational but also calls into question the reliability of generalising data on children's attitudes and motivation (e.g. from school to home contexts) where methods fail to incorporate and convey the range of situated experiences and views of the children concerned. As the project progressed, it became evident that the children's perceptions and dispositions interacted with and were influenced by their teacher's subject and pedagogic knowledge and practice, and the opportunities which were offered them to access literature, interact with one another and make connections to their everyday reading practices at home (see Chapter 9). But when the project began, knowledge about the focus children was limited to perceptions of their reading attitudes and behaviours that lacked those connections or acknowledgement of situated factors, such as the educational philosophy and culture of the school and the influence of teachers' own reading identities, beliefs, attitudes and behaviours.

Attitudes and motivation

To understand attitudes to reading from the children's perspective, all those in the focus sample of 49 in the case study classrooms were invited to take part in small discussion groups/interviews. During the first (and last) of these, the children explained how they felt about reading in their own terms. They were also asked to separately to complete a questionnaire, choosing from one of the following categories to describe their attitude to reading:

- I love reading;
- It's okay;
- I'm not bothered about it;
- I don't like reading.

Table 9.1 Three children's comments about reading at the start of the project

Attitudes to reading categories chosen by three children at the start of the project (in one school)		
Sam	Sophie	Isaac
It's okay	I don't like reading	I don't like reading

Extract from discussion with the same children near the start of the project

RESEARCHER: Why do you read?
SAM: It's fun.
SOPHIE: It helps you understand things.
ISAAC: Because I get bored – I get bored while I'm reading.
RESEARCHER: So why do it?
ISAAC: Because I have to.
RESEARCHER: Do you read the same things at school and at home?
ISAAC: Different but I can't remember what they're called.
SAM: The same – but I'm reading *Harry Potter* at home. *(He previously said he had been reading* The War Monkey *at school.)*
SOPHIE: Both [sometimes the same and sometimes different] – I'm reading one called *Pony Stable* and *Princess Diaries*.
RESEARCHER: Tell me about your best book ever.
SAM: *Jiggy McCue and the Toilet of Doom* ...
SOPHIE: I don't really have one because I don't read that much. I'm not really a fan of reading ...
ISAAC: *(Shrugs – no response)*

The questionnaire did not specify 'in school' but its completion and the discussions were located within school contexts and this could have influenced the children's responses. For example, children may have believed that researchers were only interested in finding out about reading in school; or they may have felt obliged to give responses that were more positive than they actually felt. But the discussions suggested more diverse and often more positive views of reading than their teachers had believed, and the children cited examples of independent reading pursuits outside school and their feelings about reading in school and elsewhere (Table 9.1).

Among the 49 children, more than half gave a fairly ambivalent questionnaire response ('It's okay') and seven said they loved reading. The more negative views ('I'm not bothered' and 'I don't like reading') composed the remainder. Since the focus children had been identified as learners who 'can but don't' read (Moss, 2000), their teachers were astonished to hear the children's opinions, which were fed back at an early stage, and this piqued their interest further: Were some children who seemingly disliked reading in school reading independently at home? Why were those who appeared to dislike reading telling the researchers that they loved it – or thought it was 'okay' – and describing a wide range of reading materials and activities outside school? It was possible that some of these supposedly 'reluctant readers' demonstrated disaffection and lack of interest only in school contexts, possibly in response to the range of reading material made available there and as a result of the ways in which reading was perceived and/or framed in classrooms. Perhaps they did not want to be seen by their peers to like reading, yet privately they enjoyed it.

Self-perception

The children were also asked to self-rate their reading abilities in the same way, choosing from four questionnaire response options but also talking about how they felt as readers in the discussion groups:

- I'm very good at reading;
- I'm good at reading;
- I'm okay at reading;
- I'm not very good at reading.

Only four of the children described themselves as being 'very good' and another four as 'not very good' at reading. Most said they were 'good' or 'okay'. In some respects this was unsurprising. Teachers had been asked to select the children who were known to be able to read. But the relatively positive slant among the majority of these children in terms of their perceptions of themselves as readers suggested that they continued to believe they were capable (very good/good/okay) even if they were (perceived to be) 'reluctant'. This finding resonates with that of Sainsbury and Schagen (2004) whose study highlighted a continued improvement in reading ability among primary age pupils even though their enjoyment of reading showed a decline. Sainsbury and Clarkson (2008) in deconstructing 'attitude' to reading, advise that this includes self-concept, suggesting that the motivation to read is closely linked to a child's self-perception as reader in terms of ability (see Chapter 2 for further discussion of this).

Children's perceptions of their teachers as readers

When asked at the start of the project whether they thought their teachers were readers, whilst none of the 49 focus children stated that their teachers 'definitely didn't read', over half voiced a degree of uncertainty, noting that their teacher 'probably reads' or 'probably doesn't read'. Their responses indicated that reading was done mainly by them and for the teacher, and that they were unsure if their teachers read, during the initial interviews/discussions, their observations about this included:

- 'She reads, but not enthusiastically';
- 'I don't think she ever reads';
- 'I don't really know if she likes reading';
- 'It's hard to say; she doesn't read much';
- 'She listens to us read'.

Since many of the teachers read stories or poems aloud to their classes and indeed were encouraged through the project to increase this activity, the children were also asked about their opinions of being read to by their teachers and the frequency with which this happened. Whilst not all enjoyed this at the start of the year, as many associated such reading with the literacy focus and related comprehension and written work (see Chapter 7), by the spring term nearly all the children spoke positively and excitedly about teachers reading aloud: 'I like when she reads because I can see the pictures in my head'; 'I like it because it relaxes you and she picks really good stories' (Children, interview, Suffolk). This compared much more favourably than their observations on being 'made' to read themselves (see below).

The children were also asked whether they thought their teachers liked reading or not. Looking across the children's responses to these questions in the first discussion groups, an interesting pattern began to emerge, which suggested that the frequency with which teachers read aloud correlated with the children's perceptions of them as readers. When teachers read aloud every day or several times a week the children had no hesitation in describing them as 'definitely' a reader and someone who loved reading. As the frequency of reading aloud declined, so too did children's certainty about their teachers being readers. In these cases, the children thought their teachers were 'probably' readers who thought it was okay, weren't bothered or disliked it. Although a positive correlation between frequent reading aloud and teachers being viewed as definitely readers may not be surprising, the same cannot be said for the correlation between infrequent reading aloud and children's views that their teachers probably didn't read (or like it) given all the other classroom-based reading activities, for example: 'She doesn't talk about reading. She makes us do a lot of reading and we read with her. We have guided reading' (Child, interview, Kent).

The children's initial perceptions of their teachers' reading identities appeared to be significantly and perhaps uniquely influenced by the practice of reading aloud. Their later views regarding their teachers' pleasure in reading and their knowledge of what their teachers read appeared to relate to the extent to which their teachers developed as Reading Teachers and more explicitly shared their reading lives and practices with the young readers. Those who developed this stance appeared to make a more marked impact upon the children's development as readers (see Chapter 6).

Learning with the children: Case study of Kasif

As the year progressed, many changes were observed in the focus children's attitudes about reading, themselves and their practices as readers as well as their teachers' reading identities. These will be described in more detail later. But first, the story of Kasif provides a close-up of the important relationships between the constructs, images and models that the teachers projected and promoted about reading and readers' identities and the children's evolving responses and initiatives.

Kasif's starting point

Kasif attended an inner-city primary school in Birmingham and had just entered his final year there – he was 10 years old at the start of the project. Kasif had been identified by his teacher Beverley as a bright, academic boy who was judged to be working between a secure and high level for his age at the beginning of the year. He was described as 'an academically driven reader' with good comprehension skills, and a sound understanding of how to perform well in test situations. Further comments from Beverley's assessments suggest that Kasif was secure in his understanding of the structural features of texts and able to articulate his responses to texts with confidence: 'Kasif is very vocal during discussions and is particularly keen to offer his opinions and feelings' (Teacher, observation record, autumn).

Whilst he had many strengths as a reader, his teacher chose him as a focus pupil because he avoided reading whenever he could, would never choose to read and often remarked that reading was 'dull' and 'boring'. Teacher observations show that, during free-reading time, he would sit with a book open at the same page every day, sometimes for as long as a week before he chose to swap it for another, which would receive the same treatment. Beverley noted that this negative attitude towards reading was fairly typical amongst many of the boys in the class.

Kasif's parents saw reading very much as the domain of school; they wanted him to be reading the 'right sort' of texts and to be doing well with his reading. They took great pride in his efforts and abilities, and were very eager for him to do well in national tests and to succeed in education. They were eager to ensure that he was making good progress and that all his homework was completed, including his reading homework; Beverley later observed that this tended to reinforce Kasif's view (and indeed his teacher's at the outset of the research) that reading was a school-based task.

Development of Kasif's teacher's practice

At the beginning of the project, Beverley spoke about the difficulties of finding time for reading for pleasure when 40 minutes was already required to be allocated daily to guided reading sessions. She identified Kasif as one of a group of boys who were potentially able readers. Yet she had concerns: 'They can answer the high level questions and they do read for meaning and this is seen as good reading – educationally. But they do not see themselves as readers and they do not enjoy reading' (Teacher, interview, autumn).

The project encouraged her to think about her own reading habits and she began to draw analogies between herself as a reader and the children as young readers in a much broader sense. She noted that her own reading included magazines, short non-fiction texts and a range of on-line reading, and tentatively she began to talk about her reading with the class, and encouraged them to talk about their out-of-school reading habits. She found that at home many of them chose to read cheat magazines, game magazines and comics, and much of their free choice reading was linked to popular culture such as *Dr Who*, *The Simpsons* and *Top Gear*.

As well as reflecting upon her own reading practices, Beverly, like all her project colleagues, had begun to read and share children's literature, and this had a significant impact on her perceptions of reading and on their classroom practices. Beverley noted the impact of this in her reflective research journal:

> One of the reasons the children don't read for pleasure in my class is I suppose the way I am delivering or teaching is kind of taking the fun out of books … we never really discuss reading or recommend books and I think actually I've got a role to play here.

> Some of the days we went to in London and some of the centre-days – we spent time talking about books, enjoying books and our personal responses and I thought to myself, 'I need to change my approach here. The way I use books in the classroom is just not helping this'.

> (Teacher, reflective journal, spring)

She made a commitment to herself to 'try my very best to read a whole book to the children' and, whenever she had time, to share a poem or a short story. Over the year, book talk between teacher and children increased, and recommendations for good reads started to pass between them. Reading aloud became a regular routine in Beverley's class. Reading buddies were introduced, along with a wider range of texts including joke books, quiz books, magazines and comics. This sent ripples of enthusiasm around the classroom. During the spring term, Beverley talked about how she noticed boys were starting to recommend reading to each other: 'When I talk to them now I notice that they seem to know about each other's reading. This is very new' (Teacher, interview, spring).

Later in the year it became apparent that Kasif's attitude to reading, along with that of his friends, was beginning to change. Other staff in her classroom also commented that incidental, child-initiated exchanges around reading were beginning to be heard, and later such inside-text talk was also documented in the cloakroom and on the playground.

Kasif's development as a reader

At the beginning of the project, Kasif's attitude towards reading was best described as indifferent. When asked, he couldn't remember what he was reading personally but referred to a book his teacher had been using, though again he could not recall its title: 'Well, we've been looking at a book about badgers – how they live, eat and survive. I can't remember what it's called' (Child, interview, autumn).

He explained that generally, people read to help them with English and to keep them busy and that, apart from his guided reading sessions, he read during registration, or 'maybe if the teacher has to go somewhere'.

By the spring term Kasif had become much more involved in his reading, enjoying the time his group of friends had been allocated in the library with their reading buddies. One observation found him sitting with five other boys on soft furnishings surrounded by a collection of reading materials. Kasif was sitting closely with Mazidul sharing quiz books, joke books, a Simpsons comic and a poetry book, *There's a Fly in My Soup*. Their shared engagement was striking, marked in particular by the physical contact the boys had with the reading materials. They were pointing, flicking through books and turning to contents pages to find their favourite poems, reading jokes aloud to each other and waiting for responses, asking each other quiz questions: 'What's the land of the midnight sun?' Mazidul asks: 'Arctic and Antartica' replies Kasif. The ease with which they were sharing their reading and moving around the library to select texts as they wished, reflected a noticeable change in their reading attitudes and behaviours.

As the year went on, Beverley noted further changes in Kasif's attitude to reading and found that on several occasions he *asked* if he could read. Her surprise is captured by the comments in her reflective journal: 'This is Kasif asking me if he can read in a non-reading part of the day!' (Teacher, reflective journal, spring).

As she introduced new reading material into the class reading area, Beverley also introduced a folder with a sheet and post-it notes that could be used as a comment and rating sheet. She noted that Kasif was keen to know what others were reading and was often seen to be flicking through the folder and choosing his reading according to the comments made by other boys. This behaviour was shared with many of the boys and she discussed this one day with Kasif, asking why he felt that some of the books hadn't yet been taken out and read:

> Why do you think that is?
>
> I think it's 'cos no-one has read them yet Miss and people want the ones that every-one is reading don't they... so they can join in.
>
> Perhaps, maybe if you read one of them, other people might ...
>
> Maybe.
>
> (Teacher, reflective journal, spring)

In the summer term, Kasif talked about his reading with enthusiasm and energy. He drew on shared reading experiences with his friends, reciting lines from poetry and stories that they had enjoyed together. The recommendations made by Beverley were clearly remembered by him and his friend:

> KASIF: She offers us books that she thinks we might like. She just puts them down on the side and says 'you might like that'. And one of those was *Wait til I'm Older than You.*
> WILL: And I tried that and I really liked it – but then someone nicked it. And there was another one ... *Please Mrs Butler ...*
> KASIF: Oh yeah, *Please Mrs Butler* – that's sick –
> MATTHEW: Yeah, that's sick.
>
> (Children, interview, summer)

('Sick' in this context was denoting a text which had credibility and attraction.) The boys talked about having enjoyed interviewing family members about their reading histories and noting all the different kinds of reading that happens across a weekend at home which they captured in the Reading Rivers (see Chapter 5). Beverley noted that links with home are slow but: 'We have lots of interesting information about how much reading happens in homes. So many different sorts of reading and in languages other than English. I have learnt a lot!' (Teacher, reflective journal, summer).

By the end of the year, Kasif achieved a high level in reading and writing and had reached these targets with ease. This might have happened without this project, it is not possible to know, though Beverley felt the project had significantly supported his development. However, the real gain had been in Kasif's social and emotional development and his highly positive attitude towards reading. At the close of the year he was choosing to read and to share his reading, and had become a reader of his own volition who took pleasure in reading and being part of a community of readers in the classroom.

Learning from the children as they grew as readers

Kasif was not alone in the changes that the teachers and researchers observed or that the children reported for themselves. In addition to the increasingly positive attitudes towards reading, more positive self-perceptions as readers and newly informed views about their teachers' reading identities that were noted at the end of the project in all the participating schools, the children's conversations about reading with each other, with teachers and researchers became richer, more informed and more enthusiastic.

As the project year progressed and some of the teachers actively sought the persona of Reading Teacher (see Chapter 6) evidence also emerged of children's expanding knowledge about issues relating to the act of reading and the habits, preferences and practices of different readers. In particular, it became clear that communities of readers were evolving in classrooms where the children had developed:

- their knowledge of literature and specific authors and poets;
- an increased recognition of reading diversity;
- as active participants in the shared social experience of reading;
- increased awareness of their rights as readers;
- perceptions of their teachers as fellow readers.

Children's knowledge of literature and specific authors and poets

At the start of the project, the data suggested that the children talked about a limited range of reading materials; they mainly referred to books, predominantly their guided reading book or current school reading book, and frequently in a desultory fashion. Often they referred to the number of pages or chapters it held. In addition, in the early interviews the children demonstrated a general lack of interest in or recollection of the titles of texts or writers. Several had no favourite texts or writers, and those that did name a favourite book had very little to say about it. They showed limited knowledge about authors.

By the mid- and late-phase discussions in the spring and summer terms, this had begun to change significantly. Their voices reflected a growing awareness and interest in the work of authors and poets not only in relation to the range of their work, but also with regard to the nature of their writing. The children's comments often revealed that their enthusiasm for reading and for choosing particular books originated in their teachers' read-aloud provision. It was clear their knowledge and pleasurable engagement in reading was widened through their teachers' selection of potent texts to share. In the following excerpt from a mid-phase interview, the three focus children (aged 8–9 years old) enthusiastically identified many books from the school bookshelves and showed these to the researcher. As they did so they reflected their enhanced knowledge and interest in children's literature.

(The children bring several books that their teacher recently read aloud in class.)
RESEARCHER: Did your teacher read these books to you all in class?
JOE: Yes.
THOMAS: There's a book that I want to show you.
JOE: And there's a book which I want to show you and I know where it is now but it's not a dolphin book it's even better. *(Goes to find it.)*
THOMAS: *The Dolphin Boy.* He gets a dolphin in there …
RESEARCHER: And why do you like that book?
THOMAS: Because it's got good pictures and he goes there and …
(Joe brings a book, begins to talk; Thomas continues to read The Dolphin Boy.*)*

RESEARCHER: And why do you like *Horrid Henry*?

JOE: Because he's one of my TV characters that I watch most of the time. He's on CITV.

RESEARCHER: Aha, I'll have to have a look at that.

JOE: I like *Horrid Henry* I reckon because I've got two others.

THOMAS: I know where my best one is now.

RESEARCHER: OK, do you want to show me then; where is it, is it high up?

THOMAS: No.

SABRINA: I know a book I really enjoyed.

(Thomas brings another book.)

RESEARCHER: Oh look at those aliens! What's this book called?

THOMAS: The Man on the Moon.

RESEARCHER: *The Man on the Moon*. Is this one of your new school books?

(Thomas goes through the book excitedly pointing out things in the pictures.)

THOMAS: He has things to eat … Bob goes to fetch his lunch box … this contains two sandwiches … he has an apple and nuts, sometimes he needs his friend … two of his best friends are Billy, Donna … and Sam. They talk about the stars. Briony, Josh, where's that bit, where's that bit where he doesn't think that there's any aliens?

RESEARCHER: Do you think it might be before the page where the aliens are?

THOMAS: I guess so; I'm going to have a little read through it maybe.

JOE: No the really good…

THOMAS: Oh yeah, read this bit, there's…

ALL CHILDREN IN UNISON: 'THERE'S – NO – SUCH – THINGS – AS – ALIENS'!

SABRINA: But look we'll show you the funny part. And we like this, look, see.

CHILDREN TOGETHER: ALIEN, ALIENS! There's one there. There's a little picture on … Yeah oh yeah this is good, but he's swapped the aliens. It's like *(all pointing out aliens)* – they're everywhere. Welcome to the world – aliens. Stay there aliens! Now I'll go and put this back.

(The children bring several more books, enjoy discussing them together and showing them to me. These include Baby Brains *and* Charlie Stinky Socks.*)*

RESEARCHER: So did your teacher read you this story in class?

CHILDREN TOGETHER: Yeah.

(Children, interview, Suffolk)

This typical example provides affirming evidence of the importance of the teacher reading aloud to the class. Enjoyment of reading aloud (indeed pleasure in another's reading) was a theme commonly found in the children's interviews. This excerpt demonstrates the shared knowledge that the children developed through their teacher reading aloud and reveals that reading had become for them, at least some of the time, a shared social experience.

Sabrina, Joe and Thomas not only displayed their knowledge and enjoyment of the books they chose to show, but also that they were independently capable of locating those they enjoyed on a bookcase containing hundreds of different books. Their enthusiasm was immediately noticeable as they hurried to search for and retrieve their favourites and as they collaborated to explain the story, many parts of which they were able to recall and re-voice word-for-word. They also showed in-depth knowledge of the story's development, the intricacies of the illustrations and what these added to the tale as a whole. Their energetic conversation is another example of inside-text talk which was documented across many of the case study classrooms, in particular where teachers developed as Reading Teachers (see Chapters 6–8). In contrast to the early interviews, these focus children's new and shared retelling, knowledge of authors and books, and memory of significant lines and phrases in well-known and well-loved texts in common was palpably different from the beginning of the year.

Children's increasing recognition of reading diversity

In the early interviews, children very rarely mentioned texts other than books. But, over time, children were identifying and acknowledging as acceptable in their schools a much wider range of reading materials. This more relaxed and encompassing attitude to what constituted reading helped to give them confidence and showed their extensive reading repertoires and knowledge of texts. Many began to talk about favourite comics and magazines with energy and passion, and found books which connected to current television series, sharing their interest in both narrative forms. Many also talked about different genres and about more than one book or poem by authors or poets they had encountered and enjoyed. Others described a range of reading interests and noted a wider school perspective, for instance: 'We didn't think we'd be allowed to read these [football programmes] in school – yeah, it's great!' (Child, interview, Barking and Dagenham).

In the mid- and late-phase interviews, the children often brought or mentioned a wider and more diverse range of texts. It became evident that they now felt it was legitimate to talk about examples that included comics, magazines, the Internet, maps, sweet wrappers and other texts, including those they identified in activities such as 'Twenty Four Hour Reads' and Reading Rivers (see Chapter 5). Nathan, aged nine, showed one researcher his Christmas homework, which included multiple pictures and the following writing:

> Everything I have read: Christmas cards, signs on roads, instructions in swimming pools, direction signs, high school musical book, TV programmes, menu, music, text messages, Christmas present tags, letters, crossword puzzles, instructions to play jacks, the Night before Christmas book.
>
> (Child, interview, Kent)

That reading encompassed far more than just books was celebrated in the project and this shift to greater acceptance and value of diverse reading materials and activities enabled the children to feel their everyday reading practices and the diversity inherent in their own reading was valued and validated. In several cases this enabled children to see themselves as readers for the first time in school.

Children as active participants in the shared social experience of reading

At the start of the project, many of the children showed very little interest in or knowledge about each other's reading and there was a distinct lack of engagement in collaborative or shared talk about reading during the discussion group interviews. They appeared to have little common knowledge about texts they could share and were reluctant and/or uninterested in talking about their reading alone or together.

However, with time a number of examples revealed the focus children's developing abilities to discuss different texts and to voice their views, as well as a growing awareness of one another's likes and dislikes, as shown in the example below:

HANIF: Well the book that I'm reading at the moment is the most horrifying book – it's a big book – inside it's proper scary. There's a game called Witch Board and this boy plays it with his grandad …

(He gives a long description about a magic ring and a ghost. The two boys then talk about their reading tastes.)

KARIM: He always likes to read scary books – I never read scary books – they make me have a nightmare. Once after I read a book you [Hanif] gave me I had a nightmare.

HANIF: Well, sometimes I don't read that before I go to bed, like last night I read *Spongebob Square Pants*, Miss, coz it's funny and then you can enjoy what you dream of when you go to sleep.

(Children, interview, Birmingham)

While recognising their different reading preferences, these two 10 year old boys also displayed an awareness of the aesthetic mode, their emotional reactions to different texts and the possibilities they offered readers (e.g. being horrified or made to laugh; having nightmares or pleasant dreams). This example also illustrates the boys' growing sense of their rights as readers to make choices about what and when to read (or not) and about their decisions to read for pleasure at home (even if that pleasure was derived from being scared by a story). In addition, this example demonstrates the boys' shared reading knowledge and their awareness and interest in each other as readers. Other examples of spontaneous, child-initiated talk about texts were also noted in the data, demonstrating the free flow 'inside-text talk' which was identified as characteristic of many of the children's shared social encounters with texts during the later stages of the project. In these contexts, meaning-making was shared and the children's voices resonated with interest and commitment. It is perceived that the children's capacity to talk about texts more freely, interrupting each other as they did so and making connections with other texts they knew, as well as the texts of their lives, was indicative of a more open and encompassing approach to reading for meaning and discussing literature in the project classrooms and fostered child–child reader relationships (see Chapter 8).

Children's increased awareness of their rights as readers

At the start of the project it was clear that the children felt they had little control over what they could read in school. Some were solely reading books from reading schemes, and whilst encouraged to borrow from the class or school libraries their teachers recorded that they rarely chose to do so. Indeed this apparent reluctance to read was the reason they had been identified in the first place. Of those who were 'free readers' and given the scope to choose from a colour-coded box or classroom shelf, many were observed 'reading' or 'ploughing through' the same book over very extended periods of time, whilst others appeared to swap books very frequently, although they were less than keen to discuss these and many found it hard to recall their current reading book.

Over time, however, as teachers began to appreciate the need to offer increased choice and critically to support children's choices in a variety of ways (e.g. through reading aloud, book recommendations and book-based activities) the children were encouraged to exercise more discrimination and choice as readers. The breadth of reading material validated in school also widened the options for readers. Demonstrations of their awareness of greater possibilities and flexibilities involved in the act of reading and, directly or indirectly, their rights as readers, in line with Pennac's (2006) work, were exercised. Their talk about reading later in the year showed increasing recognition of these within and outside school and they made links between these rights and the possibilities for greater enjoyment of reading. This was also reflected through their descriptions in mid- and late-phase interviews of what they were reading, as well as what they chose *not* to read.

The children's drawings of readers were a further source of their growing awareness of their autonomy and ownership of their own reading for pleasure. In the final interview activity, children were invited to draw a reader, real or imagined. In some cases they chose to draw themselves or someone imaginary who was nevertheless very similar to them (e.g. a girl of the same age), in other cases children drew Reading Teachers or close friends. They then talked to the visiting researcher about their drawing.

A précis of six children's (aged 9–11) drawings and comments from four different schools is provided below. These capture some key messages about reading and reflect their sense of agency and rights as readers, even within the context of the school where compromises are of necessity made.

- Eddie drew himself reading in bed when he can't get to sleep. It's relaxing and quiet. He's reading *Match* (a football magazine) if it's Tuesday, Wednesday or Thursday because it comes on a Tuesday. If it's another day he's reading a book. Dad or sometimes Mum will listen to him read and he sometimes calls his Dad to talk about something in *Match*.

- Natalie drew 'a random person' reading in the park because it's quiet and there's nobody around. She's reading picturebooks, fact or fiction. She's into nature. When she goes back, she tells her friends what she's been reading.

- Charlie drew an imaginary person whom he named Fred who is about 10 or 11 and is sporty and reading a football comic which he reads weekly. He's in the library. He talks to his friends about football scores and stuff he's read and he also reads the newspaper, the sports articles. Everyone in his family reads as well. Nobody in his family reads football comics, which is why he talks to his friends.

- Carl drew a Scottish, kilt-wearing, 14 year old boy called Bob reading at the New York City Reading Club on a Wednesday night. All the books overwhelm him. Nobody else is around because other people go there on different days so everyone can read in peace and have a bit of time and all the books to themselves.

- Katie drew a group of children (boys and girls) sitting around a school table all reading copies of *Ways to Live Forever* by Sally Nichols. Five children are smiling but one has a different expression and a question mark above her head. This is because she is confused by some of the words in the book. They are enjoying the book and talking about it, but haven't read to the end yet.

- Samin drew several people sprawled on floor cushions in her home. Some are friends from class, one is a cousin, her dad is there also. Most are sharing magazines, though her dad is reading a newspaper and one girl is reading a book. Samin is one of the group gathered around the magazine *Mizz*. They are having fun looking at make-up which they want to buy.

These examples show how the children's drawings and their commentaries about them revealed insights into their constructs of readers and their identities as readers. They also provide rich evidence about the relevance and importance of reading environments. It is interesting to note at least two key elements: the social nature of reading, although some do refer to their 'reader' reading alone, often there is a social element, as in Natalie's description the imagined reader returns from a peaceful sojourn reading in the park to 'tell her friends about what she has been reading'. Katie's and Samin's drawings actually showed shared social occasions in which their friends were reading together and Charlie talked to his friends about his football comics as they read them as well. A sense of personal space is also evident; some drawings deliberately excluded other people, perhaps because the reader was seeking solitude to read in quiet, private contexts. The range of textual resources they chose to read also offered further confirmation of the children's acceptance of reading diversity and their awareness of readers' rights to choose what, when and where they read and with whom. As such they demonstrate positive attitudes to reading for pleasure as a volitional act.

Teachers as fellow readers

As mentioned earlier, the initial discussions with the children revealed a striking correlation between children's perceptions of their teachers as readers (or not) and the frequency with which the teachers were reading aloud in class. It appeared that this very explicit act of reading aloud was a key factor in the focus children's recognition of their teachers as fellow readers (despite the range of other reading activities that went on in the classroom). This correlation persisted in the data collected later in the project, though in the classes of those who developed more fully as Reading Teachers, the children revealed a more layered understanding of their teachers as readers, and shared their knowledge of their teachers' reading habits, likes and dislikes as readers (see Chapter 6).

For example, they evidenced ways in which they had a clearer sense of their teachers as readers and as sources of information, advice and inspiration. Describing her drawing of children reading *Ways to Live Forever* by Sally Nicholls, Katie explained that her teacher had talked about reading the story and how it moved her. Katie and her classmates had clamoured to borrow a copy:

> It's quite good … we have two of them that are boring like the one that doesn't have any pictures in, [the proof copies] and then this one [the final published copy]. Miss got me her [Sally Nicholls'] autograph and she got it in the book as well and I've got her autograph that Miss got me.
>
> (Children, interview, Kent)

Children choosing to engage as readers and read for pleasure

The examples provided in the previous sections highlight evidence of the children's increased engagement as readers: their growing enjoyment of reading, their improved self-confidence and more positive perceptions of their abilities, as well as the significantly improved attainment that was noted in many cases. The quotes from the interviews demonstrate the enthusiasm that the children displayed in mid- and late-phase interviews. This appeared to be linked to recognition of their rights as readers, the collaborative and spontaneous nature of their talk about texts and reading and their sense that all different forms of text could be acceptable and valuable.

As already noted, identifying children's reading for pleasure is complicated and requires attention to detail and context, but many of the examples given already from the interviews and drawings reveal that children were choosing to read and making time to read in school and at home, sometimes at unexpected times or in unusual places:

EDDIE: It's the school disco tomorrow. I might bring some books as well just to read if I get bored.
RESEARCHER: Are the discos a bit boring then?
EDDIE: Sometimes.
RESEARCHER: Can you concentrate with all the music?
EDDIE: I might go in the toilets and read.

(Child, interview, Kent)

The young learners were demonstrating increased agency about what, when and how to read, positively describing and discussing their reading choices and passions, and seeing reading as an end in itself, rather than simply as a means to an end.

This finding is supported by additional evidence from the questionnaires about the children's reading habits outside school and about the reasons why they read more at home or in school. The focus children were asked whether they read more at home or at school in both the baseline and end-of-project questionnaires, and all 30 focus children for whom data were available responded to these questions. Their baseline answers revealed that more children were reading at school at that time, whereas by the end of the project more children said they were reading at home.

The increase in the numbers of children reading at home, or equally at home and school, suggested that children were *choosing* to read at home more at the end of the project than had been the case at the start. This was encouraging given that independent reading for pleasure was a core focus of the project in the light of the PIRLS evidence (Twist *et al.*, 2003, 2007). Further supporting evidence of their enhanced pleasurable engagement in reading was found in the reasons the children gave. Their explanations about why they read more at home or at school were categorised in the analysis in terms of place, key reason(s) and tone, as shown below:

- 'I read more at home because I have more books that I like.' (*Place* – home; *reason* – resources; *tone* – positive (ref. home));
- 'I read more at school because I have to do it'. (*Place* – school; *reason* – choice/control (lack of); *tone* – negative (ref. school)).

Twenty-six (of the 49) focus children offered an explanatory response in both questionnaires. The analysis showed that at the beginning of the year, when a greater proportion said they read more at school than at home, the children were roughly equal in terms of the positive and negative tones in their responses. However, at the end of the year, with roughly equal numbers reading more at home or school, nearly ten times as many children gave positive responses compared with negative ones. Of the two children who had a negative tone to their responses, one read more at home and the other at school. There was only one negative response in relation to reading at home (due to being 'made to read a lot for homework by ... parents'). Positive responses included having more choice or control over what they read and when. Having more or more preferable resources and more time to read were also common reasons given and a few children were also positive about people, such as parents or teachers who would help and encourage their reading.

The numbers of children choosing to read at home increased markedly over the course of the year. Not only this, but also more children had positive reasons for reading in both places. The data reveal a general trend towards increased independent reading for pleasure. In school, children were offered more time to read, often via the establishment or reincarnation of independent reading time, but the young learners also seized and actively created other times to read and to talk about texts with one another and with their teachers. This overt and enthusiastic desire to read and share their reading and thinking was a significant overall thread running through the project data.

Additionally, the project teachers had been asked to record the children's reading scores at the beginning and end of the project as supplementary data. Complete sets were gathered

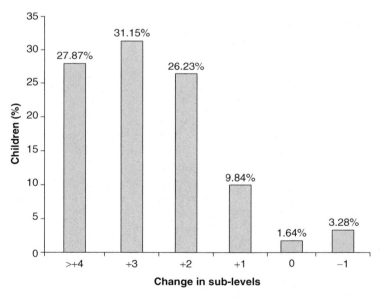

Figure 9.1 Data from teachers' records. Children's increase in sub-levels for reading attainment as measured in National Curriculum Standardised Measures

Year 3 focus children scores: Summer 2007–Summer 2008
- Charlie 2a–4c
- Robin 1a–2b
- Nicky 3c–3a

Year 3 whole class reading results:
- ✓ 2 or more sub-levels progress – 77%
- ✓ 3 or more sub-levels progress – 50%
- ✓ 4 or more sub-levels progress – 23%

Year 5 focus children scores: Summer 2007–Summer 2008
- Carrie 3c–4b
- Rohan 2b–3b
- Chris 2b–3c

Year 5 whole class reading results:
- ✓ 2 or more sub-levels progress – 70%
- ✓ 3 or more sub-levels progress – 45%
- ✓ 4 or more sub-levels progress – 19%

Figure 9.2 Teacher records: Reading results for the focus children and whole classes in one Kent school

for 61 children, including the case study group of focus children. As shown in Figure 9.1, these children made significant gains in their reading attainment over the course of the year. Around a quarter had moved up four National Curriculum sub-levels and more than half had increased by more than three. This compares with an expected norm of an increase by two sub-levels in a year. It should be stressed that these focus children were not given any special support or intervention across the year, but experienced exactly the same as their classmates; they were only focus children in terms of extra data gathered about them.

Improvements in writing were similarly noteworthy. Two teachers from one school in Kent decided to gather their own data (Figure 9.2). When they presented this to the project group as a whole, they found affirming responses from many of the other teachers who found similar gains in their own classrooms.

Conclusion

The positive changes that occurred for many children during the project's duration have been highlighted and while these did not apply to every child, they did apply to the majority. Whilst some children did not make exceptional progress in attainment, they made multiple gains in the other ways described throughout the chapter, particularly in the enjoyment they showed in reading at school. The improvements in children's attitudes, confidence and self-perceptions appear to be directly linked to the teachers' newly enriched subject knowledge and their evolving identities and practice as teachers who read and readers who teach. It would seem that the teachers' changing pedagogic practice made a marked impact upon the children, who, whilst initially being described as reluctant, uninterested and disengaged readers, began over time to enjoy reading and to choose to read independently for pleasure or to evidence this in school. The children's attainment also showed considerable improvement.

The children's increased subject knowledge was displayed in their abilities to describe and share their knowledge of authors, poets and illustrators and their experiences of a growing range of texts; this was enriched by their heightened awareness of their own and others' habits, preferences and identities as readers. The children's talk about texts was much more extended, more engaged and more spontaneous; they took pleasure in talking about their reading and in finding out what their friends and, in many cases, their teachers were reading. They were developing positive reader identities within the newly emerging reading communities in classrooms. The evidence showed that these young readers seized opportunities to exert their own choices and control over what, when and how they read, and shows how their teachers were supporting and encouraging them.

Chapter 10

Conclusion
Building communities of engaged readers

Teresa Cremin

What counts as reading and reading for pleasure in schools differs according to context. Framed and shaped by different societies' expectations, national education policies and institutional guidelines, reading and what counts as reading is socially constructed in classrooms on a moment-to-moment basis. Teachers provide the instruction, models and support that initiate children into school reading practices, and these practices influence what children think reading is and how it should be used (Levy, 2009). Teachers also shape the reader identity positions available to young people and impact upon their attitudes, interest and engagement in reading (Hall, 2012).

This final chapter revisits the reading practices developed in the Phase II project classrooms and synthesises the findings, drawing on the research reported in earlier chapters from both phases of the work. The UKLA Phase I research revealed teachers' limited knowledge of children's literature (Cremin *et al.*, 2008a, b) and this was also evident at the start of Phase II. Over time, however, the teachers in the Phase II project widened their repertoires, and, through their reflective participation came to engage in different classroom practices around reading. New communities of readers were constructed in project classrooms. These more reciprocal reading communities engaged with the diversity of children's everyday reading experiences, and, in some cases with teachers' own experiences and practices as readers. Whilst the teachers did plan for and encompass elements of what the project entitled a Reading for Pleasure Pedagogy, these elements and practices were neither uniformly developed nor regularised; they were differently shaped in each context in response to teachers' insights and children's reactions. In particular, those practitioners who developed as Reading Teachers became more conscious of the complex social processes of reading, and built new reader–reader relationships with children. These impacted positively upon the young readers' attitudes and desire to read and nurtured reader engagement and reading for pleasure. Some teachers also began to broker reader relationships beyond school.

This final chapter highlights: the coherent strategy that was identified to develop children's reading for pleasure by enhancing both teachers' subject knowledge and their pedagogic practice; new understandings about the concept of Reading Teachers as actively engaged role-models; and new knowledge about the nature and significance of creating reciprocal reading communities. It also discusses tensions and distinctions between the prevailing reading instruction agenda and the too-often side-lined reading for pleasure agenda. Recommendations in this regard are offered to schools and teachers wishing to enhance reading engagement within and beyond the classroom. The book closes with the recognition that further work is needed to create bridges across and between the reading/literacy lives of children, teachers and parents and communities.

Revisiting the projects' aims

The UKLA Phase I *Teachers as Readers* survey of 1,200 primary teachers from 11 local authorities in England, whose main responsibility was not literacy related, set out to establish practitioners' reading practices and preferences and their knowledge and use of children's literature in the classroom. The findings indicate that whilst teachers are readers who read personally for pleasure, they rely on a narrow canon of children's authors and personal childhood favourites, and have a particularly limited working knowledge of poets and picture fiction creators. Those working with older children (aged 7–11 years) read aloud much less than their counterparts working with younger children (aged 5–7 years), and both groups lean on a restricted range (Cremin *et al.*, 2008a, b). When choosing texts for use in the classroom, teachers rely heavily upon their own knowledge and make minimal use of library services. They are not therefore in a strong position to recommend texts to young readers, to match books to particular children's interests or to support the development of young readers. They are arguably unable to nurture reading for pleasure effectively.

The core goal of the Phase II project *Teachers as Readers: Building Communities of Readers* was to improve primary teachers' knowledge and use of literature in order to help them increase children's motivation and enthusiasm for reading. The project largely succeeded in this core aim across the 27 schools involved from five LAs. It achieved this through markedly extending 43 teachers' repertoires of children's literature and other texts, their pedagogic use of such texts in the classroom and their reflective awareness of the experience of being a reader (Cremin *et al.*, 2009a). Significantly, the teachers also developed awareness of children's everyday reading practices and over time new communities of readers developed; communities characterised by reciprocity, a subtle shift in the locus of control around reading and new teacher–child and child–child reader relationships. Different kinds of interactions and inside-text talk developed around children's own free-choice reading and 'texts in common'. The project also partly succeeded in its other two aims. Some teachers became Reading Teachers, and were not only more mindful of the social and affective factors involved, but also became engaged reading role-models; these teachers positively influenced children's own identities as readers. A significantly wider conception of being a reader in the twenty-first century was developed by most teachers, and some began to appreciate the social nature of reading. In addition, teachers began to build relationships with parents, carers, librarians and families, and there were some signs of boundaries beginning to be blurred between home and school practices. In the main, however, the teachers prioritised constructing communities of engaged readers in their classrooms and across the school, although several began to build foundations for increasing parental and community involvement in the future. Strong links were made by some teachers with local libraries, although this, too, was an area where development emerged slowly, after class-based relationships were established.

Children who were initially identified as reluctant, uninterested and disengaged readers became drawn into reading; their perceptions of their abilities as readers and self-confidence improved. Significantly, their talk about reading and texts became more spontaneous, informed and extended. These changes appeared to be linked to their teachers' enhanced subject knowledge and enriched pedagogic practice; it was also closely connected to their teachers' reading identities and nuanced practices as Reading Teachers. Children's attainment showed above average increases across the year. As the OECD (2002) has shown through analysis of survey data, and this project demonstrated through case studies and observational data, the 'will' to read appears to influence the 'skill'. Equally importantly, however, the focus children's commitment to and interest in reading altered; they showed increased pleasure in reading and began to read both more regularly and more independently, contributing to the construction of lively reading cultures and classroom communities of engaged readers.

Teachers' subject knowledge

Teachers' knowledge of children's literature and other texts is not commonly regarded as part of the subject knowledge required of beginning teachers, yet as this research has shown, it is significant. The Phase I survey revealed that teachers do read for pleasure themselves, but they have limited and limiting repertoires of children's authors, poets and picture fiction creators (Cremin *et al.*, 2008a, b). The Phase II project lent legitimacy to this aspect of subject knowledge. It created time and space for professional learning and personal growth through the reading of both adult and children's literature, which the teachers shared with one another and with their pupils and colleagues in school. As members of different communities of readers who talked about texts (in their local groups and on national days), the project teachers enriched their subject knowledge of children's literature and other texts, and began to take risks in their choices and respond more aesthetically. They came to recognise their professional responsibility to sustain and expand their expanded repertoires. Personally and professionally, they took considerably more pleasure in reading and in particular in reading literature. As Martin argues:

> The best teachers of literature are those for whom reading is important in their own lives and who read more than the texts they teach. Readers know how to trust the text so that it stands in its own right and does not need to be something which is used to get somewhere else. A poem is worth reading for its own sake not simply in order to teach something about poetry. Being a reader of literature gives a teacher the confidence to teach powerfully.
>
> (Martin, 2003: 16)

Readers of literature who share their pleasure in the classroom will not only be building the habits of a lifetime, but will be fostering children's personal growth, provoking and challenging them to consider the complexity of the human condition (Byatt, 1998). Additionally, as Hardy (1977) argues, narrative is a primary act of mind; humans think through story. As such, literature deserves increased professional attention and children need multiple opportunities to hear, to read and to respond to it. 'Imagination and creativity, emotional and moral engagement and humour and fun', Maybin (2013) observes, 'are all intrinsically important aspects of children's responses to fictional texts', without which she posits, the profession runs the 'risk of creating an impoverished educational experience' (p. 65). Yet education systems tend to pay lip service to the significance of children's talk and creative interactions around texts, and the importance of literature is too often taken for granted, especially in accountability cultures, where despite the policy rhetoric, reader engagement and reading for pleasure remain in the shadow of tests and targets. In such contexts the enjoyment of reading can become tokenistic, centred around celebratory events, such as author visits or annual book weeks, not woven through the fabric of school life.

Developing and sustaining teachers' knowledge of potent literature for young people is not enough however, as children bring different 'ways with words' (Heath, 1983), and different out-of-school reading practices to the classroom. Such diversity, influenced in part by the changing face of literacy in this multimedia age, needs to be recognised and built upon. So whilst acknowledging the particular power of literature, the UKLA Phase II project team sought to broaden the teachers' understanding of the wide range of texts which children choose to read in their homes and communities. Finding out about the children's everyday reading experiences and honouring and celebrating these in school, became an important early step for the project teachers. Reading fiction, while still significant, was not viewed as the only means by which young readers can find aesthetic satisfaction, and a wider range of digital and print-based texts were commonly made available in project classrooms.

Both phases of the research raise important questions about how teachers might be helped to read 'outside their comfort zones', to keep up to date with contemporary children's literature and avoid reliance upon their own childhood favourites, especially since primary teachers are generalists, not specialists or English graduates and are expected to teach across the curriculum. Reading and discussing new authors, book awards and recently published texts needs to be prioritised in professional development and could usefully be included as a regular feature of staff meetings. Consideration also needs to be given to the balance between breadth and depth of subject knowledge. Whilst practitioners need to know some literature in depth in order to teach literacy, they also need a rich repertoire of literature and other texts in order to support the development of independent young readers. The extent to which teachers' conceptions of reading are book-bound is another issue raised by this research; this is likely to shape and frame their classroom practice (Marsh, 2003b), and constrain children's access to and use of motivating reading materials. Development work that includes attention to textual diversity and connects to children's everyday reading practices is thus also recommended.

A responsive Reading for Pleasure Pedagogy

The Phase II teachers' increased subject knowledge, combined with personal reflection on being a reader and professional support enabled them to develop a Reading for Pleasure Pedagogy. This encompassed marked improvements in reading environments, read-aloud programmes, book talk and book recommendations and the provision of quality time for independent choice-led reading. As teachers became more confident, autonomous and flexible in using their enriched subject knowledge, they also began to articulate an informed and strategic rationale for selecting and using texts to support children as readers and nurture reading for pleasure. Initially it was difficult for the teachers to make the time and space within an overcrowded curriculum to profile reading engagement and pleasure. It appeared, at least at first, that a reading for pleasure agenda was incompatible with a culture of specific learning outcomes, success criteria and target setting. Furthermore, for some teachers who were relatively new to the profession, practices such as reading aloud, without later subjecting the text to scrutiny for the purposes of literacy instruction, were almost entirely new. With support and through documenting the focus children's responses to their changing pedagogic practice, these less experienced professionals, and the rest of the project teachers, became convinced of the value of more open, less structured approaches to nurturing independent readers. Readers who not only can, but *do* choose to read for pleasure. As the External Evaluator noted:

> The pedagogic approaches used within the project were significantly different from the use of reading schemes, reading instruction and criterion-based work geared to test preparation and targets that were universally followed at the start of the project. The project has served to convince teachers that 'fighting' for time for reading is worthwhile, where previously they would not have believed that there would be space in the curriculum. In these classrooms, reading has become exciting, important and personal. ... Teachers' views of pedagogy in the teaching of reading have undergone a seismic shift through the project.
>
> (Durrant, 2008: 10–11)

However, whilst a coherent Reading for Pleasure Pedagogy was established it is not simply a case of employing the four strands of quality pedagogic practice developed by the project practitioners.

In addition to a rich knowledge of children's literature and other texts, practitioners need to enrich their knowledge of children's everyday reading practices and their understanding of the experience of reading and being a reader. Without such knowledge and understanding, the establishment of reading environments, reading aloud, book talk and independent reading, might well become little more than a routine set of pedagogic procedures, void of authentic reader engagement and interaction. For example, if teachers set aside space and time for children to read independently, but offer no choice or limit choice to books available in particular boxes (assigned according to ability); or expect children to sit at school tables to read (potentially neither comfortable nor conducive to relaxed engagement); or enforce silence and require written reviews of completed books, then indifferent or even negative attitudes may be fostered. This may result in bored, listless learners who feel 'obliged' to read, and merely 'pretend' to be engaged as they turn the pages, disconnected from the text and from each other.

It is not that particular reading practices work and others do not, but that reading practices work in complex combinations. All have consequences for how reading is perceived and how children are positioned as readers. Much depends upon how opportunities are presented to young people and the context and setting in which they take place. In seeking to foster children's commitment and independence as readers, teachers who wish to reshape independent reading time have many options – discussing the current routine with the young readers will be key. The children, whose reading time it is, will have multiple ideas about creating spaces to relax in whilst reading – on floor cushions, in the reading corner, by the radiator or in a 'reading café' perhaps – and may wish to bring in their own comics, magazines or other reading material to enjoy and share with others. Negotiating new practices and positioning children as readers with agency in this context is crucial, as is the involvement of teachers and other adults in their own reading at this time and their willingness to talk about this. Such small shifts in the implementation of independent reading time will lead to different outcomes, though these outcomes cannot be guaranteed, since historical practices in the class, and differences in context and the different readers involved will influence their engagement.

The ways in which reading activities are shaped by practitioners can constrain or empower readers and will prompt different responses, impacting upon children's desire to participate as readers and as learners. In the project classrooms, whilst the four core elements of a Reading for Pleasure Pedagogy were enacted, practitioners implemented these responsively and differently, developing some more consistently and collaboratively than others. Many negotiated ways of working with their classes and sought to include children's ideas and suggestions. In the process they shaped the lived experience of readers in their classrooms.

Reading Teachers

Whilst a rich knowledge of children's literature and other texts is essential to support reading for pleasure, and teachers need be flexible in shaping supportive pedagogy, the project revealed that practitioners also benefit from drawing on their knowledge and understanding of the nature of reading and that this can be enhanced through reflection on the experience of reading and being a reader. Some teachers developed as Reading Teachers: teachers who read and readers who teach (Commeyras et al., 2003). These professionals became increasingly aware of their own reading preferences, habits, behaviours and strategies, and explored connections between their practices and those of the children and possible pedagogical consequences. They constructed reciprocal reading communities which recognised readers' rights and identities and successfully influenced both children's engagement as readers and the pleasure they derived from it. In this regard, the project significantly expanded Commeyras et al.'s (2003) conceptualisation of Reading Teachers, as the research recognised, documented and analysed the communal consequences of this personal/professional repositioning in the primary classroom.

The notion of developing as a Reading Teacher was not without challenge however. The lack of specific learning objectives related to this reader–teacher/teacher–reader stance caused concerns; some teachers were uncomfortable with and questioned the value of such personal involvement, while others were unsure how their reading persona might translate into the classroom and whether they would be imposing their particular reader's view on younger readers. Tensions developed as teachers also needed to mediate the national assessment system which focused on a narrow set of reading competencies and skills, not on readers' identities, engagement and pleasure. At the end of the project, a continuum existed with regard to the development of Reading Teachers.

This strand of the research unusually placed the teacher as reader at the centre. It sought to enable project teachers to consider their reading practices and reader relationships, with other adult readers – both those in the project groups and others in their lives – and with children. Teachers reflected upon their experience as readers, past and present, and their experience of reading, particularly reading for pleasure. Through mapping their own reading histories, keeping reading logs and ongoing discussions, and through coming to understand more about the children's everyday reading lives and practices, teachers widened their awareness of reading and being a reader. The project provided significant time and support for them as adult readers, and encouraged talk and reflection which enabled some to develop an enhanced readerly mindfulness of the significance of the texts, of meaning and of affect and the influence of social and cultural contexts. As a consequence, those practitioners who developed more fully as Reading

Teachers came to question and transform what counted as reading in their classrooms and began to reconceptualise reading in the twenty-first century.

The power of role-models in education has long been recognised; in 1966, Bruner described the value of a 'day-to-day working model' and significantly noted that the model was someone 'with whom to interact'. As knowledgeable and keen readers, Reading Teachers frequently engaged in informal dialogues with children about reading, though children and teachers did not always agree with one another; diverse views were voiced, and personal perspectives were encouraged. The Reading Teachers deliberately tried to avoid encouraging a frameset based on emulation or imitation; rather they worked to recognise diversity and difference. They encouraged children to develop their own preferences and practices as readers; readers who could choose what to read, and, where possible within the school day, when and where to read. In sharing their own identities as readers, the Reading Teachers came to consider the ways in which they framed and positioned young readers in school, and sought to offer new forms of participation and engagement. Many involved children in reshaping their reading curriculum. These teachers, aware of their own agency, offered young readers more self-direction and volition as readers, enabling them to enjoy their rights as readers. As Woods observes:

> Reading can change your life, it can inform, motivate, inspire and elevate; but it must be reading you do for yourself, at your own pace, in your own way, and that has a bearing on your own background, interests, values, beliefs and aspirations. Reading that is forced on you in a mechanistic way and formally assessed may have the reverse effect, the major purpose becoming pleasing the teacher and passing tests, and a preoccupation with form rather than substance.
>
> (Woods, 2001: 4–5)

As children became aware that their Reading Teachers were readers themselves and were interested in their own reading practices and personal affective responses, reading became a more shared, sociable, relaxed experience in school. Supported by new relationships with their teachers, the young people developed reader relationships and reader networks with one another, often framed around significant 'texts in common'. Some of these texts had been read aloud by teachers, others had been read and swapped amongst friends and amongst teachers and children. 'Texts in common' conversations between teachers and children became possible due to the teachers' widened repertoires and were recognised as salient. As Goouch and Lambirth (2011: 8) argue, it is the 'human connection between reader and text and teacher' that counts. The strengthening of this human connection through 'texts in common' prompted multiple conversations and interactions which served to create bonds between different pairs and groups of readers. These helped to build richly reciprocal reading communities.

An enhanced personal and professional awareness of what it means to be a reader and deep pleasure in reading, can, the project suggests, serve to nurture young readers, who, like their teachers, are likely to become engaged, self-motivated and interactive readers. It can also, the data indicate, influence children's attainment as readers. Nonetheless, tensions persist for teachers who wish to teach from a reader's point of view, particularly in contexts where standardised national testing and prescribed approaches to teaching and assessing phonics profess to 'fix' reading. This is additionally challenging in schools where the removal of high-quality picturebooks in early-years classrooms has been enforced to ensure that children only access phonetically regular texts. Research is needed to explore children's conceptions of reading in such literature-limited contexts, and to examine further the ways in which teachers' positions as readers influence young readers' identities and development.

Reciprocal reading communities

Structurally, the Phase II project was somewhat counter-cultural; it was not planned as an 'intervention study', nor was the focus of the work on raising reading standards. It was organised to enable teachers to come together as readers and as learners, to become more conscious of their own practices as readers, widen their knowledge of children's literature and explore ways to nurture children's reading for pleasure. Whilst there was a national structure and commonly applied methods of data collection, the work was somewhat iterative in nature. The 43 teachers were enabled to meet locally (with one another and the LA coordinator) and nationally (with other practitioners from the five local authorities, their LA coordinators and the research team). During the first term, considerable time and space was set aside in local and national groups for all involved (teachers, coordinators, and university-based researchers) to read, share and discuss literature, both adult and children's, and reflect upon their reading histories and practices. The teachers expressed surprise and satisfaction that the project afforded them time as adult readers; they also valued the space for reflection on the reading experience.

Teachers' book talk conversations, initially dominated by discussion of the use of literature for teaching literacy, gradually shifted to focus more on content and meaning and how particular books affected them personally. Over time, the role of recommendation and peer support developed markedly in local and national groups; the teachers developed the habit of sharing their reading with each other. Through discussion, debate and gradual acceptance of colleagues' diverse preferences, practices and personal responses, reading in the local and national groups became both more communal and more inclusive. Additionally, regular reading-aloud sessions and book-gifting enabled the teachers to develop a repertoire of children's 'texts in common' and webs of reading relationships developed. In these communities of practice (Lave and Wenger, 1991), teachers learnt about themselves as readers, about reading in the twenty-first century and the socially constructed nature of reading.

The project teachers began to share their increased knowledge and enthusiasm for children's texts with the young readers in their classes; conversations about texts developed and reading aloud became, for many, a kind of bonding time. New and extended opportunities for interaction around texts developed, independent reading time was established, reciprocal reader to reader recommendations ensued, and the emergence of spontaneous 'inside-text talk' was documented. Such talk was supported by more relaxed reading environments, and the presence of richly resonant class repertoires of 'texts in common'. Teachers found out about children's reading lives beyond school and widened their knowledge of children as readers and as young people, prompting many to diversify the reading material available in school and to widen their own reading of children's literature and other texts still further. Whilst differently shaped in every classroom, the social fabric of new reading communities began to be woven as commitment to reading and talking about texts developed. In such communities, in contrast to the teachers' previous and more traditional instructional practices, diversity and difference were welcomed.

Encouraging teachers in the research to participate themselves in adult reading communities and reflect upon their own literate habitus also prompted several to share aspects of their reading lives with children. These Reading Teachers appeared to shift some of the traditional boundary markers between teachers and children, and as a consequence new possibilities and relational identities opened up. The identity positions teachers claim for themselves and assign to others hold important implications not only for teachers' practices (what they can and feel they ought to do in the classroom), but also for children's access to particular identities, including the identity of an engaged reader. Viewed in this way, choosing to read for pleasure is a matter of learning, through practice, to behave in ways that others in the community do. Arguably, therefore, to become a reader who finds pleasure in reading, children need to participate in vibrant communities of engaged readers within and beyond school.

The project revealed that a reading for pleasure agenda can be developed effectively through the creation of such communities. In school, these were typically characterised by reciprocity and interaction, and in summary were seen to encompass:

- a shared concept of what it means to be a reader in the twenty-first century;
- considerable teacher and child knowledge of children's literature and other texts;
- pedagogic practices which acknowledge and develop diverse reader identities;
- new social spaces that encourage choice and child ownership of their own reading for pleasure;
- spontaneous 'inside-text talk' on the part of all participants;
- a shift in the locus of control that fosters reader agency and independence.

In these communities of engaged readers, new spaces were created for children and teachers to participate in shared talk about reading and readers' lives, and children were encouraged to bring their cultural knowledge and experiences of reading into the classroom and make more of their own choices as readers. This kindled interest, excitement and a different level of personal involvement and commitment on the part of the young learners. The cultures of these communities were typified by increased and enriched text talk, including 'inside-text talk' which was reader-led and reader-directed. A shift in the locus of control around reading for pleasure was also noticeable. The communities were also typified by the recognition and valuing of diverse reading preferences and habits; regular, extended opportunities for independent reading in modified environments; and an emphasis on reading aloud. Enjoyment in reading was placed at the centre of classroom practice. As Hitchcock, based on a study of teenage readers, argues:

> Pupils need to feel that they are part of communities where the enjoyment of reading is valued, whatever form it takes, by talking more to their teachers, family, friends, whether face to face or online. Such talk can help them see the kind of reader they are and to make choices about the kind of reader they would like to become.
>
> (Hitchcock, 2010: 59)

As has been shown, in the Phase II project, children's pleasure in reading was strongly influenced by the new reading networks and relationships which developed: between teachers;. between teachers and children; between children and children; and in some cases between children, teachers, families and communities. However, it is clear that more work is needed to foster more equivalent reading relationships with families, and to explore the potential synergy between teachers', children's and parents' reading lives and practices (see Figure 10.2 in the final section). This shared social space deserves professional attention; it may prove possible to nurture both younger and older readers through innovative work in this area.

The newly constructed reading communities that developed in classrooms fostered a sense of belonging and mutual commitment as well as increased interaction. The project revealed that reading for pleasure is a highly social process and that young readers are nurtured through their involvement in richly reciprocal communities of readers.

Balancing reading instruction and reading for pleasure

Education systems worldwide face the challenge of forging a balance between raising and measuring educational attainment and creating inclusive learning communities in which positive attitudes and an eagerness to learn prevail. Skilled professionals, engaged in reflection on policy and practice and cognisant of their own philosophies rise to this challenge. The professionals in Phase II worked hard to rebalance the reading curriculum in their schools, since at the time of the project, the policy emphasis was (and arguably still is) focused on teaching reading, not on developing reading for pleasure. In this context it was not easy to motivate and engage young readers, especially the focus children who, whilst they could read, did not choose to do so. As Dombey *et al.* observe: 'Children may develop the skills of reading, but lack the disposition to use them unless their reading experiences encourage autonomy, enthusiasm, achievement and a sense of enjoyment' (2010: 7).

Over time the teaching of reading came to be recognised by the teachers as both a deliberate act of instruction and an interactive social process woven through with enjoyment. As a Reading for Pleasure Pedagogy was developed, the teachers, and in particular those who chose to position themselves as Reading Teachers, drew flexibly from their personal and professional attributes, moving between these domains to balance instruction and enjoyment. They made decisions in the classroom both as teachers and as readers. The project demonstrated that a reading for pleasure agenda can positively impact upon both children's attainment as readers and their dispositions and desire to read. It also highlighted various ways in which a reading for pleasure agenda is distinct from, although closely related to, a reading instruction agenda. These are summarised in Figure 10.1.

To become readers who can read, children must learn to decode and comprehend a range of texts, making use of grapho-phonic knowledge and understandings about the 'word and the world' (Freire, 1985). To become enthusiastic readers, who *want* to read, children need to experience a rich 'legacy of past satisfactions' (Britton, 1977) that prompt them to engage, to respond and to persevere. As Figure 10.1 indicates, reading instruction tends to be teacher-directed and teacher-owned. It is often, though not always, tethered to reading particular schemes, and children are likely to be expected to work towards reading fluently and comprehending text (at a particular level) and alone. Such readers may, if reading for pleasure is not also fostered, learn to read in a system and for a system, not for themselves. By contrast, reading for pleasure tends to be child-directed and child-owned, with a stronger sense of volition and choice. It is likely

Reading instruction is oriented towards:	Reading for pleasure is oriented towards:
Learning to read	Choosing to read
The skill	The will
Decoding and comprehension	Engagement and response
Reading for the system	Reading for oneself
Teacher direction	Child direction
Teacher ownership	Child ownership
Solitary reading	Social and collaborative reading
Attainment	Achievement
The minimum entitlement (A set reading level)	The maximum entitlement (A reader for life)

Figure 10.1 Distinctions between reading instruction and reading for pleasure

to encompass a wider range of self-selected texts in response to children's personal interests and preferences, and in response to friends' or teachers' recommendations. Whilst reading instruction focuses on individual readers and may encourage a solitary frameset, reading for pleasure focuses more on sharing the reading experience and is sustained by conversations about texts in and through networks of social relations. Arguably the goal of reading instruction is for each child to achieve the reading level deemed appropriate by current policy diktat in their country, whereas the goal of the reading for pleasure agenda is not only for each child to develop positive attitudes and dispositions towards reading, but for them to become lifelong readers.

This conceptualisation, whilst visually creating a dichotomy between reading for pleasure and reading instruction, does not seek to polarise, rather it seeks to recognise the significance of these different orientations, the interplay between the skill and the will to read and the vital necessity of working towards a balance between them. As the PISA report *Reading for Change* concluded: 'Cognitive skills and reading motivation are mutually reinforcing ... rather than being alternatives, schools need to address both simultaneously' (OECD, 2002).

However, in education systems constrained by public assessment regimes, the pressure on teachers to conform, to 'deliver' the prescribed curriculum and ensure the required standards are reached is considerable. When teachers are expected to concentrate on reading instruction, on decoding and comprehension and developing children's knowledge about linguistic, structural or lexical aspects of texts, then the reason for reading the text in the first place may be neglected. Exhausted by endless directives and often rapidly changing imperatives, teachers have to demonstrate considerable professional commitment, personal engagement, determination and creativity to ensure reading for pleasure is coherently developed in school. In the Phase II project, the practitioners' personal engagement as readers and their involvement in different reading communities provided strong support as they took responsibility for developing reading for pleasure alongside, and as complementary to, reading instruction and worked to motivate and engage children as readers. The tension between these agendas did not cease, but the teachers, positioned as readers and as teachers, sought to enact these dual responsibilities with skill and humanity: to enable children to achieve well within the system of schooling, and to develop as engaged critically reflective readers for life.

Recommendations and ways forward

The Phase II project demonstrated that if teachers are supported to widen their reading repertoires, create a Reading for Pleasure Pedagogy and develop as Reading Teachers, they can make a positive impact upon children's desire to read, their attitudes and abilities as readers. Yet there is still work to be done to address the ever widening gap in reading experiences in and out of school and to expand conceptions of reading in the light of rapid changes in new technologies. Strategic support and guidance is also needed to enable the profession to find more equivalent and reciprocal ways of working with families and communities that connect with their everyday reading practices and experiences and to help teachers rebalance reading instruction and reading engagement and pleasure. Furthermore, as the External Evaluator of the Phase II project noted:

> A measure of trust is called for, trust that performance outcomes will continue to follow as communities of readers develop, that parental and community involvement will strengthen social cohesion and improve relationships, that children will be freed from constraints and barriers in their reading progress, motivated by the interests, excitements and challenges of reading for pleasure, leading to broader, lifelong outcomes.
>
> (Durrant, 2008: 23)

It is therefore recommended that in order to support reading engagement and reading for pleasure, schools, teachers and student teachers are enabled to:

1   Take responsibility for developing reading for pleasure, alongside and as complementary to, reading instruction, and plan systematically to achieve this;
2   Widen their conceptions of reading and being a reader in the twenty-first century;
3   Develop as Reading Teachers: teachers who read and readers who teach;
4   Make space and time to build reciprocal reading communities in their classrooms that blur the boundaries between children's home and school reading worlds;
5   Expand their knowledge of:

- literature and other texts
- everyday reading practices and experiences
- individual children as readers;

6   Develop a Reading for Pleasure Pedagogy that fosters inside-text talk and builds positive reading identities for all children;

7   Foster children's autonomy as readers who can exercise discrimination and choice within and beyond school;

8   Construct new, more equivalent reading relationships with families and community members, exploring the potential synergy between teachers', children's and parents' reading lives and practices (Figure 10.2).

Reading for pleasure and reader engagement urgently require a higher profile to foster readers who not only can, but who choose to read and who grow as readers, as learners and as young people as a result. This is not an optional extra, but a basic requirement and one which deserves increased professional attention. The significance of affect in education, the rewards and satisfaction to be found through imaginative engagement in literature and other texts and the role of reciprocal reading communities deserve to be much more widely recognised, not only by practitioners, but by parents and policy-makers.

Whilst the inclusion of a higher profile for reading engagement in various governments' documentation has recently been noted, this may be due, at least in part, to the links now established between such reading and reading attainment (OECD, 2002). As Ellis and Coddington (2013: 236) warn, if reading for pleasure is harnessed, even very loosely, to economic imperatives, then 'technocratic solutions to problems of pedagogy and curriculum design' may be imposed upon schools, teachers and children. In the new

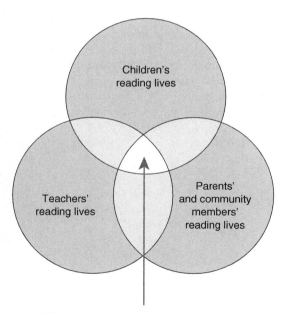

This shared social space needs expansion
to support young readers
in the 21st century

Figure 10.2 A model for the development of shared reading lives: Diversity and collaboration

National Curriculum (DfE, 2013) in England for example, imperatives are employed when referring to readers' engagement. The curriculum states that 'pupils should be taught to' develop pleasure in reading, the motivation to read and positive attitudes. As teachers are legally required to 'teach this' there is a very real danger that schools will implement a reading for pleasure curriculum that leans towards 'demanding' or 'requiring' apparent demonstrations of positive attitudes and dispositions on the part of the young. Children may be led towards masquerading as readers who 'can and do' read in order to please their teachers, whilst in reality they may be 'can but don't' (Moss, 2000), readers who are neither motivated nor engaged and who find little satisfaction in the experience. Reading for pleasure and reader engagement cannot be mandated.

Furthermore, the overriding emphasis in the early-years reading curriculum of many countries remains on phonics. In England, whilst reading for pleasure is now a statutory requirement, the National Curriculum also requires schools to ensure that young children 'read aloud accurately books that are consistent with their developing phonic knowledge and that do not require them to use other strategies to work out words' (DfE, 2013). Absurdly, this implies that children's early reading experiences in school should be limited to texts which are phonetically regular or to those books whose vocabulary corresponds to their phonemic knowledge. Whilst it is recognised in the policy documentation that children will need to hear, share and discuss a wide range of quality books to develop a love of reading and to broaden their vocabulary, there are already reports of schools and local authorities requiring the removal of all books from early-years classrooms bar the school's policy-endorsed phonic scheme. Limiting children's independent reading to phonically decodable texts will have very considerable consequences. How teachers will be able to foster pleasure and engagement in such challenging contexts remains to be seen. Young readers who do not experience a balance between reading instruction and reading for pleasure and particularly those who do not have access to a range of meaning-rich, visually engaging texts at home and at school will be seriously disadvantaged as readers and as learners.

In the light of these concerns and the ongoing decline in enjoyment and frequency of reading for pleasure among the young (OECD, 2010), and the increase in negative attitudes towards reading (Clark, 2013), sensitive nuanced ways forward need to be found to nurture desire, recognise difference, respond to diversity – of learners, texts and contexts – and build richly reciprocal and engaged communities of readers, within and beyond schools.

Appendix

The United Kingdom Literacy Association

Teachers as Readers Questionnaire

We're very grateful for your help with this survey. The background sheet will give you full details of the research project.

Local Authority: _____ **Date:** _____

Year group you currently teach: _____ **Years in teaching:** _____

Responsibility in school: _____

1. What was your favourite book as a child? _____

2. What have you read recently for your own pleasure? _____

   Please indicate when this was:
   - ☐ Within the last month
   - ☐ Within the last 3 months
   - ☐ Within the last 6 months
   - ☐ Over 6 months ago

3. What do you think is the most important book you have ever read?

   _____

   _____

4. How do you usually get hold of books for your own reading?

   You may tick more than one.
   - ☐ Library
   - ☐ Bookshop
   - ☐ On-line bookshop
   - ☐ From friend/s
   - ☐ Other (please specify) _____

5. Do you use your local library for school? Yes/No *Delete as appropriate*

   If yes, in what ways?

   _____

   _____

6. When did you last visit your local library with a class?
   - ☐ Within the last month
   - ☐ Within the last 3 months
   - ☐ Within the last 6 months
   - ☐ Over 6 months ago

7. What was the last book you read completely (or with small cuts) to your class for pleasure, not with specific objectives in mind?

   _____

   When did you read this? _____

8. How often do you read aloud to your class?
   - ☐ Daily
   - ☐ Weekly
   - ☐ Monthly
   - ☐ Infrequently

9. List 6 'good' children's book authors

_____

_____

_____

_____

_____

_____

10. List 6 'good' children's poets

_____

_____

_____

_____

_____

_____

11. List 6 'good' children's picture book authors/illustrators

_____

_____

_____

_____

_____

_____

12. How do you decide which children's books to use in your classroom?

You may tick more than one.
- ☐ Personal interest/knowledge
- ☐ Children's recommendations
- ☐ Library service
- ☐ Literacy coordinators' recommendations
- ☐ Other (please specify) _____

13. Do you import books on to the IWB (interactive whiteboard)?   Yes/No *Delete as appropriate*

Please give details _____

_____

14. How do you use literature (books, poems, picturebooks) in your literacy teaching?

_____

_____

_____

15. Do you use publishers' prepared materials in teaching literacy?
- ☐ Daily
- ☐ Weekly
- ☐ Monthly
- ☐ Infrequently

If so, what do you use them for?

_____

_____

16. Rank the following statements in order of importance (1 is most important.)

Literature is important because
- ☐ it develops reading
- ☐ it develops writing
- ☐ it widens knowledge
- ☐ it engages the emotions
- ☐ it develops the imagination

Sign (if you wish): _____

References

Aarnoutse, C. and van Leeuwe, J. (1998) Relation between reading comprehension, vocabulary, reading pleasure and reading frequency. *Educational Research and Evaluation*, 4, 143–166.

Alexander, R. (ed.) (2010) *Children, Their World and Their Education: Final Report and Recommendations of the Cambridge Primary Review.* London: Routledge.

Allington, R. L., McGill-Frazen, A., Camilli, G., Williams, L., Graff, J., Zeig, J. *et al.* (2010) Addressing summer reading setback among economically disadvantaged elementary students. *Reading Psychology*, 31(5), 411–427.

APPLG (2012) *Boys Reading Commission Final Report.* All-Party Parliamentary Literacy Group Commission, compiled by the National Literacy Trust. http://www.literacytrust.org.uk/assets/0001/4056/Boys_Commission_Report.pdf. Accessed 1 December 2012.

Anderson, R., Wilson, P. T. and Fielding, L. G. (1988) Growth in reading and how children spend their time outside of school. *Reading Research Quarterly*, 23(3), 85–303.

Applegate, A. J. and Applegate, M. D. (2004) The Peter effect: Reading habits and attitudes of pre-service teachers. *The Reading Teacher*, 57(6), 554–563.

Appleyard, J. A. (1990) *Becoming a Reader: The Experience of Fiction from Childhood to Adulthood.* Cambridge: Cambridge University Press.

Arizpe, E. and Styles, M. (2003) *Children Reading Pictures.* London: RoutledgeFalmer.

Arizpe, E., Colmer, T. and Martínez-Roldán, C. (2014) *Visual Journeys Through Wordless Narratives.* London: Bloomsbury Academic.

Arts Council England (2003) *From Looking Glass to Spy Glass: A Consultation Paper on Children's Literature.* London: Arts Council.

Ashley, B. (2003) Books in school. In C. Powling, B. Ashley, P. Pullman, A. Fine and J. Gavin (eds) *Meetings with the Minister.* Reading: National Centre for Language and Literacy, pp. 4–7.

Assaf, L. C. (2008) The professional identity of a reading teacher. *Teachers and Teaching: Theory and practice*, 14(3), 239–252.

Babalola, E. (2002) Newspapers as instruments for building literate communities: The Nigerian experience. *Nordic Journal of African Studies*, 11(3), 403–410.

Bailey, M., Hall, C. and Gamble, N. (2007) Promoting school libraries and school library services: Problems and partnerships. *English Education*, 41(2), 71–85.

Baker, L. and Wigfield, A. (1999) Dimensions of children's motivation for reading and their relations to reading activity and reading achievement. *Reading Research Quarterly*, 34(4), 452–477.

Baker, L. and Scher, D. (2002) Beginning readers' motivation for reading in relation to parental beliefs and home reading experiences. *Reading Psychology*, 23, 239–269.

Bakhtin, M. (1981) *The Dialogic Imagination* (trans. M. Holquist and C. Emerson; ed. M. Holquist). Austin, TX: University of Texas Press.

Barrs, M. and Thomas, A. (1991) *The Reading Book.* London: CLPE.

Barrs, M. and Cork, V. (2001) The reader in the writer. *Reading Literacy and Language*, 34(2), 54–60.

Bartlett, L. (2007) To seem and to feel: Situated identities and literacy practices. *Teachers' College Record*, 109(1), 51–69.

Barton, D. and Hamilton, M. (1998) *Local Literacies: Reading and Writing in One Community*. London. Routledge.

Barton, D., Hamilton, M. and Ivaniĉ, R. (eds) (2000) *Situated Literacies: Reading and Writing in Context*. London: Routledge.

Bearne, E. (2003) Rethinking literacy: Communication, representation and text. *Reading Literacy and Language,* 37(3), 98–103.

Bearne, E. (2005) Multimodal texts: What they are and how children use them. In J. Evans (ed.) *Literacy Moves On: Using Popular Culture. New Technologies and Critical Literacy in the Primary Classroom*. London: David Fulton.

Bearne, E., Grainger, T. and Wolstencroft, H. (2004) *Raising Boys' Achievements in Writing*. Joint Research Project, United Kingdom Literacy Association and the Primary National Strategy. Baldock: United Kingdom Literacy Association.

Benevides, T. and Stagg Peterson, S. (2010) Literacy attitudes, habits and achievements of future teachers. *Journal of Education for Teaching,* 36(3), 291–302.

Benton, M. and Fox, R. (1985) *Teaching Literature 9–14*. Oxford: Oxford University Press.

Ben-Yosef, E. (2010) Reading to fly: Creative reading as pedagogical equalizer. *Encounter: Education for Meaning and Social Justice,* 23(1), 46–51.

Block, C. and Mangieri, J. (2002) Recreational reading: 20 years later. *The Reading Teacher,* 55(6), 576–580.

Book Marketing Ltd (2000) *Reading the Situation: Book Reading. Buying and Borrowing Habits in Britain*. London: Library and Information Commission.

Bourdieu, P. (1991) *Language and Symbolic Power*. Cambridge: Polity Press.

Bowers, J. and Davis S. (2013) *Why Teachers Should Read More Children's Books*. Guardian Network Teacher Professional. http://www.theguardian.com/teacher-network/teacher-blog/2013/jul/25/teachers-read-more-childrens-books. Accessed 6 August 2013.

Boyne, J. (2008) *The Boy in the Striped Pyjamas*. London: Definitions.

British Educational Research Association (2004) *Revised Guidelines for Educational Research*. http://www.bera.ac.uk. Accessed January 2006.

Britton, J. (1977) The third area where we are more ourselves: The role of fantasy and the nature of the reader's satisfaction, and response to literature. In M. Meek, A. Warlow and G. Barton (eds) *The Cool Web*. London: Bodley Head.

Bromley, H. (2000) Never be without a Beano: Comics, children and literacy. In H. Anderson and M. Styles (eds) *Teaching Through Texts*. London: Routledge.

Brown, S. and McIntyre, D. (1993) *Making Sense of Teaching*. Buckingham: Open University Press.

Bruner, J. (1966) *Towards a Theory of Instruction*. London: Oxford University Press.

Burgess, T., Fox, C. and Goody, J. (2002) *When the Hurly Burly's Done: What's Worth Fighting for in English in Education*. Sheffield: National Association for the Teaching of English.

Burgess-Macey, C. (1999) Classroom literacies: Young children's explorations in meaning making in the age of the literacy hour. *Reading,* 33(3), 120–125.

Burnard, P. (2002) Using image-based techniques in researching pupil perspectives. *The ESRC Network Project Newsletter,* 5, 2–3.

Burns, C. and Myhill, D. (2004) Interactive or inactive? A consideration of the nature of interaction in whole class teaching. *Cambridge Journal of Education,* 34, 35–49.

Butler, K., Simpson, E. and Court, J. (2011) Promoting excellence: Shadowing the CILIP Carnegie and Kate Greenaway medals. In J. Court (ed.) *Read to Succeed: Strategies to Engage Children and Young People in Reading for Pleasure*. London: Facet Publishing, pp. 131–152.

Byatt, A. S. (1998) Hauntings. In B. Cox (ed.) *Literacy Is Not Enough: Essays on the Importance of Reading*. Manchester: The Books Trust.

Cameron, E. (1972) McLuhan, youth and literature. *The Horn Book Magazine,* October.

Chambers, A. (1973) *Introducing Books to Children*. London: Heinemann.

Chambers, A. (1985) *Booktalk: Occasional Writing on Literature and Children*. London: Bodley Head.

Chambers, A. (1993) *Tell me: Children. Reading and Talk*. Stroud: Thimble Press.

Childress, K. (2011) What does research say about the benefits of reading aloud to children? Seminar in Reading and Language Arts Research, Appalachian State University, New York. http://www.app-state.edu/~koppenhaverd/rcoe/s11/5710/question1/kathleenchildress.pdf. Accessed August 2013.

Clark, C. (2011) *Setting the Baseline: The National Literacy Trust's First Annual Survey into Reading – 2010.* London: National Literacy Trust.

Clark, C. (2012) *Children's and Young People's Reading Today.* Findings from the 2011 National Literacy Trust's annual survey. London: National Trust.

Clark, C. (2013) *Children's and Young People's Reading in 2012.* Findings from the 2012 National Literacy Trust's annual survey. London: National Literacy Trust.

Clark, C. and Foster, A. (2005) *Children's and Young People's Reading Habits and Preferences: The Who, What, Why, Where and When.* London: National Literacy Trust.

Clark C. and Rumbold, K. (2006) *Reading for Pleasure: A Research Overview.* London: National Literacy Trust.

Clark, C. and Osborne, S. (2008) *How Does Age Relate to Pupils' Perceptions of Themselves as Readers?* London: National Literacy Trust.

Clark, C. and Phythian-Sence (2008) *Interesting Choice: The (Relative) Importance of Choice and Interest in Reader Engagement.* London: National Literacy Trust.

Clarke, C. and Douglas, J. (2011) *Young People's Reading and Writing: An In-Depth Study Focusing on Enjoyment, Behaviour, Attitudes and Attainment.* http://www.literacytrust.org.uk/assets/0000/8266/Attitudes_towards_Reading_Writing_Final_2011.pdf. Accessed 31 May 2011.

Clark, C. and Hawkins, L. (2011) *Public Libraries and Literacy: Young People's Reading Habits and Attitudes to Public Libraries, and an Exploration of the Relationship Between Public Library Use and School Attainment.* London: National Literacy Trust.

Clark, C., Torsi, S. and Strong, J. (2005) *Young People and Reading.* London: National Literacy Trust.

Clark, C., Osborne, S. and Akerman, R. (2008) *Young People's Self-Perceptions as Readers: An Investigation Including Family, Peer and School Influences.* London: National Literacy Trust.

Clark, C., Woodley, J. and Lewis, F. (2011) *The Gift of Reading in 2011: Children and Young People's Access to Books and Attitudes Towards Reading.* London: National Literacy Trust.

Cliff Hodges, G. (2010) Rivers of reading: Using critical incident collages to learn about adolescent readers and their readership. *English in Education,* 44(3), 180–199.

Coffey, A. and Atkinson, P. (1996) *Making Sense of Qualitative Data Analysis: Complementary Strategies.* Thousand Oaks, CA: Sage.

Collins, F. M. (2005) 'She's sort of dragging me into the story!': Student teachers' reading experiences of reading aloud in Key Stage 2 classes. *Literacy,* 39(1), 10–17.

Collins, F. M. and Safford, K. (2008) 'The right book for the right child at the right time': Primary teacher knowledge of children's literature. *Changing English,* 15(4), 415–422.

Collins, F. M. and Kelly, A. (2013) Primary student teachers' attitudes towards poetry and poetry teaching. In *Making Poetry Matter: International Research on Poetry Pedagogy.* London: Bloomsbury.

Comer Kidd, C. D. and Castano, E. (2013) Reading literary fiction improves theory of the mind. *Science,* 342(6156), 377–380.

Commeyras, M. and Inyega, H. N. (2007) An integrative review of teaching reading in Kenyan primary schools. *Reading Research Quarterly,* 42(2), 258–281.

Commeyras, M., Bisplinghoff, B. S. and Olson, J. (2003) *Teachers as Readers: Perspectives on the Importance of Reading in Teachers' Classrooms and Lives.* Newark, NJ: International Reading Association.

Corden, R. (2003) Writing is more than 'exciting': Equipping primary children to become reflective writers. *Reading Literacy and Language,* 37(1), 18–26.

Court, J. (ed.) (2011) *Read to Succeed: Strategies to Engage Children and Young People in Their Reading for Pleasure.* London: Facet Publishing.

Cox, K. E. and Guthrie, J. T. (2001) Motivational and cognitive contributions to students amount of reading. *Contemporary Educational Psychology,* 26(1), 116–131.

Cox, R. and Schaetzel, K. (2007) A preliminary study of pre-service teacher as readers in Singapore: Prolific, functional or detached. *Language Teaching Research,* 11(3), 300–316.

Cremin, T. (2007) Revisiting reading for pleasure: Diversity, delight and desire. In K. Goouch and A. Lambirth (eds) *Understanding Phonics and the Teaching of Reading*. Reading, MA: McGraw Hill, pp. 166–190.

Cremin, T. (2009) Teachers as readers: Building communities of readers research. *Literacy Today*, 58(March), 32–33.

Cremin, T. (2010a) Reconceptualising reading in the 21st century. In T. McCannon (ed.) *Reading in the 21st Century*. Dublin: Reading Association of Ireland.

Cremin, T. (2010b) Poetry teachers: Teachers who read and readers who teach poetry. In M. Styles and M. Rosen (eds) *Poetry and Childhood*. Stoke on Trent: Trentham Books, pp. 219–227.

Cremin, T. (2010c) Motivating children to read through literature. In G. Gillon, J. Fletcher and F. Parkhill (eds) *Motivating Literacy Learners in Today's World*. New Zealand Council for Educational Research.

Cremin, T. (2013a) Exploring teachers' positions and practices. In S. Dymoke, A. Lambirth and A. Wilson (eds) *Making Poetry Matter: International Research on Poetry Pedagogy*. London: Bloomsbury, pp. 9–19.

Cremin, T. (2013b) Teachers researching literacy lives. In A. Goodwyn, L. Reid and C. Durrant (eds) *International Perspectives on Teaching English in a Globalised World*. London: Taylor & Francis/Routledge.

Cremin, T. and Myhill, D. (2012) *Writing Voices: Creating Communities of Writers*. London: Routledge.

Cremin, T., Bearne, E., Mottram, M. and Goodwin, P. (2007) *Teachers as Readers Phase 1 (2006–7) Research Report*. http://www.ukla.org/downloads/TARwebreport.doc.

Cremin, T., Bearne, E., Mottram, M. and Goodwin, P. (2008a) Primary teachers as readers. *English in Education*, 42(1), 1–16.

Cremin, T., Bearne, E., Mottram, M. and Goodwin, P. (2008b) Exploring teachers' knowledge of children's literature. *Cambridge Journal of Education*, 38(4), 449–464.

Cremin, T., Mottram, M., Collins, F. and Powell, S. (2008c) *Building Communities of Readers*. London: UKLA and the Primary National Strategy.

Cremin, T., Mottram, M., Collins, F., Powell, S. and Safford, K. (2008d) *Teachers as Readers: Building Communities of Readers Research Report 2007–8*, for the Esmée Fairbairn Foundation.

Cremin, T., Mottram, M., Collins, F., Powell, S. and Safford, K. (2009a) Teachers as readers: Building communities of readers. *Literacy*, 43(1), 11–19.

Cremin, T., Bearne, E., Mottram, M. and Goodwin, P. (2009b) Teachers as readers in the 21st century. In M. Styles and E. Arizpe (eds) *Acts of Reading: Teachers, Text and Childhood*. Stoke on Trent: Trentham Books, pp. 201–218.

Cremin, T., Mottram, M., Collins, F., Powell, S. and Drury, R. (2012) Building communities: Teachers researching literacy lives. *Improving Schools*, 15(2), 101–115.

Cremin, T., Mottram, M., Collins, F., Powell, S. and Drury, R. (forthcoming, 2014) *Building Communities: Researching Literacy Lives*. London: Routledge.

Cunningham, A. and Stanovich, K. (1998) What reading does for the mind. *American Educator*, 22(1 and 2), 8–15.

Darling-Hammond, L. (2011) Effective teaching as a civil right: How building instructional capacity can help close the achievement gap. *Voices in Urban Education*, No. 31, Fall. http://vue.annenberginstitute.org/sites/default/files/issuePDF/VUE31.pdf. Accessed 6 May 2014.

DfE (2013) The National Curriculum in England framework document for consultation, February. http://www.education.gov.uk/nationalcurriculum. Accessed 6 August 2013.

DfEE (1998) *The National Literacy Strategy Framework for Teaching*. London: DfEE.

DfES (2006) *Primary Framework for Literacy and Mathematics*. Nottingham: DfES Publications.

Dombey, H. (1998) Changing literacy in the early years of school. In B. Cox (ed.) *Literacy Is Not Enough: Essays on the Importance of Reading*. Manchester: Manchester University Press and Book Trust, pp. 125–132.

Dombey, H. with Bearne, E., Cremin, T., Ellis, S., Mottram, M., O'Sullivan, O., Öztürk *et al.* (2010) *Teaching Reading: What the Evidence Says*. Leicester: United Kingdom Literacy Association.

Dreher, M. J. (2003) Motivating teachers to read. *The Reading Teacher*, 56(4), 338–340.

Dungworth, N., Grimshaw, S., McKnight, C. and Morris, A. (2004) Reading for pleasure?: A summary of the findings from a survey of the reading habits of year 5 pupils. *New Review of Children's Literature and Librarianship*, 10, 169–188.

Durrant, J. (2008) Evaluation of teachers as readers: Building communities of readers. Report submitted to the Esmée Fairbairn Foundation. http://www.ukla.org/research/previous_ukla_funded_research/ukla_research_on_teachers_as_readers. Accessed on 10 October 2013.

Edmunds, K. M. and Bauserman, K. L. (2006) What teachers can learn about reading motivation through conversations with children. *Reading Teacher*, 59, 414–424.

Education Standards Research Team (ESARD) (2012) *Research Evidence on Reading for Pleasure*. May. http://www.eriding.net/resources/pri_improv/121004_pri_imp_reading_for_pleasure. Accessed on 10 October 2012.

Ellis, D. (2000) *The Breadwinner*. Oxford: Oxford University Press.

Ellis, S. and Coddington, C. (2013) Reading engagement research. In K. Hall, T. Cremin, B. Comberand and L. Moll (eds) *International Handbook of Research on Children's Literacy, Learning and Culture*. Oxford: Wiley Blackwell, pp. 228–240.

English, E., Hargreaves, L. and Hislam, J. (2002) Pedagogical dilemmas in the National Literacy Strategy. *Cambridge Journal of Education*, 32(1), 9–26.

EU (2012) *Final Report of the EU High Level Group of Experts on Literacy*. Luxembourg: Publications Office of the European Union, September.

Eurydice (2011) *Teaching Reading in Europe: Contexts. Policies and Practices*. Brussels: European Commission.

Evans, M. D. R., Kelley, J., Sikora, J. and Treiman, D. J. (2010) Family scholarly culture and educational success: Books and schooling in 27 nations. *Research in Social Stratification and Mobility*, 28, 171–197.

Fisher, D., Flood, J., Lapp, D. and Frey, N. (2004) Interactive read-alouds: Is there a common set of implementation practices? *The Reading Teacher*, 58(1), 8–16.

Fisher, R. (2005) Teacher–child interaction in the teaching of reading: A review of research perspectives over twenty five years. *Journal of Research in Reading*, 28(1), 15–27.

Flick, U. (2006) *An Introduction to Qualitative Research*. London: Sage Publications.

Flouri, E. and Buchanan, A. (2004) Early father's and mother's involvement and child's later educational outcomes. *British Journal of Educational Psychology*, 74, 141–153.

Flynn, N. (2007) What do effective teachers of literacy do? Subject knowledge and pedagogical choices for literacy. *Literacy*, 41(3), 137–146.

Frater, G. (2000) Observed in practice. English in the National Literacy Strategy: Some reflections. *Reading*, 34(3), 107–112.

Fredricks, J., Blumenfeld, P. and Paris, A. (2004) School engagement: Potential of the concept, state of the evidence. *Review of Educational Research*, 74, 59–109.

Freire, P. (1985) Reading the world and reading the word: An interview with Paulo Freire. *Language Arts*, 62(1), 15–21.

Furlong, T. (1998) Reading in the primary school. In B. Cox (ed.) *Literacy Is Not Enough: Essays on the Importance of Reading*. Manchester: Manchester University Press and Book Trust, pp. 133–141.

Gamble, N. (2000) Teaching literature. In T. Cremin, and H. Dombey (eds) *Handbook on the Teaching of Primary English in Initial Teacher Education*. London: UKLA/NATE.

Gambrell, L. (1996) Creating classroom cultures that foster reading motivation. *The Reading Teacher*, 50, 14–25.

Gambrell, L. (2011) Seven rules of engagement: What's most important to know about motivation to read. *Reading Teacher*, 65(3), 172–178.

Gannon, G. and Davies, C. (2007) For the love of the word: English teaching, affect and writing. *Changing English*, 14(1), 87–98.

Gennrich, T. and Janks, H. (2013) Teachers' literate identities. In K. Hall, T. Cremin, B. Comber and L. Moll (eds) *International Handbook of Research on Children's Literacy: Learning and Culture*. Oxford: Wiley Blackwell, pp. 456–468.

Giroux, H. A. (1987) Introduction: Literacy and the pedagogy of political empowerment. In P. Freire and D. Macedo, *Literacy: Reading the Word and the World*. Westport, CT: Bergin and Garvey, pp. 1–28.

Goodwin, P. (2011) Creating young readers: Teachers and librarians at work. In J. Court (ed.) *Read to Succeed: Strategies to Engage Children and Young People in Their Reading for Pleasure*. London: Facet Publishing.

Goodwyn, A., Reid, L. and Durrant, C. (2014) *International Perspectives on Teaching English in a Globalised World*. Oxford: Routledge.

Goouch, K. and Lambirth, A. (2011) *Teaching Early Reading and Phonics*. London: Sage.

Gordon, J. (2012) More than canons: Teacher knowledge and the literary domain of the secondary English curriculum. *Educational Research*, 54(4), 375–390.

Graham (1997) The Initial Teacher Training National Curriculum for primary Education 1997: A most unnecessary document. *Changing English*, 4(2), 241–249.

Grainger, T., Goouch, K. and Lambirth, A. (2005) *Creativity and Writing: Developing Voice and Verve in the Classroom*. London: Routledge.

Gregory, E. and Williams, A. (2000) *City Literacies: Learning to Read Across Generation and Cultures*. London. Routledge.

Gregory, E., Mace, J., Rashid, N. and Williams. A. (1996) *Family Literacy History and Children's Learning Strategies at School*. End-of-award report, ESRC Project R000–22–1186. London: Goldsmiths College.

Guthrie, J. T. and Alvermann, D. E. (1999) *Engaged Reading: Processes, Practices, and Policy Implications*. New York. Teachers College Press.

Guthrie, J. T. and Wigfield, A. (2000) Engagement and motivation in reading. In M. L. Kamil, P. B. Mosenthal, P. D. Pearson and R. Barr (eds) *Handbook of Reading Research* (3rd edn). New York: Longman.

Guthrie, J. T. and Davis, M. H. (2003) Motivating struggling readers in middle school through an engagement model of classroom practice. *Reading and Writing Quarterly*, 59(5), 414–424.

Guthrie, J. T., Wigfield, A., Humenick, N. M., Perencevich, K. C., Taboada, A. and Barbosa, P. (2006) Influences of stimulating tasks on reading motivation and comprehension. *Journal of Educational Research*, 99(4), 232–245.

Hall, C., Thomson, P. and Russell, L. (2007) Teaching like an artist: The pedagogic identities and practices of artists in schools. *British Journal of Sociology of Education*, 28(5), 605–619.

Hall, K. (2004) Reflections on six years of the National Literacy Strategy in England: An interview with Stephen Anwyll, Director of the NLS 2001–2004. *Literacy*, 38(5), 119–125.

Hall, K. (2008) Leaving middle childhood and moving into teenhood: Small stories revealing identity and agency. In K. Hall, P. Murphy and J. Soler (eds) *Pedagogy and Practice: Culture and Identity*. London: The Open University and Sage Publications, pp. 87–104.

Hall, K. and Harding, A. (2003) *A Systematic Review of Effective Literacy Teaching in the 4 to 14 Age Range of Mainstream Schooling*. Research Evidence in Education Library. London: EPPI-Centre, Social Science Research Unit. Institute of Education. University of London.

Hall, K., Myers, K. and Bowman, H. (1999) Tasks, texts and contexts: A study of reading and metacognition. In *English and Irish Primary Classrooms Educational Studies*, 25(3), 311–325.

Hall, L. A. (2012) Rewriting identities: Creating spaces for students and teachers to challenge the norms of what it means to be a reader in school. *Journal of Adolescent and Adult Literacy*, 55, 368–373.

Hall, L. A., Johnson, A., Juzwik, M., Stanton, E., Wortham, F. and Mosley, M. (2010) Teacher identity in the context of literacy teaching: Three explorations of classroom positioning and interaction in secondary schools. *Teaching and Teacher Education*, 26, 234–243.

Hardy, B. (1977) Towards a poetics of fiction: An approach through narrative. In M. Meek, A. Warlow and G. Barton (eds) *The Cool Web*. London: Bodley Head.

Harrington, C. and Mills, W. (2011) The sport of reading. In J. Court (ed.) *Read to Succeed: Strategies to Engage Children and Young People in Their Reading for Pleasure*. London: Facet Publishing.

Heath, S. B. (1983) *Ways With Words: Language, Life and Work in Communities and Classrooms*. Cambridge: Cambridge University Press.

Heisey, N. and Kucan, L. (2010) Introducing science concepts to primary students through read-alouds: Interactions and multiple texts make the difference. *Reading Teacher*, 63(8), 666–676.

Hitchcock, G. (2010) An exploration of how reading for pleasure is perceived and experienced by engaged readers at Key Stage 3. Unpublished MA dissertation. Kings College, London.

Hitchcock, G. and Hughes, D. (1995) *Research and the Teacher* (2nd edn). London: RoutledgeFalmer.

Holden, J. (2004) *Creative Reading*. London: Demos.

Holland, D. and Lave, J. (2001) History in person. In *Enduring Struggles: Contentious Practice, Intimate Identities*. Santa Fe, NM: School of American Research Press, pp. 1–32.

Holland, D., Lachicotte, W., Skinner, D. and Cain, C. (1998) *Identity and Agency in Cultural Worlds*. Cambridge, MA: Harvard.

Hopper, R. (2005) What are teenagers reading? Adolescent fiction reading habits and reading choices. *Literacy*, 39(3), 113–120.

Hosseini, K. (2008) *A Thousand Splendid Suns*. London. Bloomsbury Publishing.

Hughes-Hassell, S. and Rodge, P. (2007) The leisure reading habits of urban adolescents. *Journal of Adolescent and Adult Literacy*, 51(1), 22–33.

Hunt, P. (1993) Finding the right book for a reader. In P. Pinsent (ed.) *The Power of the Page. Children's Books and Their Readers*. London: David Fulton.

Hunt, R. A. and Vipond, D. (1987) Aesthetic reading: Some strategies for research. *English Quarterly*, 20(3), 178–183.

Hurd, S., Dixon, M. and Oldham, J. (2006) Are low levels of book spending in primary schools jeopardising the National Literacy Strategy? *The Curriculum Journal*, 17(1), 73–88.

Innocenti, R. (1985) *Rose Blanche*. London: Jonathan Cape. (2004 edn, text by I. McEwan. London: Red Fox.)

Iser, W. (1978) *The Act of Reading: A Theory of Aesthetic Response*. Baltimore, MA: Johns Hopkins University Press.

Ivey, S. J. and Guthrie, J. T. (2008) Struggling readers: Boosting motivation in low achievers. In J. T. Guthrie (ed.) *Engaging Adolescents in Reading*. Thousand Oaks, CA: Corwin Press, pp. 115–129.

Kalb, G. and van Ours, J. C. (2013) Reading to young children: A head-start in life? Melbourne Institute of Applied Economic and Social Research Working Paper No. 17/13. Available at SSRN: http://ssrn.com/abstract=2267171 or http://dx.doi.org/10.2139/ssrn.2267171. Accessed 7 May 2014.

Kaufman, D. (2002) Living a literate life, revisited. *The English Journal*, 91(6), 61–57.

King, C. (2001) 'I like group reading because we can share ideas' – the role of talk within the literature circle. *Reading. Literacy and Language*, 35(1), 32–36.

Krashen, S. (1993) *The Power of Reading*. Englewood, CO: Libraries Unlimited.

Krashen, S. (2004) *The Power of Reading: Insights from Research*. Portsmouth, NH: Heinemann.

Kwek, D., Albright, J. and Kramer-Dahl, A. (2007) Building teachers creative capabilities in Singapore's English classrooms: A way of contesting pedagogical instrumentality. *Literacy*, 41(2), 71–78.

Lafontaine, D. and Monseur, C. (2009) Gender gap in comparative studies of reading comprehension: To what extent do the test characteristics make a difference? *European Educational Research Journal*, 8(1), 69–79.

Landay, E. and Wootton, K. (2012) *A Reason to Read: Linking Literacy and the Arts*. Cambridge, MA: Harvard University Press.

Lave, J. and Wenger, E. (1991) *Situated Learning: Legitimate Peripheral Participation*. Cambridge: Cambridge University Press.

Lawson, M. A. (2003) School–family relations in context: Parent and teacher perceptions of parent involvement. *Urban Education*, 38(1), 77–133.

Lepper, M. R. and Henderlong, J. (2000) Turning 'play' into 'work' and 'work' into 'play': 25 years of research on intrinsic and extrinsic motivation. In C. Sansone and J. M. Harackiewicz (eds) *Intrinsic and Extrinsic Motivation: The Search for Optimal Motivation and Performance*. San Diego, CA: Academic Press, pp. 257–307.

Levy, R. (2009) 'You have to understand words ... but not read them': Young children becoming readers in a digital age. *Journal of Research in Reading*, 32(1), 75–91.

Lewis, D. (2001) *Reading Contemporary Picturebooks*. London: Routledge.

Lincoln, Y. S. and Guba, E. G. (1985) *Naturalistic Inquiry*. Beverley Hills, CA: Sage Publications.

Lindsay, J. (2010) *Children's Access to Print Material and Education-Related Outcomes: Findings From a Meta-Analytic Review*. Naperville, IL: Learning Point Associates.

Littleton, K. and Mercer, N. (2013) *Interthinking: Putting Talk to Work*. London: Routledge.

Lockwood. M. (2008) *Promoting Reading for Pleasure in the Primary School*. London: Sage Publications.

Logan, S. and Medford, E. (2011) Gender differences in the strength of association between motivation, competency beliefs and reading skill. *Educational Research*, 53(1), 85–94.

Luke, A. (1988) *Literacy. Textbooks and Ideology: Postwar Literacy Instruction and the Mythology of Dick and Jane*. London: Falmer.

Lupton, R. and Hempel-Jorgansen, A. (2012) The importance of teaching: Pedagogical constraints and possibilities in working class schools. *Journal of Education Policy*, 1–20, iFirst article.

Lutz, S. L., Guthrie, J. T. and Davis, M. H. (2006) Scaffolding for engagement in learning: An observational study of elementary school reading instruction. *Journal of Educational Research*, 100, 3–30.

Mackey, M. (2002) *Literacies Across Media: Playing the Text*. London: Routledge.

Manzo, A. V. and Manzo, U. C. (1995) *Teaching Children to Be Literate: A Reflective Approach*. Fort Worth, TX: Harcourt Brace College.

Marks, H. M. (2000) Student engagement in instructional activity: Patterns in the elementary, middle and high school years. *American Educational Research Journal*, 37(1), 153–184.

Marsh, J. (2000) Teletubby tales: Popular culture in the early years language and literacy curriculum. *Contemporary Issues in Early Childhood*, 1, 119 –133.

Marsh, J. (2003a) Contemporary models of communicative practice: Shaky foundations in the foundation stage? *English in Education*, 37(l), 38–46.

Marsh, J. (2003b) Early childhood literacy and popular culture. In N. Hall, J. Larson and J. Marsh (eds) *Handbook of Early Childhood Literacy*. London: Sage, pp. 112–125.

Marsh, J. (2003c) One way traffic? Connections between literacy practices at home and in the nursery. *British Educational Research Journal*, 29(3), 369–382.

Marshall, B. (2001) Creating danger: The place of the arts in education policy. In A. Craft, B. Jeffrey and M. Liebling (eds) *Creativity in Education*. London: Continuum.

Martin, T. (2003) Minimum and maximum entitlements: Literature at Key Stage 2. *Reading Literacy and Language*, 37(1), 14–17.

Maybin, J. (2013) What counts as reading? PIRLS, EastEnders and the man on the flying trapeze. *Literacy*, 47(2), 59–66.

Maybin, J. and Moss, G. (1993) Talk about texts: Reading a social event. *Journal of Research in Reading*, 16(2), 138–147.

Maynard, S., MacKay, S., Smyth, F. and Reynolds, K. (2007) *Young People's Reading in 2005: The Second Study of Young People's Reading Habits*. NCRCL Roehampton University, London and LISU, Loughborough University.

McCarthey, S. J. and Moje, E. J. (2002) Identity matters. *Reading Research Quarterly*, 37(2), 228–238.

McDermott, R., Goldman, S. and Varenne, H. (2006) The cultural work of learning disabilities. *Educational Researcher*, 35, 12–17.

Medwell, J., Wray, D., Poulson, L. and Fox, R. (1998) *Effective Teachers of Literacy: A Report of a Research Project Commissioned by the Teacher Training Agency*. Exeter: University of Exeter.

Meek, M. (1982) *Learning to Read*. London: Bodley Head.

Meek, M. (1988) *How Texts Teach What Readers Learn*. Stroud. Thimble Press.

Meek, M. (1991) *On Being Literate*. London. Bodley Head.

Meek, M. (1998) Important reading lessons. In B. Cox (ed.) *Literacy Is Not Enough: Essays on the Importance of Reading*. Manchester: Manchester University Press and Book Trust, pp. 116–124.

Meek, M. (2002) What more needs saying about imagination? Address at the 19th International Reading Association World Congress on Reading, Edinburgh, Scotland.

Mercer, N. (2000) *Words and Minds: How we Use Language to Think Together.* London: Routledge.

Meyers, E. (1999) The coolness factor: Ten libraries listen to youth. *American Libraries,* 30(10), 42–49.

Millard, E. (1997) *Differently Literate: Boys, Girls and the Schooling of Literacy.* London: Falmer Press.

Moje, E. B., Overby, M., Tysvaer, N., and Morris, K. (2008) The complex world of adolescent literacy: Myths, motivations, and mysteries. *Harvard Educational Review,* 78, 107–154.

Moss, G. (2000) Raising boys' attainment in reading: Some principles for intervention. *Reading,* 34(3), 101–106.

Moss, G. (2003) Analyzing literacy events: Mapping gendered configurations of readers, texts and contexts. In S. Goodman, T. Lillis, J. Maybin and N. Mercer (eds) *Language, Literacy and Education: A Reader.* Stoke on Trent: Trentham Books, pp. 123–137.

Moss, G. and McDonald, J. W. (2004) The borrowers: Library records as unobtrusive measures of children's reading preferences. *Journal of Research in Reading,* 27, 401–412.

Moundlic, C. (2011) *The Scar,* illustrated by O. Tallec. Somerville, MA: Candlewick Press.

Mour, S. I. (1977) Do teachers read? *The Reading Teacher,* 30, 397–401.

Mullis, I. V. S., Martin, M. O., Kennedy, A. M. and Foy, P. (2007) *Progress in International Reading Literacy Study in Primary Schools, 2006.* Chestnut Hill, MA: TIMSS & PIRLS International Study Center, Boston College.

Mullis, I. V. S., Martin, M. O., Foy, P. and Drucker, K. T. (2012) *Progress in International Reading Literacy Study in Primary Schools,* 2011 Chestnut Hill, MA: TIMSS & PIRLS International Study Center, Boston College.

Nathanson, S., Pruslow, J. and Levitt, R. (2008) The reading habits and literacy attitudes of inservice and prospective teachers: Results of a questionnaire survey. *Journal of Teacher Education,* 59(4), 313–321.

National Literacy Trust (2005) *Children's and Young People's Reading Habits and Preferences: The Who, What, Why, Where and When.* The National Literacy Trust, December.

National Literacy Trust (2012) *Boys' Reading Commission: The Report of the All-Party Parliamentary Literacy Group Commission.* London: The National Literacy Trust (www.literacytrust.org.uk).

Nell, V. (1988) The psychology of reading for pleasure: Needs and gratifications. *Reading Research Quarterly,* 23, 6–50.

Ness, P. (2011) *A Monster Calls.* London: Candlewick Press.

Nestlé Family Monitor (2003) *Young People's Attitudes Towards Reading.* Croydon: Nestlé.

Nicholls, S. (2008) *Ways to Live Forever.* London: Scholastic.

Nystrand, M., Wu, L., Gamorgan, A., Zeiser, S. and Long, D. (2003) Questions in time: Investigating the structure and dynamics of unfolding classroom discourse. *Discourse Processes,* 35(2), 135–198.

OECD (2002) *Reading for Change: Performance and Engagement Across Countries: Results From PISA 2002.* New York: Organisation for Economic Co-operation and Development.

OECD (2009) *What Students Know and Can Do: Results from PISA 2009.* http://www.oecd.org/edu/pisa/2009. Accessed 9 November 2012.

OECD (2010) *PISA 2009 Results: Learning to Learn – Student Engagement, Strategies and Practices,* Vol. III. http://dx.doi.org/10.1787/9789264083943-en. Accessed 7 May 2014.

Ofsted (2004) *Reading for Purpose and Pleasure: An Evaluation of the Teaching of Reading in Primary Schools.* London: Ofsted.

Ofsted (2007) *Poetry in Schools: A Survey of Practice, 2006/7.* London. Ofsted. http://www.ofsted.gov.uk/resources/poetry-schools. Accessed 7 May 2014.

Ofsted (2011) *Excellence in English: What We Can Learn from 12 Outstanding Schools* (100229). http://www.ofsted.gov.uk/resources/100229. Accessed 9 November 2012.

Pahl, K. (2002) Ephemera, mess and miscellaneous piles: Texts and practices in families. *Journal of Early Childhood Literacy,* 2(2), 145–166.

Panteleo, S. and Sipe, L. (eds) (2008) *Postmodern Picturebooks: Play. Parody and Self-Referentiality.* London: Routledge.

Parker, M. and Hurry, J. (2007) Teachers' use of questioning and modelling comprehension skills in primary classrooms. *Educational Review*, 59(3), 299–314.

Pavlenko, A. and Blackledge, A. (2004) *Negotiation of Identities in Multilingual Contexts*. Clevedon: Multilingual Matters.

Pennac, D. (1994) *Reads Like a Novel*, trans. D. Gunn. London: Quartet Books.

Pennac, D. (2006) *The Rights of the Reader*. London: Walker Books.

Peters, M., Seeds, K., Goldstein, A. and Coleman, M. (2007) *Parental Involvement in Children's Education 2007*. London: BRB International for the DCSF.

Pihl, J. (2011) Literacy education and interprofessional collaboration. *Professions and Professionalism*, 1(1), 52–66.

PIRLS (2006) *Progress in International Reading Literacy Study*. International Association for the Evaluation of Educational Achievement. http://timss.bc.edu/pirls2006/intl_rpt.html. Accessed 7 May 2014.

PIRLS (2011) *Progress in International Reading Literacy Study*. International Association for the Evaluation of Educational Achievement. http://timss.bc.edu/pirls2011/index.html. Accessed 7 May 2014.

Powell, S. and Tod, J. (2004) *A Systematic Review of How Theories Inform Learning Behaviours in the Classroom*. London: EPPI-Centre.

Pressley, M. (1998) *Reading Instruction That Works: The Case for Balanced Reading*. New York: Guilford Press.

Protherough, R. (1983) *Developing Response to Fiction*. Milton Keyes: Open University Press.

Pullman, P. (2004) The war on words. *Guardian Review*, 6 November.

Rees, D. (1988) Dahl's chickens: Roahl Dahl. *Children's Literature in Education*, 19(3), 143–154.

Robinson, M. and Mackey, M. (2003) Film and television. In N. Hall, J. Larson and J. Marsh (eds) *Handbook of Early Childhood Literacy*. Thousand Oaks, CA: Sage Publications.

Rogers G. and Hathorn, L. (2003) *Way Home*. London: Andersen Press.

Rosenblatt, L. (1978) *The Reader, the Text, the Poem: The Transactional Theory of Literary Work*. Carbondale, IL: South Illinois University Press.

Ross, C. S., McKechnie, L. and Rothbauer, P. M. (2006) *Reading Matters: What Research Reveals About Reading, Libraries and Community*. Westport, CT: Libraries Unlimited.

Rothbauer, P. M. (2004) 'People aren't afraid any more but it's hard to find books': Reading practices that inform personal and social identities of self-identified lesbian and queer young women. *Canadian Journal of Information and Library Science*, 27(4), 53–74.

Rudland, N. and Kemp, C. (2004) The professional reading habits of teachers: Implications for student learning. *Australasian Journal of Special Education*, 28(1), 4–17.

Rummel, M. K. and Quintero, P. (1997) *Teachers'/Reading Teachers' Lives*. Albany: State University of New York Press.

Sainsbury, M. and Schagen, I. (2004) Attitudes towards reading at ages nine and eleven. *Journal of Research in Reading*, 27(4), 387–400.

Sainsbury, M. and Clarkson, R. (2008) *Attitudes to Reading at Ages Nine and Eleven: Full Report*. Slough: NFER. http://www.nfer.ac.uk/nfer/publications/RAQ01. Accessed 29 October 2013.

Sanacore, J. (1999) Encouraging children to make choices about their literacy learning. *Intervention in School and Clinic*, 35, 38–42.

Sanacore, J. (2002) Questions often asked about promoting lifetime literacy efforts. *Intervention in School and Clinic*, 37, 163–168.

Schaffner, E., Schiefele, U. and Ulferts, H. (2013) Reading amount as a mediator of the effects of intrinsic and extrinsic reading motivation on reading comprehension. *Reading Research Quarterly*, 48(4), 369–385.

Schoon, I., Parsons, S., Rush, R. and Law, J. L. (2010) Childhood language skills and adult literacy: A 29-year follow-up study. *Pediatrics*, 125(3), 459–466.

Schraw, G., Flowerday, T. and Reisetter, M. F. (1998) The role of choice in reader engagement. *Journal of Educational Psychology*, 90, 705–714.

Schunk, D. H. (2003) Self-efficacy for reading and writing: Influence of modeling, goal setting, and self-evaluation. *Reading and Writing Quarterly: Overcoming Learning Difficulties*, 19, 159–172.

Sheldrick-Ross, C., McCechnie, L. and Rothbauer, P. M. (2005) *Reading Matters: What the Research Reveals About Reading, Libraries and Community*. Oxford: Libraries Unlimited.

Shulman, L. S. (1987) Knowledge and teaching: Foundations of the new reform. *Harvard Educational Review*, 57(1), 1–21.

Smith, V. (2005) *Making Read Mean*. Leicester: UKLA.

Sonnenschein, S., Baker, L., Serpell, R. and Schmidt, D. (2000) Reading is a source of entertainment: The importance of the home perspective for children's literacy development. In K. A. Roskos and J. F. Christie (eds) *Play and Literacy in Early Childhood: Research from Multiple Perspectives*. Mahwah, NJ: Earlbaum, pp. 125–137.

Spufford, F. (2002) *The Child that Books Built*. London. Faber & Faber.

Stanovich, K. E. (1986) Matthew effects in reading: Some consequences of individual differences in the acquisition of literacy. *Reading Research Quarterly*, 21, 360–407.

Strauss, A. and Corbin, J. (1990) *Basics of Qualitative Research: Grounded Theory Procedures and Techniques*. London: Sage Publications.

Strauss, A. and Corbin, J. (1998) *Basics of Qualitative Research: Techniques and Procedures for Developing Grounded Theory* (2nd edn). Newbury Park, CA: Sage Publications.

Street, B. V. (1984) *Literacy in Theory and Practice*. Cambridge: Cambridge University Press.

Street, B. V. (2008) New literacies, new times: Developments in literacy studies. In B. V. Street and N. Hornberger (eds) *Encyclopedia of Language and Education*, Vol. 2: *Literacy*. New York: Springer, pp. 3–14.

Styles, M. (1992) Just a kind of music: Children as poets. In M. Styles, B. Bearne and V. Watson (eds) *After Alice*. London. Cassell.

Sulentic-Dowell, M., Beal, G. D. and Capraro, R. M. (2006) How do literacy experiences affect the teaching propensities of elementary pre-service teachers? *Reading Psychology*, 27, 235–255.

Sullivan, A. and Brown, M. (2013) Social inequalities in cognitive scores at age 16: The role of reading. CLS Working Paper 2013/10. London: Centre for Longitudinal Studies.

Thomson, P. (2002) *Schooling the Rustbelt Kids: Making the Difference in Changing Times*. Stoke on Trent: Trentham Books.

Tonne, I. and Pihl, J. (2012) Literacy education, reading engagement, and library use in multilingual classes. *Intercultural Education*, 23(3), 183–194.

Topping, K. (2010) *What Kids Are Reading: The Book-Reading Habits of Students in British Schools*. London: Renaissance Learning UK.

Topping, K., Valtin, R., Roller, C., Brozo, W. and Lourdes Dionsiso, M. (2003) *Policy and Practice Implication of PISA 2000: Report of the PISA Task Force to the International Reading Association Board of Directors*. International Reading Association.

Trelease, J. (2013) *The Read-Aloud Handbook* (7th edn). New York: Penguin.

Trong, K. L. and Kennedy, A. M. (2007) Reporting PIRLS 2006 questionnaire data. In M. O. Martin, V. S. Mullis and A. M. Kennedy (eds) *PIRLS 2006 Technical Report*. International Association for the Evaluation of Educational Achievement (IEA) Boston College, TIMSS & PIRLS International Study Center. Lynch School of Education. http://timss.bc.edu/PDF/P06_TR_Chapter13.pdf. Accessed 7 May 2014.

Twist, L., Sainsbury, M., Woodthorpe, A. and Whetton, C. (2003) *Reading all Over the World: The Progress in International Reading Literacy Study*. Slough: NFER.

Twist, L., Schagan, I. and Hogson, C. (2007) *Progress in International Reading Literacy Study (PIRLS), Reader and Reading National Report for England 2006*. London: NFER and DCSF.

Twist, L, Sizmur, J., Bartlett, S. and Lynn, L. (2012) *PIRLS 2011 Reading Achievement in England*. Research Brief DFE-RB262 http://www.education.gov.uk/publications/standard/publicationDetail/Page1/DFE-RB262. Accessed 7 May 2014.

UKLA/QCA (2007) *Reading on Screen*. London: UKLA/QCA.

Urrieta, L. (2007) Figured worlds and education: An Introduction to the Special Issue. *The Urban Review*, 39(2), 107–116.

Villers, H. (2011) The six dimensions of the 'Honeycomb' model, and its implications for literacy, libraries and literature in NZ. In J. Court (ed.) *Read to Succeed: Strategies to Engage Children and Young People in Their Reading for Pleasure*. London: Facet Publishing.

Wadsworth, R. (2008) Using read alouds in today's classrooms: Read alouds benefit children of all ages and in all subjects. *Leadership Compass,* 5(3), 1–3. http://www.naesp.org/leadership-compass-archives-0. Accessed on 4 September 2013.

Wang, M. and Holcombe, R. (2010) Adolescents' perceptions of school environment, engagement, and academic achievement in middle school. *American Educational Research Journal,* 47(4), 633–662.

Waugh, D., Neaum, S. and Waugh, R. (2013) *Children's Literature in Primary Schools*. London: Sage.

Weber, C. (2013) Reading for pleasure with training primary teachers. *English 4–11,* 48, 13–15.

Weisner, D. (2006) *Flotsam*. New York: Clarion Books.

Wigfield, A. and Guthrie, J. T. (1997) Relations of children's motivation for reading to the amount and breadth of their reading. *Journal of Educational Psychology,* 89, 420–432.

Winchester, D. (2008) Rivers of reading. *English 4–11,* 33, 19–22.

Woods, P. (2001) Creative literacy. In A. Craft, B. Jeffrey and M. Liebling (eds) *Creativity in Education*. London: Continuum, pp. 62–79.

Wyse, D. and Styles, M. (2007) Synthetic phonics and the teaching of reading: The debate surrounding England's Rose Report. *Literacy,* 41(1), 35–42.

Younger, M. and Warrington, M. (2005) Raising boys' achievement. In *Department for Education and Skills Research Report 636*. http://www-rba.educ.cam.ac.uk/report.html (accessed October 15, 2011).

Zevin, G. (2005) *Elsewhere*. London: Bloomsbury.

Index

Printed in Great Britain
by Amazon

83087541R00113